SURVIVING

THE STORMS OF LIFE

Dr. Bill Myers

SURVIVING

THE STORMS OF LIFE

AND 100 STORM DEVOTIONS FOR SURVIVAL

PLUS 365 MINI DAILY DEVOTIONS

TATE PUBLISHING
AND ENTERPRISES, LLC

Published by Tate Publishing & Enterprises, LLC
127 E. Trade Center Terrace | Mustang, Oklahoma 73064 USA
1.888.361.9473 | www.tatepublishing.com

Tate Publishing is committed to excellence in the publishing industry. The company reflects the philosophy established by the founders, based on Psalm 68:11,
"The Lord gave the word and great was the company of those who published it."

Book design copyright © 2015 by Tate Publishing, LLC. All rights reserved.
Cover design by Junriel Boquecosa
Interior design by Gram Telen

Published in the United States of America

ISBN: 978-1-63185-980-9
1. Self-Help / Motivational & Inspirational
2. Self-Help / Recovery
14.12.05

STEFFAN DAVID MYERS
1989-2010

Son, not a day goes by that I don't think of you. You were and will always be a part of me. Losing you left a hole in my heart that only God can fill. It's a day to day journey of living my life without you.

When I was first reminded after losing you of Romans 8:28 "And we know that in all things God works for the good of those who have been called according to His purpose," I wanted to rip it out of the Bible. I thought to myself, "Nothing good is coming from losing you, my son!" But after a period of grieving, my eyes were opened to some good. This book was birthed from my pain and I'm praying it will help others who are suffering. Also, many lives were touched and changed from your earthly death. Of course, I believe you know all this. Yes, I believe God told you so you could join in the heavenly celebration.

I look forward to the day we see one another again! I'm very thankful for the spiritual dreams God has given me over the past four years of seeing and hugging you. Your happiness in Heaven encourages me to keep living each day.

I love you, Steffan. Thank you for inspiring me to write this book.

Dad

ACKNOWLEDGEMENTS

There are so many wonderful family and friends I'd like to express my appreciation to for inspiring, encouraging, and praying for me to pursue this dream of writing my first book.

To my wife Teri, I say thank you! This journey has been the toughest one to travel. In the past four years, we have held each other up in the darkest of days. We have cried together, laughed together, and encouraged each other to keep moving forward and not give up. You have always been the love of my life and this book wouldn't be possible without your love and support. You gave me two precious gifts, Steffan and Lydia, and I truly love you.

To my precious daughter Lydia, I say thank you! When I didn't think I would survive losing Steffan, you gave me reason to live. You have always brightened up any room you've entered and loved unconditionally. I've watched you encourage others who have suffered. The light of Jesus in you has been a light house for many. I'm excited to see the next chapter in your life. Lydia, you will always be the best Ariel (Little Mermaid), Belle (Beauty and the Beast), and Elsa (Frozen) that I will ever know. You're my shining star and I love you.

To Cale, Lydia's boyfriend, I say thank you! You came into our lives a year ago (2013) and brought joy and laughter to our home. Like Lydia, you bring a smile each time you enter a room.

You helped us truly enjoy this past Christmas (2013) for the first time since losing Steffan. I just know my son would love you. I don't know what the future holds for you, but thank you for loving us in the time we have known you. I love you, Cale.

To my loving family and many Facebook friends (5,000), I say thank you for reading my daily devotions and praying for me. Your request and desire for me to write a book has truly inspired me. I pray you will be blessed as you read <u>Surviving the Storms of Life</u>. God bless and thank you, family and Facebook friends. I love you all!

Contents

FOREWORD

As a pastor with a ministry that began in the sixties and now spans into six decades, I've watched as the storms of life have challenged and battered many homes and, more importantly, the lives of those who lived there. I've stood with hundreds of families in their time of grief and personal loss and, at least ten times, had the difficult task of officiating funerals to speak words of comfort to parents whose young children had been taken from them in untimely deaths.

I can unequivocally say that there is a marked difference between the families whose faith in God sustains and undergirds them and the families who have no life–giving relationship with Christ. I've watched many that simply couldn't take the brunt of the storm and they failed to survive.

When Jesus shared the parable of two houses that faced brutal storms, he was not teaching us how to avoid storms but how to survive them. The difference between the home that stood and the one that didn't wasn't the fierceness of the storm; it was the foundation of the structure. Houses, dreams, and hopes built on rock are subject to the same floods, winds, and forces of nature that also pound those built on sand.

As a South Mississippian, I joined others in bracing for a major hurricane nine years ago that challenged our communities in ways we had not imagined. Although 100 miles inland, our county endured several hours of 90–100 mph sustained winds with gusts of 120 mph. In the aftermath, many chose to leave and move to some hurricane–free part of the nation where I presume they will have to deal with mudslides, earthquakes, or ice storms. There is no such thing as a storm–free life; the issue is how well we prepare for them.

I watched Bill, Teri, and Lydia up close as they faced one particular "Katrina" tearing away at their home and soul. Yet they survived, continue to survive, and even thrive.

The principles Bill shares are not untested theory; they are bedrock principles that will work in your life just as they've worked in the Myers' home. We all have our own "storm stories;" but as Bill shares his, you will come to admire, as I have, the peace and faith that took over when their strength was gone. May you be blessed, inspired, and be a survivor of your storm.

—David L. Hagan
Senior Pastor—Life Church, Laurel, MS

INTRODUCTION

No! No! Please! Tell me he's alive! Oh dear God, this has to be a dream! I must wake up. This can't be happening! Sir, you must be mistaken. It can't be my son!! No, no, it just can't be. Just can't be.

I can't breathe. I can't focus. I can't think. God, help me! Please! Where are you?

What seemed a perfect day had now suddenly turned into the most horrific nightmare!

For those of you who have lost a child or a loved one, you understand the shock and pain that accompanies the initial news. At that particular moment, you feel numbness all through your body and mind.

Through my anguish and intense pain of suffering, God led me to write this book on surviving the fiercest of storms. Everyone will face a storm in their life. No one is excluded. Of course, everyone's storms are different and each deal with pain differently. Some major storms that people face are death, divorce, job loss, broken relationships, and health issues. I urge you to never minimize someone's storm. Pain is pain. I can't compare my pain of losing my son, Steffan, to someone who just lost their job. It's different, but it's still painful for the one going through it.

In this book, I share various storm stories that I experienced through my life that are full of good and bad decisions, pain, humor, survival, and a heart to follow God. I purposely wrote my book to be easy reading for every one of all ages. Since the first year of someone's tragedy seems to be the most difficult, I also included some valuable heart–felt devotions at the close of my book to help in your daily struggles. I pray each page and chapter of this survival book will speak to your heart and offer you comfort in your pain and a hope to keep living your life one step at a time.

Dear friend, I made it through my storm, and you will too! With God's help, we will overcome life's fierce storms and once again, we will live a life full of joy and happiness.

God, Are You There?

I am looking back over this beautiful Sunday, January 10, 2010. I recall my morning prayer time with God and how anointed it had become. I arose at 4:00 a.m., poured a cup of coffee to wake me, curled up in my recliner, and opened my sleepy eyes to my Bible and began my fellowship time with God. Getting up at 4:00 a.m. gave me a couple of quality hours of only God and me before anyone would begin stirring. I loved praying and interceding in the mornings. I have always felt it was the best way to begin a day. I knew it was vital as a Christian, husband and dad to be a prayer warrior. As the spiritual head of my home, I felt responsible to pray for my family daily. This particular early January morning, I felt so close to my Heavenly Father and could sense his presence all around me. My prayer was mixed with times of quietness and listening but also some intense spiritual warfare. At one point during my prayer and crying out to God that morning, I felt sweat rolling down my back. But no matter how intense my prayer time would get each morning, it always seemed to end with that loving, peaceful feeling that only Abba Father (Daddy) could give. Mmm, that sweet, sweet Spirit. There's nothing better and more satisfying than knowing you're beginning your day communing with your Father, and knowing He's listening.

After a couple of hours of seeking God, and two cups of coffee, my beautiful prayer time concluded with the feeling that He was in control of my life, I had victory regarding my prayer requests and petitions, and my prayers would be answered. I have known since a young boy that God hears our prayers and will answer.

Soon after my prayer, my wife Teri and daughter Lydia awoke and got ready for church. It was sometime after my morning prayer with God that I realized our son, Steffan, had not come home from the night before. I was disappointed, but not particularly shaken. There had been previous times he would choose to stay at a friend's house instead of driving home late at night. But he usually texted Teri if he wasn't coming home, and since she was asleep during my prayer time, I just figured he was upstairs sound asleep. When Teri woke, she told me that he hadn't come home and she hadn't received a text or call from him. Again, we weren't terribly anxious because he spent the night with friends many times on Saturday evenings. But she was disappointed that he hadn't texted her and let her know his plans.

We went about getting ready for church as usual. I left the house early to rehearse with the church choir before service, and Teri and Lydia came a bit later. I was still feeling peaceful. The Sunday service was wonderful on this amazingly warm day in January. The praise and worship at Life Church in my hometown of Laurel, was always awesome, but this Sunday morning it seemed to be the best. It sounded as if the angels in heaven were singing along with the choir. I remember standing on the front row of the choir worshiping as we sang "Revelation Song," which concluded with the entire Life Church congregation standing to their feet, hands lifted in adoration and praise to God. Teri, who was in the congregation, recalled noticing our dear friend Denisea Marengo in the choir. She had lost her son Zac in a terrible automobile accident just a couple years before. Teri thought to herself, *Only God could restore the peace and joy Denisea is experiencing after losing her son.* As the choir worshiped through the special music, Denisea displayed the most peaceful look on her face that declared God was in control. Looking back on that day, sometime after our own tragedy, Teri shared with me that she believed God had allowed her to observe Denisea's peace to prepare her for her own nightmare to come. Yes, He was already working in Teri's heart to offer her hope for the major storm that was headed our way.

It had been a beautiful Sunday morning service full of worship, an aspiring message from Pastor David Hagan, and loving fellowship time among the people. Of course I thought, the icing on my cake for a perfect day would be if our son Steffan would have joined us instead of sleeping in at a friend's house. Well, he wasn't sleeping in at all. He was actually worshiping God with joy, peace, and love at the same time we were, but in a different location.....heaven.

During my tragedy, God gave me the illustration of storms to help me understand and relate to my emotional state during our crisis. If you've ever sailed or been on a cruise, you know that storms can be dangerous and even life threatening. When a storm hits on water, the ocean can be fierce, causing vessels to fight for survival. Unfortunately throughout centuries, many ships have crashed and sank to the bottom of the ocean due to gigantic storms and inexperienced sailors. But many ships have survived due to a wise, experienced captain and sailors navigating their ship through the fierce storm to safety.

Life's experiences teach us valuable lessons that can't be learned from a classroom. As Teri, Lydia, and I were experiencing the major storm of Steffan's death in our lives, we gave ear to those who had successfully been through the same storm. Their experience of survival during the darkest of nights, offered us hope that we could and would make it. Listening to those who have experienced tragedies reminded me of an illustration I have often thought of. If I had to venture to the Everglades, Florida, and live for a period of time, I would definitely seek out those who have experienced living around poisonous snakes and crocodiles. I would want to gather as much information as I could for survival. (I probably still wouldn't go to the Everglades!) Talking and listening to wisdom from those individuals who have survived storms as we have experienced, have helped the most.

"I will turn their mourning into gladness; I will give them comfort and joy instead of sorrow, declares the Lord." Jeremiah 31: 13 NIV.

Yes, our loving Father desires to help us through our storms by providing people who have valued experiences of survival. I believe each of us would rather receive advice from someone with similar experience than one who truly didn't have a clue about our feelings or how to relate to what we were going through. Here in the south, we sometimes hear the old timers' expression, "Been there, done that." Even though I do not enjoy hearing that phrase, it does ring true. People often relate to others who have already experienced the same. You somehow feel in your heart that there's someone in this world who might understand your intense pain. That's true empathy, my friend.

In our particular case of losing our precious son, God provided several dear saints who had been through a similar storm and survived. Because these precious saints of God had also lost their teenagers in accidents, we listened intently, desperate for help. I'm not sure if Teri and I would have made it as parents had it not been for these survivors. Some of them came to our home the very night we had received the news to offer comfort. Through several visits, they helped us understand our roller coaster emotions with words of hope and encouragement that helped us move forward by taking one step at a time. I thank God for precious saints like Denisea Marengo who lost her precious son, Zac, in a tragic auto accident; Mike and Karen Mulkey, who lost their loving daughter, Tiffany, only a year before we lost Steffan; and our dear long time friend Alicia Dewitt Craft who lost her beautiful Natalie several years before our tragedy. These individuals offered advice and hope for survival through their own experience and pain. Teri, Lydia, and I are survivors because of their love, prayers, and countless hours of conversation.

The Lord is close to the brokenhearted and saves those who are crushed in spirit. Psalm 34:18 NIV.

Questions to ponder:

1. Has this storm I'm experiencing caused me to feel hopeless, at the end of my rope?

2. As I face my storm, have I turned the control of my ship over to God or have I tried to navigate alone?

"Praise be to God and Father of our Lord Jesus Christ, the Father of compassion and the God of all comfort, who comforts us in all our troubles, so that we can comfort those in any trouble with the comfort we ourselves have received from God." 2 Corinthians 1:3–4 NIV.

Let's pray:

Father God, I pray you will open my eyes as I read this book. I pray you will heal the brokenness in my heart as I go through each chapter, and help me relate this book to my own storm. Teach me to rely on you, the anchor of my ship. I thank you, Father, for offering me hope in my pain and encouraging me to begin taking small steps with my life. I choose to move forward because I am a conqueror through Christ Jesus! I love you, God. In Jesus's name, amen.

BEGINNING TO GROW

The question has probably already run through your mind, "Who the heck is Bill Myers?" Over the years of teaching school and working with church youth groups, students have asked my age to which I would laughingly reply, "I was teaching young people on Noah's ark." Sadly, I had to stop using that phrase after one student honestly replied, "Really?"

Students in today's generation do not understand the concept of nicknames. They are usually clueless how my nickname Bill came from William, or even someone with the nickname Dick derived from the name Richard. Confusing, huh? After explaining to no avail to the youth today about nicknames, I usually just reply, "It is what it is."

My younger years weren't too colorful. I was born in Meridian, Mississippi and then when I turned one year old, we moved to Laurel. Laurel became my home and the place where I finished school. As long as I could remember in my younger years, my family lived within the city of Laurel and always attended Wildwood Baptist Church, until they moved to the country many years later on family land that had been in our family many generations. I had already graduated from high school when they decided to move. With the move to the country the decision was made for them to attend a community church near their home.

My parents, Elsie and Ercle, married very young. Actually they eloped, which only lasted sixty–two years, until my mom's departure into Heaven. I never witnessed my parents fighting. I'm sure they disagreed over issues, but I never experienced them arguing or fighting between themselves in my presence. They always seemed so much in love, even in their older years. Dad was a butcher/manager in the local A & P Grocery store most of his life. He was excellent at his trade and enjoyed it immensely. He was a giver of himself and never seemed to meet a stranger. He would help anyone without complaining. Even today as I write, my ninety–one year old dad hasn't changed. He's still a giver (and an excellent golfer).

As long as I could remember, Mom worked at the Office Supply Company, later becoming the vice president. Her store in Laurel was actually across the street from my dad's grocery store. Mom was loving, kind, and beautiful. She, in my opinion, was a classy true southern belle who taught me much about life. She was a hugger, a compassionate mother, a good listener, and definitely an advice giver, which sometimes I didn't want to listen to. Bless her, I still miss that excited, exuberant smile she always gave me when we would see each other. She's now in Heaven enjoying my son Steffan and her many loved ones that were waiting for her.

Growing up, I recall our household income was average, our vehicles were average, and I guess my two brothers and I were also average. None of us were superstar athletes or academic wizards while in school, but we were a family who loved one another very much. We had what we needed, but weren't rich.

At the young age of nine, I asked Jesus into my heart while attending Wildwood Baptist Church's Vacation Bible School. I knew what I was doing and was confident of the decision I was making. Many adults feel that children don't understand the concept of salvation at their young age. I totally disagree. Children aren't clueless. Jesus said to come to him with childlike faith. He loves children.

Everyone (young or old) who calls on the name of the Lord will be saved. Acts 2:21 NIV.

If we try to shove religiosity down their young throats, I'm sure it can get confusing. The way to Jesus Christ is simple. We're to come to Him as we are. I encourage pastors, church leaders, and teachers to make the most of their VBS time. Singing songs and making crafts are fun, but it's the Bible and prayer time the teachers have with children that is most important. Many children do not receive Bible teaching at home; therefore events as VBS are vital for reaching young lives for Jesus. VBS is a wonderful evangelical tool! It worked for me!

Whoever welcomes one of these little children in my name welcomes me; and whoever welcomes me does not welcome me but the one who sent me. Mark 9:37 NIV.

It's a special calling from God to work with children and teenagers. We have the honor to input into their lives, not just education, but more importantly, Christian life skills.

I literally take my teaching job seriously as I stand in front of my students each day. I know they are listening to the positive life skills I share. They might not remember as adults which song they sang while in my music groups, but they will remember the encouraging words I gave them and how I handled day to day storms in my life. It's already proven true with many testimonies from students over the years in my school and church work.

Whether we're a school teacher, daycare worker, or Sunday school teacher, God has called us to mentor the young lives before us. They will learn more by watching and observing our lives than material from a textbook. We are called to encourage, not discourage. We are called to be cheerleaders, cheering them on to reach their goals, and we are called to love them unconditionally. Friends, most conduct problems that we encounter from a student are usually the result of crying out for a need in his/her life.

We must remind ourselves daily that God created each child or teen and they are precious to Him. He loves each one dearly and has created a plan especially for them that is unique.

God has called all adults to mentor and model the life of Jesus before the young. Let's allow them to see Jesus in us by the way we live, treat others, and how we handle situations and circumstances. As we pray, let's receive our daily instructions from our Heavenly Father and choose to make a difference in someone's life!

Jesus said, "If anyone gives even a cup of cold water to one of these little ones because he is my disciple, I tell you the truth, he will certainly not lose his reward." Matthew 10:42 NIV.

Remember, we are teachers, counselors, ministers, missionaries, and mentors to those around us. Let's thank God for the ones we have to work with and pray for them daily. We might be the ONLY Bible they ever read, our lives.....

I always loved going to church and participating in all the activities, including the music program. Wildwood had an awesome youth choir where I made many memories and great friends as a teen. Music at church, school, or home seemed important to me. I recall various times in my younger years gathering all the neighborhood friends together in my garage for a talent show, starring me. How I retained my friends through those young years, I'll never know. I would sing and dance until I exhausted everyone from watching.

As I grew a bit older somewhere around the eighth or ninth grade, I made the decision in my heart to choose the music ministry for my life. I truly felt God speaking to me that this was the path to follow. I never changed my career pattern through high school and college. No matter what type of music I was involved in, sacred or secular, my heart was to reach others for Jesus.

Looking back, I'm thankful for the various churches and schools that allowed me to serve in my music ministry. Honoring God and touching lives was and still is my priority.

My love for God was always strong even though I didn't know much about the Bible. I did participate in church Bible drills throughout junior high and high school, which helped me learn where to find various scriptures. I don't know if churches today still have Bible drills, but it helped me get familiar with the Bible and understand the importance of memorizing and learning God's Word. I'm so thankful I participated in the Bible drills, even though at the time it seemed like only a contest. Even today when I hear a pastor give a scripture reference, I can easily find that verse due to my previous experience in Bible drills.

I'm sure as a kid my prayer life was childish, but I've learned as an adult that God loves to hear children pray from their hearts, even if it is about the carrots and peas on their lunch plate. He truly cares. Parents, I encourage you to teach your children how to pray from their heart instead of reciting pointless prayers. Teach them how to use the Bible. It's an actual manual to live by. When we buy a new car, it comes with a how–to manual to operate. The Bible is our manual for life. God's Word shows us how to live a life like Jesus. Our Father expects us as parents and leaders to teach our children His ways which encompasses reading His Word and establishing a beautiful prayer life. It's a charge. It's a challenge. It's beneficial and rewarding. It's our calling!

"Your Word is a lamp to my feet and a light for my path" Psalm 119:105 NIV.

His Word will give us direction and hope. Have you ever wandered down a dark path at night without a light? It can get dark and scary without seeing where you are going. God's Word is the light that will show us the path to follow even in the darkest nights. If you're not a regular reader of God's word, begin now with a heart to absorb all that God would share with you. You'll notice a difference in your life immediately. It will change you, I promise.

I've always been somewhat a dreamer, night and day. My parents laughingly joked over the years about the many times they entered my bedroom only to find me sitting in the middle of my bed thinking or as they would phrase it, gazing into space. I've always enjoyed creating in my head and could plan an entire musical revue, play, or story in a short time. I'm not sure that my parents felt my day dreaming was an asset. I recall as young baseball player playing in right field and day dreaming about music only to miss a flying ball that was hit my way. Even with the team and coaches yelling at me to get the ball after it hit the ground, I was still dreaming about music. Needless to say, my baseball career quickly came to an abrupt end. I've been blessed to have night dreams also. My first spiritual dream occurred when I was young after I got saved. I dreamed that Jesus entered my bedroom and sat in a chair between the twin beds in my room. I was so excited about His visit and asked Him many questions which He answered. When I awoke, I couldn't remember what we talked about. I just remember His loving visit. It left a lasting impression in my life. I don't think anyone believed my dream because of my age, but it didn't matter because I knew what I had dreamed and knew in my young heart that Jesus had come to visit with me.

We should never discount a child's spiritual dream. God speaks to children just as He speaks to adults. Children have the same Holy Spirit as adults. No one's spirit is any bigger than anyone else's. We should encourage children to share their dreams. You never know when it could be God speaking to us through their dreams. God also uses ordinary people who maybe you and I wouldn't use, but He sees the heart that we don't see. If someone gives you a spiritual Word from God, listen and meditate on what they've said, but make sure it lines up with His Word. Sometimes you have to put the word someone gives you on a shelf and wait for God's timing. A word or dream from God may be for now or for a later date. If it's from God, you'll receive His peace.

After high school graduation, my parents allowed me to attend Clarke College in Newton, Mississippi, a remote Christian junior college approximately sixty miles from home. Because it was a private junior college, they sacrificed financially to allow me to attend so I wouldn't have to rely on student loans. I think back with so much gratitude and love for my sweet parents for helping their children. They loved us deeply. Unfortunately, it was years before I truly realized their sacrifices for me. They continuously and sacrificially gave to their children out of love. It's a great lesson to live by.

I loved my two years at Clarke College. It literally changed my life. I grew in the Lord by leaps and bounds. Even though my parents were loving and giving, they didn't offer me much spiritually, with the exception of regularly attending church. Unfortunately, they weren't grounded spiritually themselves and therefore wasn't able to guide me spiritually. But God supplied all my needs (Philippians 4:19). He placed just the right people in my life to help encourage me to grow spiritually.

When I arrived on the college campus and began classes, I didn't know anyone except my roommate, Bill, who was from my hometown of Laurel. Bill was a superb singer and guitarist. He was extremely handsome and could woo the ladies on campus with his guitar and velvet voice. I, on the other hand, weighed about 110 lbs, wasn't that great of a singer, but very comical. He'd woo the ladies and I'd make them laugh. We were much like the old Dean Martin and Jerry Lewis movies. He was the handsome leading man and I was the comical side kick. We had a wonderful time at Clark and made valuable friendships. I remember my first impression of the college was that everyone seemed to love everyone. There didn't seem to be cliques or social groups. No one cared about an individual's social or financial status or any previous awards from high school. They exemplified the love of Jesus to everyone. I learned so much about who I was at Clarke. Sadly, over the years, Clarke closed and is no longer there.

The second semester of my first year at Clarke, I was hired as the part-time minister of music and youth for Mt. Horeb Baptist Church, Meridian, where I was able to work at the church and continue college. It was a small Baptist church with loving people and a large youth group. I learned so much during my tenure there. My mind still remembers those special youth services when the youth choir would sing, testify, perform drama, and end with an alter call. Young and old would flood the aisles giving their hearts to Jesus or rededicating their lives. God truly used us during those awesome services. Already at the age of eighteen, I could feel God's hand on me. It was a great feeling.

Again, I urge parents to encourage their children in the Lord. Pray for them. Love them. Listen to them. Convey your confidence in them to accomplish their goals. Our children and youth desire our approval for their tasks. Let's not leave them hungry. God has called us as adults to be "cheerleaders," cheering them to greatness. We are mentors, good or bad, in everything we say and do. Children watch and learn from our actions and reactions, so we must be Christlike teachers and mentors for them, sowing into their lives the love of Jesus. The children and youth today yearn for heroes and mentors. They crave someone to look up to. Many have been let down by Hollywood celebrities and national sports stars. We should become the ones they look up to, whether we are parents, grandparents, aunts, uncles, or just church members. Let's allow Jesus to shine through us to the children and youth today and become the light house for them, showing them the way (Jesus). What a compliment to our lives when someone shares that they saw Jesus in us, in the way we handled certain situations and other people.

I have decided to follow Jesus. No turning back, no turning back.

Questions to ponder:

1. Is my life pleasing to God and a positive, spiritual testimony to others?

2. Am I doing what He desires for me to do with my life?

Jesus said, Be faithful......and I will give you the crown of life. Revelation 2:10 NIV.

Let's pray:

Oh dear God, let me be the light house in someone's life with the way I live. Whether it's decisions I make or the way I treat people around me, may others see Jesus in me. Help me to be a living testimony, a walking Bible, offering hope to the hopeless. In Jesus's name, amen.

STORM WITHOUT WARNING

In November 1973, I experienced my first major storm, the death of my younger brother Stephen (Stevie) David Myers. He was only seventeen years old, a junior in high school and football player. I remember it was homecoming day at his high school. This day consisted of a big pep rally, parade downtown, and the big football game. It was such a big event with many school clubs and bands participating in the day's events. The football players weren't allowed to attend the parade as they needed to get ready for the big game. Stevie had come home to get ready for the game. He had brought his girlfriend home with him to visit and hang out until he had to report to the school field house for the game. One of the reasons he brought her home was to show her his new rifle that Dad had purchased for him. Because of our family land in the country, Dad and my brothers loved to hunt, fish, etc. Stevie, my dad, and my older brother, Buddy, loved to hunt and shoot their guns. They were very good hunters. Remember, while they were in the country hunting, I was at home performing talent shows for the neighborhood gang.

My dad always had a standard rule about guns. No one was ever allowed to enter our house with a loaded gun. They would come home from hunting or target practice and immediately unload and clean their guns before entering the house. This was standard procedure. But for some unknown reason, Stevie's new rifle didn't get unloaded or cleaned. No one knows how it happened as he was so careful with all his guns.

He walked his girlfriend to the doorway of his bedroom and got the rifle that was hanging on the post of his bed and began to show her with pride his new toy. In the conversation, he cracked a joke thought the 22 rifle down, allowing the butt of the gun to bump the floor. The bump of the gun caused it to accidently discharge, and it shot him under his chin. His girlfriend panicked, grabbed the phone in shock and tried calling for help. In 1973, there was no 911. She called the operator, but gave the wrong address and the ambulance couldn't find them. Horrified and in a state of shock, she frantically ran across the street and got help from a neighbor, who called the ambulance with the right address and in turn, called my dad.

It was a tragic day for our family. I was in Jackson, Mississippi, at the time of the accident attending a church conference. My older brother, Buddy, and his wife were living in Jackson and I was staying with them for the short visit. When the call came in, we didn't think it was too bad. We were just told by a family friend that Stevie had a little gun accident, and we could come home if we wanted to. They either didn't know the details at the time or were trying to protect us since we weren't there. We quickly packed our clothes, but just before leaving my brother's apartment, we decided to call and get an update. We called the emergency room at the hospital and waited for what seemed like eternity. My sister-in-law placed the call while we were packing. I'll never forget her gasp and the shocked look on her face when my dad came to the phone and in a broken voice said, "Take your time coming home. Stevie's already gone." I had never experienced death of this nature before. Death had completely eluded me up until this point. I was speechless. The almost two hour drive home to Laurel seemed to last forever. I kept thinking it was a dream. I remember when we pulled into the driveway of our house, I saw cars everywhere. At that point, the horrid reality of his death kicked in. I immediately burst into tears, realizing my baby brother was truly gone and I'd never see him again in this lifetime.

No one knows how the gun fired. It was never cocked nor was the trigger pulled. The butt of the gun just bumped the floor and it fired. Investigators filed the report as a freak gun accident.

I will never forget that night as I entered my home where I had grown up and witnessed my parents in a state of shock and devastation. My poor mother was lying on the couch weeping and weeping. Stevie was the only one of us three boys who still lived at home, and it made it even more difficult. He was literally snatched from their lives without warning. It was a nightmare.

Stevie's best friend was a football player also and had kept wondering throughout the homecoming football game that night where he was. When the coaches received the official word about Stevie, they decided to withhold the information from the team as it was game time. During the latter part of the game, the word leaked out through the football stands, and the crowd began to get quieter and quieter. Testimonies from the football team revealed they knew something was wrong because the fans weren't cheering as usual.

The football team was told by the coaches to head straight to the field house immediately after the game and not to speak to anyone on the way. The boys knew something was wrong but weren't sure until the coaches closed the field house doors and began sharing the news of the tragedy. Many boys wept and immediately came by the house after leaving the school. I will never forget the look on Stevie's best friend's face as he stood on the steps of my house weeping. He had frantically raced to our home still in his uniform. I can't recall his name, but even in my pain, my heart broke for him and all his close friends. They loved my brother. We never had much contact with his girlfriend after the funeral. I always worried about her emotional state. I'm sure it was devastating for her to witness the whole scene of Stevie being shot.

The entire high school football team served as honorary pallbearers. It was so touching and emotional to see all the young people that came to show love and support.

The road to recovery was very long for my parents. My dad finally submitted to counseling, which helped him express his emotions. I honestly believe he went back to work too quickly after Stevie's death. He didn't want to stay in the house where Stevie had died any more than he needed to, so he jumped back into work quickly to ease the pain. And after an extended leave of absence from work and much encouragement, my mom reluctantly went back to work. In the end, it proved to be good therapy for her.

I loved my little brother. He was three years younger, but we were very close as brothers and enjoyed hanging out, except when it came to hunting and fishing, which I did neither. He had given his heart to Jesus several years before the accident, so I knew in my heart he was in heaven. Of course, that didn't change the "missing" factor we experienced. I eventually resigned from my church in Corinth and moved home to be with my parents, which proved to be a good thing. I hated to leave my church but knew in my heart that mom and dad needed me. I believe God used me to bring laughter and joy back into our house. My parents seemed to enjoy my friends when they would come over. God is good in how He comforts us during our storms.

Even though I walk through the valley of the shadow of death, I will fear no evil, for you are with me; your rod and staff, they comfort me. Psalm 23:4 NIV.

After Stevie's death, I heard the recording of the musical rock group The Hollies' "He Ain't Heavy, He's My Brother" and always thought of Stevie. Many times after his death, I cried, wishing I could have been there to possibly help him, even though the doctors shared that he died immediately after arriving at the hospital. But he was still my baby brother, my good friend.

I heard a story in regards to this song about the time of Stevie's death, which I'm sure is fictional. A mother and her two young sons were headed to visit family during Christmastime when their car veered off the road and crashed. It was a major snowstorm and ice on the road had caused the crash. The older brother, who was only about nine years old, realized his mom was dead and his four year old little brother was unconscious, but alive. He carried his brother in his arms to a nearby farmhouse. The farmer and his wife opened the door with astonishment and immediately offered to relieve the boy of the burden of carrying his brother down the long snow–covered road. The little nine year old looked into the farmer's eyes and replied through his tears, "It's okay mister. He ain't heavy, he's my brother."

I still miss you, brother. Can't wait to see you again…

"He Ain't Heavy, He's My Brother"
By The Hollies

The road is long
With many a winding turn
That leads us to who knows where
Who knows where.
But I'm strong
Strong enough to carry him
He ain't heavy, he's my brother.

So on we go.
His welfare is my concern.
No burden is he to bear
We'll get there.
For I know
He would not encumber me

He ain't heavy, he's my brother.

If I'm laden at all
I'm laden with sadness
That everyone's heart
Isn't filled with the gladness
Of love for one another

It's a long, long road
From which there is no return
While we're on the way to there
Why not share
And the load
Doesn't weigh me down at all
He ain't heavy, he's my brother

Stephen David Myers 1955–1973

Questions:

1. Do I love my family, appreciate what they do for me, and forgive them when they hurt me?

2. Knowing that time on this earth is short, do I pray for my family daily?

Even though I walk through the valley of the shadow of death, I will fear no evil, for you are with me. Psalm 23:4 NIV.

Prayer:

Our Heavenly Father, I thank you for family. I thank you for the time we have on earth to enjoy one another. God, I thank you for salvation and eternal life. I pray now for family members and close friends who don't know you as their personal savior. Let my life be a lighthouse of hope to them. I pray in Jesus's name. Amen.

ON THE ROAD...

In 1976, I moved to Nashville, TN to live with my relatives, gospel music greats Henry and Hazel Slaughter. They were such a sweet family and a wonderful influence in my life. They allowed me to travel with them for a season to help sell records and set up equipment. It was fun to learn about the gospel music business. At that time, they were traveling with the Bill Gaither Trio. Their concerts were always coliseum filled and wonderful to attend. I recall God's anointing would be so strong and intense at some concerts as the audience would stand to their feet and worship God with great songs such as "Because He Lives" and "The King Is Coming." I received a valuable education while traveling and was able to visit most states in America, seeing many beautiful sites. Most of that concert season encompassed living on the Slaughter bus on the road. When we would arrive home in Nashville, it was just enough time to wash our clothes, take a breather, and head out again. It was an adventure. After our busy season was over, I decided to stay in the Music City.

During one of our concert travels, Aunt Hazel and I decided to experience the "Daniel fast" which consists of eating only fruits and vegetable. I had never experienced a spiritual fast before and I can't recall if we fasted for twenty one or forty days, but it was the first time that I had willingly given up something for God. It changed my life and created a deep hunger to learn more about Jesus.

I'm not sure how it came about, but one night while in Nashville, I attended a Full Gospel Business Men's Association convention. I'm not sure who I was with, but it was there in that big auditorium that I saw my first physical miracle. God began healing many different sick and afflicted people who came expecting a miracle. I was in the back of the auditorium and out of curiosity, began making my way down to the front by the side aisle of the auditorium. Looking back, I believe it was the Holy Spirit wooing me to the front. I had never actually witnessed anyone getting physically healed before and honestly, I was pretty much a skeptic.

Just as I arrived to the front to get a close–up view of what was taking place, I saw several men of God praying for a crippled man in a wheel chair. I don't remember the men who prayed or remember the man in the wheel chair except that after praying, this elderly gentleman slowly stood up from the chair and walked! More evidence of his prior crippled condition was revealed when they raised the leg of his pants and revealed thin, tiny legs. They looked like two tooth picks attached to a body. It was obvious that this man had never walked before. Shocked and in total awe of what God had done, my heart began to weep with joy and compassion for this man. I had witnessed a miracle from God! When the service finally concluded, I'm not sure if I walked or floated from the auditorium. After arriving home, I couldn't get the image of the elderly man out of my mind. Reflecting over the events left me sleepless that night, thinking about what God had done. I had actually witnessed someone being physically healed! God was so loving and awesome to heal that man. My heart began to ponder, if He did it for this man, would He do it for others? This was unusual for me as I was raised in a denominational church where one didn't experience healings. I knew God could heal but wasn't sure if it was for today. A little research in God's

Word can clear that confusion. It's clear He does heal today and instructs us to pray in faith for those who are sick.

I will restore you to health and heal your wounds, declares the Lord. Jeremiah 30:17 NIV.

Do you need a miracle in your life? Is it financial, health, job, relationship, etc.? When we need a miracle and are praying for that "mountain" that's standing in the way to be removed, we should know that the devil will work hard to make us doubt, worry, and fear. He will even super-size the problem to make us think there's no way we'll get our miracle. But the devil is a liar and a deceiver. He continuously tells us that God's too busy to be concerned about our miracle, or it's not going to happen, or we're not good enough to receive a miracle. If you were given a present, would you open it or just leave it on a table to look at? We know the answer. We'd open it to receive our gift. God's blessings and favor are like presents given to us. They are free, but we must choose to open them.

God's Word tells us, I am the Lord, the God of all mankind. Is there anything too hard for me? Jeremiah 32:27 NIV.

Truth spoken! NOTHING is too difficult for God. He loves and cares about our every need! He's the God of more than enough! When Jesus fed the multitude of five thousand who gathered to hear Him teach, He was given five loaves of bread and two fish. The situation looked hopeless. But God is a God of more than enough! He fed all five thousand men, plus women and children! (Matthew 14: 13–21) Do you think that God can't supply your needs? We have favor with God! We are His children!

God's favor surrounds us like a shield. Psalm 5:12 NIV.

Christians do not need to cross their fingers or desperately look for 4-leaf clovers, wishing and hoping that something will happen, but instead put their faith, hope, and trust in Jesus. I love the old hymn that speaks truth, "My hope is built on nothing less than Jesus' blood and His righteousness. I dare not trust the sweetest frame but wholly lean on Jesus's name. On Christ the solid Rock I stand, all other ground is sinking sand." The world will offer temporary, superficial solutions and hopes, but we must trust our Heavenly Father's Word, which is eternal. Please do not give up! Trust God and His timing. Give Him thanks for all He has done, is doing, and will do in your life. Your miracle is on its way!

With God ALL things are possible. Matthew 19:26 NIV.

While on the road with the Slaughters, traveling all across the United States, I began to experience major headaches almost every day. They weren't migraines, but painful enough to make me miserable and ruin my day. These headaches were considered a major storm in my life. One particular day while experiencing another headache, sweet Hazel asked everyone on our bus to gather around and pray for God to heal me of these headaches. Immediately my mind went back to the miracle service where I had witnessed the man in the wheel chair being healed. I thought, *Would God heal ME?* Well, I'm here to tell you, my friends, that after they prayed, the daily headaches quickly went away. Yes, I was healed! God had healed me! It made a total believer out of me. Yes, God still heals! I thought to myself, *What else about Jesus am I missing?*

At that point in my life, a hunger grew in my heart for more of God. I had finally come to a place where I wasn't concerned about denominations or religions; I just wanted to know more about Jesus. I began reading almost every Christian book I could get my hand on. Hazel gave me a Katherine Kuhlman book on healing, which was full of testimonies of healings. I had never heard of this woman before or read any of her books. I recall reading how God healed so many in her healing services. As I read, I would have to stop and cry. I was so moved in my heart that God loves us so much. Yes, God loved Bill too. I knew in my heart that my eyes were being opened to a greater power of God than I had known before.

Now some of you might disagree with my beliefs on God's amazing power to heal today. Sorry, no debate. I'm just sharing with you what I experienced. I don't think we'll completely understand and comprehend the ways of God until Heaven. Let's continue in our daily walk with God to pray for the sick and those hurting, believing His Word.

And a woman was there who had been subject to bleeding for twelve years. She had suffered a great deal under the care of many doctors and had spent all she had, yet instead of getting better she grew worse. When she heard about Jesus, she came up behind him in the crowd and touched his cloak, because she thought, "If I just touch his clothes, I will be healed." Immediately her bleeding stopped and she felt in her body that she was freed from her suffering.

At once Jesus realized that power, had gone out from him. He turned around in the crowd and asked, "Who touched my clothes?"

"You see the people crowding against you," his disciples answered, "and yet you can ask, 'Who touched me?'"

But Jesus kept looking around to see who had done it. Then the woman, knowing what had happened to her, came and fell at his feet and, trembling with fear, told him the whole truth. He said to her, "Daughter, your faith has healed you. Go in peace and be freed from your suffering." Mark 5:25 NIV.

If you are suffering with pain or a major life storm, pray and believe! Go back to the scripture of Jesus healing all that were sick and oppressed. He also instructed His disciples that greater things would they do than He. Wow! That's big! Please don't give up on your prayer life. Don't give up on your miracle! God cares about you. Pray and believe no matter what you're facing. Jesus will bring you through your storm! Your faith will bring forth your miracle!

Ask and it will be given to you; seek and you will find; knock and the door will be opened to you. For everyone who asks receives; he who seeks finds; and to him who knocks, the door will be opened. Matthew 7:7 NIV.

Soon after my study on healings and God's miracles, I began to hunger for more of God. My second spiritual dream was during this time of hunger. I dreamed I was lying on my back in my bed, telling God how much I loved Him when suddenly I began to rise toward the ceiling. It was an awesome feeling! When I reached the ceiling of my bedroom, I knew it was stopping me from receiving all I craved, so I immediately begin begging for more of Jesus. Suddenly, I went through the ceiling! That's almost like a rapture experience! I then awoke, humbled and blessed that I had experienced God in another spiritual dream!

Questions:

1. Do I really believe that God heals today?
2. Have I fully trusted Him for my healing and the healing of those I love?

The prayer offered in faith will make the sick person well; the Lord will raise him up. James 5:15 NIV.

Let's pray:

Father, I pray you will help me grow in you. You are the potter and I am the clay. Place me on the potter's wheel and mold and make me into the image of Jesus so I can make a difference in others' lives. Teach me your ways, oh Lord. I believe that you heal today! I desire more of you. In Jesus's name, amen.

HOME AGAIN

Near the end of 1976, the Holy Spirit began speaking to me about moving back to Mississippi. I believed in my heart God had wanted me in Nashville for a season to gain revelation and insight into His Word, but now it was time to take what I had learned home.

After leaving Nashville, I was hired as a minister of music and youth in a Mississippi church about five hours from my home. I enjoyed the church and worked hard to build my music and youth program. But friends, if we don't keep our spiritual fire lit, it can go out. When I took the church position, I was on fire for God. I desired to change the world for Jesus. But I was not grounded in the Word like I needed to be. Eventually, my strong desire and passion began to fade due to long hours of church work, eventually causing burnout. Yes, if ministers aren't careful, they can lose their passion for God even doing church work. We should always begin our day with Jesus and remain in His presence, which I wasn't doing. The devil loves for us to get side-tracked with various activities, especially with exhaustion.

God tells us that His Word, the Bible, is a lamp unto our feet and a light unto our path. His Word will show us the way. We shouldn't have to spend our days confused about His will. His Word is available to show us the path to travel. Think of God's Word as a flashlight shining down a dark path. If we keep the light turned on, we'll be able to see the path we're walking down and find our way. Unfortunately, many Christians never open their Bible. My friend, prayer and God's Word go hand in hand. They work together, not separately. Think of God's Word as an anchor for your ship. When the storms of life hit, it will hold you steadfast. I encourage you to begin reading and meditating on the Word accompanied with prayer. It will completely change your life and help you grow stronger in your Christian walk. When we become grounded in His Word, we're better equipped to face the storms that hit us. And trust me, we will all be hit with storms. Thank God, Jesus will be with us through each storm and each step we take afterwards. That's a promise!

I believe God used me in my time with this church to plant spiritual seeds into the lives of the young people. I desired to see their lives change for Jesus. He opened the door for me to counsel and mentor many youth. Being young, I felt I did a good job with the church. Of course, many mistakes and bad decisions were made along the way, but that's part of growing. Thank God for grace.

The church was kind to me, but I truly missed my Laurel home and family. So my being homesick and allowing the pressures of daily church work to weigh me down, I finally resigned and moved home to Laurel where I began to teach music in a local high school.

I tried to pray daily but didn't discipline myself to study God's Word and pray on a daily basis. Instead of getting up early to spend time with God, I chose to sleep late. Because of the lack of being daily grounded in God's Word, my relationship with God and others stayed on a roller coaster ride. There would be days that I would be up and feeling spiritually powerful and then days where I would plummet into the valley. I'm sure you know what I'm talking about. Good moods, bad moods. This emotional roller coaster ride really took a toll on many of my relationships. I look back and recall being so lonely at times. I was grasping at straws, trying to fulfill my emotional needs. Not only did I jump from one relationship to another, I also spent a lot of money trying to make myself happy. There were times I tried to buy friendships by being the big spender and paying for everyone's fun times. I wanted to be the life of the party and I deeply desired for everyone to like me, but it only got worse. I ended up broke and lonelier. I felt like the prodigal son.

There was a man who had two sons. The younger one said to his father, "Father, give me my share of the estate." So he divided his property between them. Not long after that, the younger son got together all he had, set off for a distant country and there squandered his wealth in wild living. After he had spent everything, there was a severe famine in that whole country, and he began to be in need. So he went and hired himself out to a citizen of that country, who sent him to his fields to feed pigs. He longed to fill his stomach with the pods that the pigs were eating, but no one gave him anything. When he came to his senses, he said, "How many of my father's hired men have food to spare, and here I am starving to death! I will set out and go back to my father and say to him: father, I have sinned against heaven and against you. I am no longer worthy to be called your son; make me like one of your hired men." So he got up and went to his father. But while he was still a long way off, his father saw him and was filled with compassion for him; he ran to his son, threw his arms around him and kissed him. The son said to him, "Father, I have sinned against heaven and against you. I am no longer worthy to be called your son." But the father said to his servants, "Quick! Bring the best robe and put it on him. Put a ring on his finger and sandals on his feet. Bring the fattened calf and kill it." Let's have a feast and celebrate. For this son of mine was dead and is alive again, he was lost and is found. So they began to celebrate. Luke 15:11 NIV.

I didn't realize at the time but the lonely prodigal days were storms in my life and they were rough. I caught myself crying and feeling lonely, seeing others happy in their relationships while I felt miserable. I recall one late evening as I was getting exercise by walking the football track in our local stadium, I began to feel that lonely, empty feeling. My feeling so sorry for myself reached its pinnacle and I just leaned against the brick wall in the stadium and cried. The pain was real. I was hurting. I look back and ponder why didn't I just go to my knees and look to God who desired to fulfill my every need, even the loneliness? I was praying, but just not spending enough fellowship time with my Father.

The biggest problem I discovered was that I wasn't listening and trusting. A relationship with God isn't based on us doing all the talking; it's a two–way conversation between us and God. I had experienced many moves of God over the years. At times, I would feel so close to Him and other times felt far away. Goodness, He was patient with me! I think back and realize that I wasn't able to love, forgive and care for others the way He did for me. I really wasn't that good of a friend to others. But my God loved me before I was born and still loved me unconditionally. My Savior, my Redeemer, my Counselor, my Friend, my Companion...... Jesus.

Come near to God and he will come near to you. James 6:8 NIV.

Now let me stop here and state that I will take all the blame for my past failed relationships. Some of it was due to bad choices, but mostly I knew deep in my heart that this particular person wasn't God's will for me. Yes, I was involved in quite a few relationships. One dear lady once told me that I had been involved in relationships more times than most people would go to Wal–Mart. Okay, this subject on relationships goes back to seeking God about all aspects of our life. If I had really been praying and studying God's Word, I could have avoided hurting many friends and also avoided being hurt. You see, God has a plan for each of us. He has a plan just for you! Think of life as a journey traveling down a major road filled with many turnoffs and detours. If we will consult our GPS (the Holy Spirit) we can stay on a clearly designed road which will bring us to our calling (destination) sooner.

But when he, the Spirit of truth, comes, he will guide you into all truth. John 16:13 NIV.

If we'll look to the Holy Spirit to guide us in each area of our lives, we can avoid many pitfalls and wrong turns down the road of life. He desires for us to see truth and follow after it. What is truth? Jesus.......

Jesus said, I am the way, and the truth, and the life. John 14:6 NIV.

A successful relationship with God comes from spending time with Him daily. In my opinion, attending church once a week isn't sufficient to maintain a deep relationship with God. It's choosing to spend time with Him daily in worship, prayer, and His Word. Please don't misunderstand me, attending church is good, but talking to God should be part of our daily life and not just once–a–week corporate prayer. Many feel by attending church once a week, they are okay. The problem is they are missing out on a beautiful relationship with Jesus. I know in my life, I got to a place that I wanted more. I thought, *If this is all there is, why keep going to church?* I kept reading in the Bible about the passion the disciples had and realized it was that passion that I desired. I truly wanted to be different from so many of my friends, who were miserable much of the time. Bottom line: I wanted more of God.

If we're going to have successful relationships, we must put God first.

Beloved, let us love one another for love is of God. Everyone who loves has been born of God and knows God. Whoever does not love does not know God, because God is love. 1 John 4: 7–8 NIV.

True love comes from God because God is love. If we don't have love flowing between God and us, what do we have to give to others? When we put God first and spend quality time with Him, the love that's flowing between God and us will flow into others. This revelation is important. Have you noticed that when you are worshiping God in church, you have so much love to give? You will see many men with their arms lovingly around their wives. We're happy and peaceful because we feel the love of God. There's no desire to argue, fight or demand our own way. When we're worshiping with our whole heart, we begin taking on the character of Jesus. Friend, we could avoid a lot of turmoil in our lives if we would just put Him first and allow Him to handle our problems.

I felt in my heart that I had taught the students well, not just in the area of music, but also spiritually. I recall there were many prayers prayed before various shows I directed. My heart was to see lives changed for the better. I desired for my students to recognize where their talents had come from and how God wanted to use them. As time allowed, I helped them receive music scholarships and also spiritual food that would stay with them into their adult life.

In May 1986, after six years of teaching, I decided it was time to resign from my teaching position and discover a new adventure. I was literally exhausted from teaching school. I had tried to do it all. I taught and coached students in show choir, dance team, cheerleaders, beauty pageants, pep rallies, etc. My ship was facing storms, and I had neglected to rely on God to navigate me. I look back over those sweet years realizing that even though I worked hard to instill spiritual values into my students, I had taken on too much, feeling the need for approval from others to build my own self–worth. I was, what you would label, a people pleaser. I wanted so much for everyone to like me that I would go out of my way to make it happen. I understand now that my approval comes from God, not man. If you have been looking to things to man for self–worth and approval, decide today that you will surrender to Jesus and allow Him to fulfill you. Only Jesus can satisfy your soul.

After resigning my teaching position, I felt the wooing from the Holy Spirit to come back to Nashville again (ten years later after the time before). I made the decision to temporarily live with Henry and Hazel Slaughter again until I could find work and get my own apartment. Now, I say "work," but I actually moved to Nashville with the thoughts that God would probably make me a star! Reflecting back over that particular time, I realize that my loving Father actually brought me back to Nashville to show more revelation to me. What was it about Nashville? It seemed to be my oasis for spiritual refreshing. The Holy Spirit was drawing me closer to Him, but I was confused and felt that being a star in Nashville would give me a platform to speak about Jesus and that would be a good thing! I do admire celebrities who will take a stand for Christ. They can be very influential. But God had different plans for me.

Questions:

1. Have I truly prayed and trusted God in each step of my life?

2. Do I believe I am important enough to God that He has specific plans for me?

Jesus said, I am the light of the world. Whoever follows me will never walk in darkness, but will have the light of life. John 8:12 NIV.

Let's pray:

Father, forgive me for the times I have neglected you. My time with you is vital to my growth as a Christian. Help me discipline myself to daily fellowship with you. I recognize that I need you in my life. Your decisions should be my decisions and Your will, my will. I love you, God. In your precious son Jesus's name, amen.

Nashville Again?

Upon my arrival in Music City (Nashville) for the second time, I began taking acting and modeling classes. I noticed that every time I went to an interview or audition for a showbiz gig, I would be faced with other male contenders that were tall, and handsome with a head full of hair. (This was the late eighties.) I couldn't fix my height problem but I went to a wig store in Nashville and discovered thick hair. I bought a full–haired wig for my auditions. I thought I was so cool–looking that I began to wear it more and more until eventually it was full time. After taking several classes, I decided to compete in a national commercial writing/modeling contest in Nashville, thinking this could open many stardom doors for me. In spite of my eyes being full of stars, God blessed me. I competed and won second runner–up in runway modeling and first place commercial writing and production. I was so excited, believing this would be the start of something very big! I accepted my trophies and accolades at a beautiful awards dinner where several country stars were in attendance, and was then off to become famous. I was positively convinced my phone would be ringing with many top agencies begging to book me for work. I actually remember sitting on my couch staring at the house phone waiting for it to ring. I was convinced my stardom had arrived! I thought, *Here I am, world! I'm ready!*

But negative.

The phone seemed to be very, very silent. I did get called by one lone agency who "loved me" so much that they wanted me to sign up for various modeling and acting classes. I was to pay them to become famous? I decided against the idea and actually joined a smaller agency who finally called and booked me for my first "famous" modeling job. I was to model restaurant clothing for a convention of buyers at the Opryland Hotel. Yes, I was modeling aprons and kitchen uniforms. Really famous, wasn't I? I think I might have made $125 for my first big gig! Later, I did pick up one commercial print for a hotel chain's spring and summer brochure where I had to sit by a pool in the dead winter dressed in a swimsuit with my feet dangling in the pool. I was to appear like it was summertime sitting casually by the poolside. They barely paid anything, and I finished the shooting with my feet half frozen. And not to forget the infamous cable commercial about retail hot tubs where I sat boiling in a hot tub for hours not able to verbally say anything. Do you know how challenging it is to act cool in a hot tub for hours, with a smile on your face? I felt like a lobster in a boiling pot. Yeah, that cable commercial didn't cause the phone to ring much or open any doors for big jobs. I soon began to realize that my Hollywood star and my appearance on the red carpet weren't in the making at that time; so I ended up substitute-teaching in the Nashville school system to make financial ends meet.

While living in Nashville I decided to attend church with Henry and Hazel, who were members of Belmont Church near Music Row. The church had an "early bird" prayer time each morning, Monday through Friday, to begin the day with worship and prayer. Hazel really encouraged me to go with them to the prayer time. So one morning I reluctantly staggered out of bed, putting on the nearest clothes I could find, and fell into the back seat of their car for the ride to Belmont Church. To my surprise, it was great. I felt the anointing of God moving among the people that were present. The group was an eclectic group of musicians, ministers, and average Joes like me. I felt the anointing of God moving among the people that were present. I almost hated to leave when it concluded. After just a morning or two, I began to feel the Lord tugging at my heart to draw closer to Him. I knew then I was hooked and began to crave more of God.

You will call upon me and come and pray to me, and I will listen. You will seek me and find me when you seek me with all your heart. I WILL be found by you, declares the Lord. Jeremiah 29: 12–14 NIV.

Those special prayer times changed my life for the better, and I looked forward to them each morning. Each day that I attended, I could feel my life changing for the better. I began to feel peace about my life, knowing my Father God was in control. I even attended Sunday mornings and Wednesday evening services at Belmont. I ceased worrying about my life and the direction I was to go. I began leaning on God to guide me. This gave me a sweet peace that I hadn't experienced before. Each service, I would find myself seeking God for my life which included praying for a godly wife. I was very lonely and realized I was tired of making a mess of my life and making my own decisions. I wanted to give God my whole life. It was a sweet time of surrender, desiring God's will. When I decided to move to Nashville this time, I made a conscious decision to not date anyone until I knew that it was from God. Did you know that He's calling each of us to that very thing, surrender? It's the way to peace. When we finally decide to step aside and allow God the freedom to steer our ship, we can avoid much heartache and turmoil. This time, I was determined to rely on him for every decision and determined to get grounded in His Word.

But seek first his kingdom and his righteousness, and all these things will be given to you as well. Matthew 6:33 NIV.

It's so easy to have our attention on what we are praying for, whether it's our needs or wants. But our loving Father asks that we seek him first. It's a trust factor. God is lovingly telling us to trust Him in what we are praying for and desiring by putting our attention on Him, and not on our circumstances and situations. With our focus on worshiping and thanking Him, we don't have time to ponder over how to help God solve our problems. We begin to trust that He will take care of us. He always answers our prayers according to His will. Like a parent, He does what's best for His children. Today, I urge you to continue believing for your miracle, but make your time with your Father a priority. Trust Him with all your heart and let Him handle your prayer requests.

Questions:

1. Have I surrendered each part of my life to God, including career, relationships and hurts by laying them at the foot of the cross?

2. Have I allowed myself to think that God doesn't care about the small areas of my life, and instead expects me to handle and make decisions regarding these?

I am confident of this very thing that he who began a good work in you will carry it on to completion until the day of Christ Jesus. Philippians 1:6 NIV.

Let's pray:

Dear God, I believe you will supply all my needs according to your will. I surrender my life to you. Father, I acknowledge that I need you in my life. I desire the plans that you have for me, knowing you love me and always do what's best for me. I love you, God! In Jesus's name. Amen.

LOVE

L is for the way you look at me

O is for the only one I see

V is very very extra ordinary

E is even more than anyone that I adore

One Sunday morning while in worship at Belmont Church, I looked across the mass auditorium which held a couple thousand members and saw this beautiful young woman worshipping God. I just couldn't take my eyes off her. How I spotted her in the large crowd of a couple thousand church members had to have been God. I just felt in my heart something was right about this young lady. I caught myself glancing over at her throughout the worship. I should have been paying attention to the service! I just couldn't get her image out of my mind. Was this the girl for me? Standing there in the midst of the service I began to pray that if she was the one for me, she would come to church on Wednesday evening, which was a much smaller crowd, and I would introduce myself to her. I waited with great anticipation for Wednesday evening to arrive. That afternoon, I took a lot of time getting dressed. But to my dismay, she wasn't there! I was so disappointed and thought to myself that I had missed God on this one. Friends, our plans aren't always God's plans. There's a lesson in trust here.

The following Sunday morning, I went to church as usual. I was a bit early. While I was sitting there waiting for the service to begin, this same beautiful lady who hadn't been at church on Wednesday evening came in the building and sat directly in the seat in front of me! In that large auditorium of people, she sat right in front of me! To make matters more exciting, Pastor Don Finto began the service by asking everyone to stand and greet those around us! This was an unusual request for the service. Again, it just had to be God! This beautiful woman immediately stood up, turned around, looked me in the eyes, shook my hand and said, "Hi, I'm Teri Braddy." I wanted to reply, "Hi, I'm Bill, your future husband!" Of course, I did refrain from that comment. Needless to say, I didn't concentrate on the sermon that morning either. All I could think of was, *Wow! She is sitting right in front of me! God, this is so cool!*

After service, we chatted, and she invited me to the church singles Thanksgiving meal that she was involved in. During that week, I called her several times asking questions about the Thanksgiving meal. Of course, I didn't care about the details of the dinner; I just wanted to talk to her. I went to the Thanksgiving gathering and really got to know her. She worked hard helping to prepare the festive meal for all the singles that weren't going home for the holidays.

My family chuckled that I must have really liked her to choose to stay in Nashville and eat a Thanksgiving meal with her instead of coming home to be with family. I hardly ever missed Thanksgiving with the family. After the blessing was spoken, she plopped on the couch in exhaustion, allowing everyone else to go through the line first. I thought this was my big chance to make an impression, so I prepared her plate first and brought it to her. And, it worked! She was impressed!

More phone conversations during the week and meals after church services developed. I just felt in my heart that Teri was the one that God had chosen for me. Unfortunately, being a woman, she didn't feel the same at first. She felt I was rushing things. She even left me a voice message one Wednesday afternoon on my answering machine that explained that I was moving too fast with my emotions and needed to slow down so our relationship could develop and we could get to know one another better. Well, as a man, I just thought, when you know, you know! Ha!

At first, I was offended with her message and decided, in my pride, that I would go to church that night but wouldn't sit with her. Yep, I'd show her! If she desired for me to slow down in our relationship, that's what I'd do! I thought, *She'll be saving a seat for me, but I'll just smile, politely decline and sit somewhere else.* When I arrived and looked around I couldn't find her. At that same moment in my prideful thinking, I felt a tap on my shoulders and guess who? It was Teri who had been running late. She whispered, "Sorry I'm late. Find a seat and I'll follow." God quickly squelched my prideful "I'll-show–you" attitude. We sat together and had a wonderful time. During the service I asked God to forgive me of pride. I was already realizing she was a true gift to me from my Heavenly Father. He loved me! Teri and I regularly prayed together as a couple for His will to be done in our lives and from that, we developed a deep love for each other.

Okay, remember reading about the wig? Well, one night near Christmas 1986, we had planned to attend a formal church banquet held at the gorgeous Opryland Hotel. We were so excited and really planned for the event. The night before the banquet, I was baking cookies in my apartment. When the timer rang, I opened the oven to remove the cookies. The oven was hot and my face was hit with heat, but I thought nothing of it. As I previously mentioned, I had begun to wear the modeling wig full time. After removing the cookies from the oven, I went to the bathroom to wash my hands. When I looked into the mirror I was horrified to find that my synthetic wig was burned up! Yep, the front was all melted off from the heat of the oven! I stood there staring at myself in the mirror with complete panic! What would I do? The banquet was the next night! I frantically began trying to call the owner of the wig store to no avail. The next morning, I called her when she opened her business and shared my story. (I think she secretly laughed.) But unfortunately, she was out of the particular color of wig I had been wearing. All she had available in this style was black. Ugh! I had no choice but to wear it. I did call Teri and forewarn her that my "hair color" had changed! (Teri knew all the time I was wearing the wig but didn't want to bring up the subject.) That night at the banquet, I looked like an Elvis impersonator. I believe Teri was thankful the day I quit wearing the synthetic poof. Bottom line, we should always be honest and truthful. It makes life much easier.

As you make decisions as important as marriage, relationships, and etc., pray and seek your loving Father. Read in the Bible about Abraham who desperately wanted a son. God spoke to him and told him he would give him a son. But, Abraham got weary of waiting on God's perfect timing, so he and his wife Sarah took matters into their own hands and developed their own plan to have a son. You see, they felt the need to "help" God with the matter. Well, they got a son all right. It was Ishmael, which wasn't God's blessing. After repenting, they waited on God and received their beautiful son, Isaac, God's choice. There is a major lesson to be learned here about waiting on God to provide the best.

Wait for the Lord; be strong and take heart and wait for the Lord. Psalm 27: 14 NIV.

Receiving God's best for us can be completely opposite of what we think it should be. For example, I always wanted a wife who would sing duets with me. Yep, I thought we make great music together and travel the world. But my loving God gave me a beautiful wife who really wasn't a musician but had a great appreciation for it. Instead, Teri is analytical where I'm creative.

She's strong in financial planning where I'm not. Bottom line, God gave me my opposite to complete me. God's Word states the two shall become one. That's exactly what He did for me. For every area I'm weak in, she is strong and vice versa. We complete each other. Friends, when we decide to trust God in all matters of our lives, we can receive a beautiful blessing. I encourage you, young and old, to seek God with your whole heart regarding decisions that you normally make such as schools, jobs, marriage, and relationships. God will not steer you wrong....His way is always the best.

All the days ordained for me were written in your book, O Lord, before one of them came to be. Psalm 139:16 NIV.

Nothing surprises God! Sometimes we feel He gets shocked over our sins and bad choices. Friends, He knew before we were born what choices we would make. Our loving Father is never surprised, caught off guard, or shocked over our decisions. He's the Alpha and Omega, the beginning and the end, and He has beautiful plans for us!

I know the plans I have for you, declares the Lord, plans to prosper you and not to harm you, plans to give you hope and a future. Jeremiah 29:11 NIV.

God's plans for us are always beautiful, full of prosperity and hope. We have to "choose" to follow His direction or follow ours. Sometimes our minds can get very independent when it comes to choices and decisions, feeling we know what's best. That independence will cause us to avoid seeking God's guidance through prayer and His Word. We've all heard the old saying, "God gave us a brain and we should use it." Yes, He did give us a brain, but he desires for us to follow Him. Personally, there were times in my past when I would get weary and exhausted from making my own choices, desperately trying to open a closed door. If I had only taken time to seek God with a listening ear and heart, I would have avoided many bad decisions which gave me much heartache. Through the years, I have learned to rely on my

Heavenly Father by trusting His will for my life. He definitely knows more than me and His ways are much better than mine.

The Lord is good to those whose hope is in Him, to the one who seeks Him; it is good to wait quietly for the salvation (wholeness) of the Lord. Lamentations 3: 25–26 NIV.

Waiting and relying on God is worth it. He desires to direct us down the right path that will bless us. Today, let's begin by seeking His will for our lives. Because He has a special plan for us daily, let's not waste a single day by ignoring Him.

Dear friends, His plans for us can also be fun! Yes, following God's will can give us joy, peace and a good time!

Questions:

1. Have I truly sought God regarding my decision making?
2. Do I believe in my heart He has a chosen path designed especially for me to follow?

O Lord, you have made known to me the path of life. Psalm 16:11 NIV.

Let's pray:

God, I know in my heart you have specific plans for me and you always want the best for me. My life is yours, O Lord. I pray I will stay close to you and not pull away from your will for my life. Thank you for helping me grow spiritually. I desire all of you. I pray in Jesus's name. Amen.

WILL YOU MARRY ME?

As the following Valentine's Day, 1987 approached, I knew I wanted to ask Teri to marry me, but my financial resources were zero. My only income at this particular time was substitute teaching. After paying rent for my apartment, my extra cash was very scarce. I prayed about what to do. My past history of trying to impress would have driven me to take her to the finest restaurant in Nashville with flowers, but God had been changing me. Yes, I was on the Potter's wheel, and He was molding me to be more like Jesus. Knowing all I had to offer was myself, I planned an inexpensive spaghetti dinner out of a jar and box at my apartment. There were also a few left-over crepe paper streamers available to hang around the apartment to make the Valentine holiday "romantic."

From the moment Teri arrived at my tiny apartment this Valentine's night, I tried very hard to make the evening special. We ate our store–bought spaghetti dinner with candlelight and music in the background (tape player). My heart was racing and beating so loudly because this would be the night I would ask her to be become my wife. I hardly had any appetite.

After our dinner, we sat on the couch sharing our feelings, hopes, and dreams. When I felt the moment was right, I went to the kitchen and brought back a large basin of water and a cloth. I shared with her that I loved her with all my heart and wanted us to spend the rest of our lives together. I then humbly knelt down on the floor in front of her as she sat on the couch. I explained how Jesus loved His disciples and chose to wash their feet as a sign of laying His life down for them through love. I then removed her shoes and gently and lovingly began to wash her feet, telling her what she meant to me and praying for us as I washed. We both cried many tears of love and thankfulness. When I finished, I asked her to marry me. Praise God, through our tears, she answered yes! The Spirit of God was in my apartment that night, and He was blessing our relationship. Even though there was zero money available in my bank account to purchase an engagement ring, we felt so happy and complete. I could have looked at my poor financial situation as a major storm in my life hindering me from giving her an expensive romantic evening, but instead chose to be thankful that my loving Father had answered my prayers about giving me a Godly woman who would soon be my wife. I am sharing this story to encourage you in whatever you're facing. What He did for me, He'll do for you.

It was just before the Passover Festival. Jesus knew that the hour had come for him to leave this world and go to the Father. Having loved his own who were in the world, He loved them to the end.

The evening meal was in progress, and the devil had already prompted Judas, the son of Simon Iscariot, to betray Jesus. Jesus knew that the Father had put all things under his power, and that he had come from God and was returning to God; so he got up from the meal, took off his outer clothing, and wrapped a towel around his waist. After that, he poured water into a basin and began to wash his disciples' feet, drying them with the towel that was wrapped around him.

He came to Simon Peter, who said to him, "Lord, are you going to wash my feet?"

Jesus replied, "You do not realize now what I am doing, but later you will understand."

"No," said Peter, "you shall never wash my feet."

Jesus answered, "Unless I wash you, you have no part with me."

"Then, Lord," Simon Peter replied, "not just my feet but my hands and my head as well!"

Jesus answered, "Those who have had a bath need only to wash their feet; their whole body is clean. And you are clean, though not every one of you." For he knew who was going to betray him, and that was why he said not every one was clean.

When he had finished washing their feet, he put on his clothes and returned to his place. "Do you understand what I have done for you?" he asked them. "You call me 'Teacher' and 'Lord,' and rightly so, for that is what I am. Now that I, your Lord and Teacher, have washed your feet, you also should wash one another's feet. I have set you an example that you should do as I have done for you. Very truly I tell you, no servant is greater than his master, nor is a messenger greater than the one who sent him. Now that you know these things, you will be blessed if you do them. John 13:1–17 NIV.

To be like Jesus is my desire.

From February to August we planned our wedding and married August 15, 1987, in Nashville. God provided the finances for us to purchase the beautiful ring she had wanted the spring before the wedding (another answer to our prayer). To us, our wedding was beautiful. All our planning was centered on God. For our ceremony, we chose a historic Methodist church in downtown Nashville because of its beauty and historical pipe organ.

The day of our wedding, I felt quiet and subdued. I was extremely happy and peaceful, but didn't want to say much. I basically felt like crying. Our godly pastor, Don Finto, sat with me just before the ceremony and explained that what I was feeling was the anointing of God upon my life. It was beautiful and peaceful. The anointing was strong, causing me to be humble in His presence. Yes, I believe humility describes what I was feeling. Waiting for the service to begin, I felt His love, His comfort, direction, and approval that I was in His will. I don't believe I will ever forget the awesome feeling of His presence.

Through prayer and a desire for a spiritual wedding service, the beautiful hymn "Holy, Holy, Holy" was chosen to be played on the pipe organ for Teri's entrance. The foyer doors opened at just the right moment, on the arm of her dad, my bride entered the sanctuary looking beautiful and radiant. I will always remember her smiling at me with such love in her eyes. From the moment she took her first step into the sanctuary, it seemed the anointing became stronger, and tears began running down my cheeks. All I could think was how much I truly loved Teri and was so blessed to have her become my wife. I was engulfed with a heart of thanksgiving to my loving Father God. Looking back at the video of our wedding, it seemed that my tears caused every woman in the sanctuary to cry with me.

My dad stood beside me as my best man, and my older brother Buddy, who was a minister, took part in the ceremony. Henry and Hazel Slaughter sang several selections, one of which Henry had written especially for our wedding. The wedding was full of beautiful memories.

Our Wedding Song

Words and music by Henry Slaughter

Lord, we gather here in your presence, as before and will again; to worship, praise and adore You, and glorify Your name. Declaring our love to each other, making these solemn vows, to love and serve forever through all the days of our lives.

In our home we will lift up Jesus, and look to Him each day, to guide us in each step we take, following in all His ways. Walking in His precepts, obeying his commands, establishing His kingdom in our hearts as together we will stand.

And He will be Lord in our home.

Thank you, Uncle Henry.

Just after our beautiful honeymoon to Disney World, we were snuggled in our home, and I was watching a Christian TV show. I began to feel in my heart God speaking to me to sow a large financial seed into this particular television ministry. I knew I heard from God and obeyed, but I failed to discuss the plan with Teri. Oops! Being new in our marriage, I literally wasn't thinking. Thank God for Teri's forgiveness and my Father's grace. She desired God as much as I did, but it was a good marriage policy to discuss spending big amounts before actually doing it! Thank God for grace. Just after sowing the financial seed, somewhere around three weeks after our wedding, Teri was offered a promotion and pay raise with BellSouth. The only obstacle was that the job would require a transfer to Birmingham, Alabama. After praying about the matter, she took the promotion and we moved to Birmingham. This was a blessing since my family lived in Mississippi. Remember, I sowed a seed and it grew into a blessing of a harvest. I truly believe God blessed us. Hint: Always discuss matters of spending with your spouse before taking action.

It was neat how God began our marriage by moving us away from all our loved single friends in Nashville. Even though we missed them terribly, we instantly met and bonded with other married couples in Birmingham and thus began our new journey as a married couple, Bill and Teri Myers.

We bought a new house under construction in the south Birmingham area. Before the painter began painting the walls, we went into the house and wrote our names on the living room wall as a declaration of our love and marriage. We loved our first house and felt right at home. Of course, we knew we needed a church, so I went to a local Christian bookstore in the area and inquired about churches that were on fire for God. We were told to visit a particular church, Pelham Christian Fellowship, which met in an old store front.

We decided to visit and immediately got hooked. We felt peace the moment we entered the doors of the church. Pelham

Christian Fellowship became home to us. God opened the door for us to develop friendships with many married couples. I also discovered the church hosted early morning prayer meetings, so I quickly joined them and became part of the prayer group. I remember experiencing some wonderful spiritual answers to prayers during those morning meetings, which brought back memories of the Belmont morning prayer meetings I had experienced in Nashville. Prayer changes everything!

As the church outgrew the store front, the decision was made to build a new church building down the street, and the church became Covenant Life Church. Many wonderful relationships and memories were made in this church.

One day, when I had too much time on my hands, I came across a piano store in downtown Birmingham that restored old pianos and was run by a blind man. He was a very kind and gentle man who was fascinating to watch as he tuned pianos. He had a seventy-five year old baby grand piano for sale that he had personally refinished and tuned. It was historic and completely beautiful. I had always wanted a baby grand, so I bought it right there on the spot! When Teri got home from work, I asked, "Guess what I bought today?" She thought for a minute and noticed the sheer curtain on the kitchen window. When I told her I had bought a baby grand piano, there was stunned silence. I look back and realize that wasn't a very smart move on my part. What was I thinking? I did it again! I bought a major investment without discussing it with my wife. The problem I had was that my brain was still thinking as a single instead of a married partner. If I saw something I wanted, my first thought was purchase it instead of calling Teri and discussing whether we could afford it. It wasn't that she had to give me permission, but we had chosen to become one in our marriage and it was the right thing to do to discuss matters with her first. Oh, the lessons I learned the first few years of marriage adjustments!

Communication, my friends, is the key to a successful marriage. No two people are going to think alike. Everyone's different. Couples need to communicate regularly to avoid pitfalls in their marriage or relationships. If someone tells you their marriage is problem–free, they lied and don't have much of a marriage. Any two people living under the same roof will have conflict every now and then. People just think differently. This also applies to roommates sharing the same living space, people that work together, etc. We're all programmed to think we're right; but others think and do things differently. This doesn't mean that either is wrong, just different. I have always laughed about newlyweds discussing whether commode lids stay in the up or down position. This goes back to communication. There isn't necessarily a right or wrong way. Couples should talk about matters and reach a compromise. Coming from ministry background where I counseled many couples, Teri and I talked about this issue before we were married and agreed to adjust as we go. If it's up and you need it down, then put it down, and vice versa. We decided to get separate sinks as soon as we could to avoid toothpaste tube issues, etc. Communication, my friends, is the key.

Your attitude should be the same as that of Christ Jesus. Philippians 2:5 NIV.

Most of us have heard the old cliché, "I am who I am and that's just the way it is, and people can get over it!" Being a teacher, I've heard this statement often from students who make excuses for what they say or do. As Christians, we should be conscience of what we say and do. When we allow ourselves to be molded by God into the image of Jesus, we take on the same characteristics and nature of Jesus. We learn to refrain from being negative and gossipers. We begin to look for the best in others, instead of tearing them down.

God also encourages us in Ephesians 5:1 to be "imitators of Christ as dearly beloved children." As children love to imitate what they see and repeat what they hear; we also are charged to imitate and model Christ's behavior and to be clear reflections of the Lord (Matthew 5:16)."

To be Christ–like is freedom. To desire to be like Jesus is to feel as if the heavy weights of the world have been removed from our shoulders. Freedom!

How we choose to treat others is a witness to the world, good or bad. Yes, each of us represents a fruit bearing tree. We either bear good fruit like love, joy, peace, kindness, gentleness, etc., or our tree bears bad fruit which is the opposite of good fruit. Friends, we are known by our fruit. Do we really have to "tell and convince" people that we are a Christian or can they see it in our lives in the way we treat others and handle life's problems.

Facing problems and storms doesn't make us strong. But rather how we handle the problems and storms and what attitude we display can make us strong and a witness to the world for God.

Do nothing out of selfish ambition or vain conceit. Rather, in humility value others above yourselves, not looking to your own interests but each of you to the interests of the others. Philippians 2: 3–4 NIV.

How does this work? No, we can't make it happen. But as we spend time daily with our Heavenly Father, our attitude will change for the better. The time in worship and prayer we spend with God will cover us with love for Him which will flow from us to others. You can't give to others what you don't have. Just as a car can run out of gas and need to be refueled, we need to refresh ourselves with God daily.

The steadfast love of the Lord never ceases, his mercies never come to an end; they are new EVERY MORNING; great is your faithfulness. Lamentations 2:2–3 NIV.

Let's not run on yesterday's fuel, but spend time with God each day and allow Jesus to shine through us to others! Our time with God will help us be better communicators.

Questions:

1. When in confrontation with someone, do I believe I am always right?

2. Do I get frustrated because others do not think and act the same way as I do?

The Lord's unfailing love surrounds the man who trusts in him. Psalm 32:10 NIV.

Let's pray:

Father, help me to listen to your voice today. Help me do what you desire of me today as I come in contact with others. Help me to be sensitive to your voice and be loving to others. I lay my life down as a servant of Christ. Use me to make a difference. In Jesus's name, amen.

BABY LOVE, MY BABY LOVE

We were new in our marriage and really desired children but just couldn't seem to get pregnant. There were doctors' visits, prayer, a lot of old wives' tale remedies to get pregnant, but nothing seemed to work. I'm sure many of you who have desired children and needed a bit of help, have tried some of the remedies that we tried. Maybe your methods worked, but honestly we now look back and just laugh at some of the craziness that we put ourselves through. But as the months rolled on, discouragement began to creep into our home. And this is where we felt the love of God kick in. A couple from our church, Judy and Larry Brasher, called us one night and basically invited themselves to our home for dinner and fellowship time with us. They knew in their hearts it was God's will for them to come. Isn't it wonderful how God chooses to use us when we submit ourselves to him?

After our meal, they asked if they could pray for us. I clearly remember gathering together in front of our living room fireplace, joining hands with the Brashers and praying. Being led by the Holy Spirit, Larry asked us if we were fighting discouragement of some sort. We began to cry and replied, "YES!" He shared with us that God had sent them to us because He loved us and that our loving Father, Jehovah Jireh (our provider) cared about our needs very much. I knew in my spirit that this particular dinner was a God–ordained meeting and that my Heavenly Father loved us enough to send servants of God to us.

Larry instructed his wife Judy to gently lay her hands on Teri's abdominal area as they prayed in the name of Jesus. I have to admit, in the beginning of the prayer, I was a typical doubting Thomas, but as they prayed, Teri felt something move and adjust on the inside of her body. The doubts quickly faded. The prayer was so anointed and we conceived that week! Now that's a miracle! Isn't God great? It quickly reminded me of the miracle healing of my headaches I had received many years before while traveling on the road with Henry and Hazel. God is our Jehovah Rapha, our healer!

Listen my dear friend, I encourage you to seek your loving Father for your every need. If you're going through a storm in your life, and it has caused you to be discouraged, please understand that He cares deeply about every aspect of your life. I believe Jesus will come to you in the midst of your storm no matter how big or small. To Jesus, it's important. He's a miracle-working God! Also, He's no respecter of persons. What He did for Bill and Teri, He'll do for you, if you will trust him with your whole heart. Study and meditate on biblical scriptures so His Word will come alive in you. The Bible says your faith can move mountains! Don't waver! God's Word is sharper than a two–edged sword! It's powerful! Don't allow the devil to discourage you. Don't listen to the lies as he whispers to you that it'll never happen. God can do anything!

I shall decree a thing, and it shall be established in my life. Job 22:28 NIV.

From that moment on, we knew our lives were for a purpose and God would supply our needs and give us the desires of our heart—a baby!

And I will do whatever you ask in my name, so that the Father may be glorified in the Son. You may ask me for anything in my name, and I will do it. John 14: 13–14 NIV.

This verse assures us that Jesus loves and cares about every part of our lives. What are you dealing with that seems overwhelming? Do you feel stuck in your job, desiring something new, but feeling hopeless? Is it your health? You have prayed and prayed but feel there's no light at the end of the tunnel? Is it your marriage or a relationship that you're in that feels dead and over? Is it problems with your children, finances, or brokenness?

God's Word offers hope and answers to our heart's cry. He will NOT forsake us! His Word encourages us to ask and believe. He can and will do anything for us according to His will. He stands at our heart's door knocking. We should open the door and receive.

If you believe, you will receive whatever you ask for in prayer. Matthew 21:22 NIV.

Some people feel they shouldn't bother God with small, trivial matters. That's nonsense! Nothing is too small or big for God. There's nothing He wouldn't do for His children according to His will. He loves US!

Whatever you ask for in prayer, believe that you have received it, and it will be yours. Mark 11:24 NIV.

Believing you have it before you actually receive it is faith, which incorporates trust!

In the day of my trouble I will call to you, O Lord, for you will answer me. Psalm 86:7 NIV.

This is love. This is God..

The pregnancy announcement came as a total shock and surprise to me. It was Christmas of 1988, and I was teaching music at Pelham Christian School in Alabama. The school was part of our church. We had a big Christmas musicale planned to be performed by all the students. Teri decided to hold off from telling me that we were going to have a baby until all the musicale hoopla was over. There were major planning sessions and rehearsals, which took so much of my time, and she knew in her heart she wanted my full attention with no distractions. Yes, it was to be a momentous occasion.

The morning after the big musical show, we were home resting. She had just decided to surprise me with the big news when I received a long–distance call from a dear friend of mine that her elderly husband had passed away. The news broke my heart. They had always called me son since they didn't have children of their own. Because of my sadness, Teri decided to delay the baby news for a few hours. She knew I loved this couple, but also knew I had wanted to be a father most of my life, and her news would be a great Christmas gift to me. So she allowed me time to grieve. What love!

Since we lived in Birmingham, Alabama, and usually visited family in Tennessee and Mississippi for Christmas, we scheduled a celebration between just the two of us for a day or two earlier. I always enjoyed opening our presents from each other when it was just us. To me, it was romantic and special.

Just before packing our bags for Christmas in Mississippi, Teri planned a morning Christmas celebration for just us. I was totally unaware of what was in store for me. After breakfast, we moved to our basement den where we sat on the floor surrounded by our gifts. She asked to open her gifts first. It took her a while since I had overspent and gave her quite a bit. Please understand that at that particular time in my life, I was still fighting the urge to impress others. Teri has never been one to want expensive gifts. She managed the household budget and knew exactly how much we should spend on gifts and bills. Of course, smart, know–it–all Bill wouldn't listen and I would hit the mall. Christmas usually put us in debt. You see, the truth is, I should have been looking to Jesus for approval instead of looking to others.

If you are looking for approval from others and feel a need to impress, stop now. First of all, the keeping up with the Jones' mentality will cause you to be defeated and exhausted. Second, you'll end up spending more than you need to spend on gifts which will be forgotten quickly. If you're a parent, you know what I'm talking about. We give so many gifts to our children for Christmas and birthdays, and what do they do? They usually play with the simplest item or the kitchen pots and pans. More importantly, they desire our time. Jesus gave of himself. He loved and cared for those around Him. What a beautiful lesson for us. I encourage each of you to think about what I've just shared. Love is not about how much we spend, but more about giving of ourselves. Maybe it's time to reprioritize our lives. You can't buy love. When will we ever learn that lesson? Teri would have been so much happier in the earlier years of our marriage over some simple gift that she knew I had spent time creating or looking for. She just wanted to know that I loved and cared about her. Over the years I have found that she would rather have the house cleaned and laundry folded than an expensive gift! Time is another beautiful gift to give.

After opening her den full of gifts, it was my turn. I have always felt I had the gift of guessing my presents before opening them. The excitement of many holidays had been spoiled by me guessing the gift before opening it. Because this really disappointed Teri, she would go to great lengths to surprise me. But I still could basically figure out the shirt, pants, sweaters, etc. But this time it would be different. Over time, I learned to keep my mouth shut and not verbally guess what was inside the wrapping. This made for a happier holiday. Lesson learned.

I opened the gifts in the order she had arranged. I was smiling but thinking to myself, *This is nice but not nearly as impressive money-wise as I had spent, lavishing her with expensive gifts.* The mental gift–guessing was successful until I came to the final gift. The last gift was a cardboard dollhouse. It really puzzled me as she wouldn't allow me to shake it. I thought and pondered for a minute but finally gave up. Yep, she had me on this one, but I still didn't think much about it. Maybe it was a bottle of cologne or a new book to read. But a doll house? As I opened the lid of the house and looked inside, a tiny baby doll wearing a diaper was looking up at me. Attached to the diaper was a little note saying, "Dear Daddy, I'm coming to see you in nine months." Do you remember reading back a few pages that I had wanted to be a dad most of my life?

Stunned, I stared at the doll, looked at Teri for assurance that it was what I thought it was, then collapsed to the floor crying joyous buckets of tears. Poor Teri was sitting there wondering whether she was even going to get a hug. Overcome with thanks and praise to God, my mind couldn't think of anything else! I was finally going to be a daddy. For the first time in a while, my life had new meaning. What a gift from my loving Father God. This would be a Christmas never to forget. Thank you, God, for loving us enough to send the Brashers to our home earlier to pray for us. God's timing and plans are awesome!

And I will do whatever you ask in my name, so that the Father may be glorified in the Son. You may ask me for anything in my name, and I will do it. John 14:13–14 NIV.

If you believe, you will receive whatever you ask for in prayer. Matthew 21:22 NIV.

Whatever you ask for in prayer, believe that you have received it, and it will be yours. Mark 11:24 NIV.

Our Heavenly Father WILL answer your prayers just as He answered ours. His Word promises that He will not break His promise.

This is the confidence we have in approaching God: that if we ask anything according to his will, He hears us. And if we know that He hears us—whatever we ask—we know that we have what we asked of Him. 1 John 5:14–15 NIV.

God allows us to come boldly before His throne with our prayers. Boldly isn't pride, but instead confidence in His Word. When we pray, we should pray in faith (confidence), believing and trusting Jesus that He will answer.

Then you will call on me and come and pray to me, and I will listen to you. You will seek me and find me when you seek me with all your heart. Jeremiah 29: 12–13 NIV.

What a friend we have in Jesus…

Are you in need today? Have you felt all is lost? Do you feel like God has forgotten you?

Jesus said, I will do whatever you ask in my name, so that the Son may bring glory to the Father. You may ask me for anything in my name, and I WILL do it. John 14:13 NIV.

We shouldn't limit God in our minds. Many feel they aren't good enough to receive blessings and answers to prayers. Well, who is? Romans 3:23 tells us that we have all sinned and come short of the glory of God. We are covered in God's grace and can approach the throne of grace with boldness and confidence (Hebrew 4:14–16). God hears the cries of His children and will answer.

If you believe, you will receive WHATEVER you ask for in prayer. Matthew 21:22 NIV.

The more time we spend with our Father, the more He molds us into the image of Jesus. As we grow closer to Him, our desires will align more with God's will for us. We begin to desire His will for us in every decision we need to make . When our desires line up with His will, our prayers will line up with His will.

This is the confidence we have in approaching God: that if we ask anything according to His will, He hears us. And if we know that He hears us–whatever we ask–we know that we have what we asked of Him." 1 John 5: 14–15 NIV.

Prayer changes EVERYTHING! Do you need a change or miracle in your life today? Don't lose hope! Your loving Father is ready to answer. You don't have to earn God's attention. He's always with us.

In the day of trouble I will call to you, O Lord, for you WILL answer me. Psalm 86:7 NIV.

Believe in prayer! Believe in miracles! Believe in God!

Questions:

1. Do I truly trust God in all matters of my life?
2. Do I believe He can and will perform a miracle in my life?

Jesus said, I tell you the truth, if you have faith as small as a mustard seed, you can say to this mountain, "Move from here to there" and it will move. Nothing will be impossible for you. Matthew 17:20 NIV.

Let's pray:

Father, please forgive me for my doubts and fears. I choose to trust you in the good times as well as the storms in my life. Strengthen me, Father, so I will not waver in my faith. In Jesus's name, amen.

SHE'S HAVING MY BABY

Having a little girl was always a dream of mine. Being a music major in college and involved in the arts , I had experience in grooming young ladies for pageants and talent shows. I thought it would be great to have a daughter! God would give me a Miss America! Yay!! I had dreamed and fantasized about being the proud parent of a beautiful girl. Assuredly, we were ready for this easy challenge. The plan seemed to be laid out (or at least in my mind).

When the time finally arrived for the official sonogram, we were so excited. We had our friends, Larry and Judy, who had prayed for us, to accompany us on the celebration trip.

It's a boy!

Needless to say, there was shock and disappointment from me. The tears began to flow down my cheeks. To me, having a girl would be perfect. A fashionable pink bow for her to wear home from the hospital had already been selected. In the midst of my selfish dismay, Larry, again led by the Holy Spirit, lovingly put his arm around me and shared that God was giving me the perfect gift I needed. I looked at him with my "poor-pitiful-me face" and told him I didn't know how to fish, hunt, or coach sports, which boys learn from their dads. My background was music.

He smiled and said, "Bill, God has called you to love him and teach him the Word of God so he will have a strong personal relationship with Jesus Christ. As far as all the sports areas you are worried about, God will supply the rest."

I felt at that moment the Spirit of God touch my heart and confirm what Larry had shared. Peace flooded my heart. God was giving me a son for a purpose. He had chosen me to raise this child as his dad. All the extracurricular activities that had caused me to worry seemed unimportant at that moment. My purpose in life was to love him with all my heart and teach him the ways of God. That was a job responsibility I could and would do. This was my calling!

Dear Saints of God, it's comforting to know that God loves and knows what's best for us. You see, He knew what was needed in my life. Trust has been the key to conquering the storms when they would hit.

God didn't say "if" we will walk through the valley of the shadow of death, He said "as" we walk through the valley of the shadow of death (storms), He will be with us. The problem is, we say we trust Him, but instead we feel this need to help God solve our problems.

Are you experiencing disappointments? discouraged? Are you feeling like a failure because of something in your past? Have you lost a race, failed a test, been turned down for a promotion, or just emerged from a broken relationship? If you have answered yes to any of these questions, then God is speaking to you to move forward, no longer focusing on the past and its failures. We must look ahead and continue striving to do our best.

Forgetting what is behind and straining toward what is ahead, I press on toward the goal to win the prize for which God has called me heavenward in Christ Jesus. Philippians 3:13–14 NIV.

Friends, we can't change the past. It's done. Once a sports event is over, it's over. One team wins, one team loses. If we experience a loss or a broken heart, we must continue moving forward with God, step by step. We can't allow the past to affect our future. Just because we failed in the past, doesn't mean we must fail in the future. If we will allow God to teach us valuable lessons that are derived from our failures and disappointments, we will gain strength and wisdom. It's okay to be disappointed or hurt over a loss or broken heart. We shouldn't feel guilty for our emotions. The key is not to stay down when we are knocked down!

Your attitude should be the same as that of Christ Jesus. Philippians 2:5 NIV.

Walking with God is a journey. There will be days we will experience sunshine and days we experience storms.

Being confident of this, that He who began a good work in you will carry it on to completion until the day of Christ Jesus. Philippians 1: 6 NIV.

Our confidence is in knowing that God has a specific plan for us.

We left the hospital that day with joy and excitement, trusting God. It was a new day, a new adventure, and I knew there would be many new challenges ahead.

Questions:

1. Do I trust that God desires the best for me?
2. Do I truly believe that I'm God's child, an heir of God and joint heir of Jesus?

Trust the Lord with all of your heart, lean not to your own understanding, in all your ways praise Him and He will direct your path. Proverbs 3:5 NIV.

Let's pray:

Father, forgive me for the times I've taken situations into my own hands without seeking you. I know that you love me and know what's best for me. I surrender my life to you now. I give you my family, job, and every part of my life. It's yours. God, help me each day to trust you. I declare that I love you with my whole heart. In Jesus's name, amen.

I'm a Daddy!

Teri's pregnancy was wonderful. She loved being pregnant and basically eased through her pregnancy. She doesn't recall ever getting sick or having any problems beyond some swelling in her feet. Don't throw stones at us! Ha! It was an exciting nine–month journey. We had great anticipation about our new arrival.

We had attended a Christian healing service at our church where Teri was prayed for. We believed that God would give her an easy delivery that would last no more than two hours.

When Teri went into labor, we rushed to the hospital with excitement. We just believed that our son would be born quickly with no problems. I actually thought it would be a piece of cake. If you're a mother reading this, you're beginning to laugh! The delivery wasn't what we thought it was going to be. Teri was in labor for about twelve hours and finally the nurse told me to dress in scrubs as they were going to use forceps to help her deliver. This wasn't what I had hoped for, but my ways aren't always God's ways. Bottom line: Steffan was born a healthy eight pounds, eight ounces and twenty–one inches long.

A month after he was born, we dedicated him to God at Covenant Life Church in Pelham, AL. (It's now called Life Church and is pastored by our good friends, Rev. Rick and Debra Bishop.) We took this dedication very seriously. My parents even traveled from Mississippi to attend. God inspired me to write a beautiful song for the occasion, which I titled "Steffan's Song." Our anointed pastor, Rev. Jerry Bishop, who is now in heaven with Steffan, held our son in his arms, lifted him up to God and literally gave him to the Father. Little did I know that God would loan him to us for only twenty years. Yes, we all cried during the dedication service. The same anointing that I had felt at our wedding was upon us now, the presence of God. We knew in our hearts, as many did, that God had his hand on Steffan David Myers. Steffan's name is derived from Stephen, which means "crowned one." David means "beloved one." We named our son after my beloved brother, Stephen David Myers. We felt this would honor the memory of my brother, and bless my parents, and we basically just liked the name Steffan.

Parents, always pray and seek God before choosing names for your children. Names have specific meanings.

The tongue has the power of life and death. Proverbs 18:21 NIV.

We should speak positive, life–filled words over our children. Names are important to God. He even changed Jacob's name to Israel and Abram's name to Abraham. That's why we have to be so very careful what we speak over our children and family members. Children aren't ever stupid or dumb. Their action or decision might be bad, but they should never be called negative words. It will affect them, I promise. Start now speaking good things over your family. Tell your spouse, your children, and even your grandchildren that they are a blessing from God. You will see a difference!

Questions:

1. Do I truly understand that God's Word is truth and will guide me each step I take?

2. Do I believe that there's power in the words we speak?

Do not let any unwholesome talk come out of your mouths, but only what is helpful to building others up according to their needs, that it may benefit those who listen. Ephesians 4:29 NIV.

Let's pray:

Father, today I make the decision to watch the words that come from my mouth as I speak. I choose words of life. Help me to trust You in all areas of my life. In Jesus's name, amen.

Hairspray!

After teaching music for several years, I began to feel limited in my abilities. Teri and I prayed and decided it was time for me to change careers for a season. I just wanted to try something different, so I enrolled in a local cosmetology school and began my new career as a hairdresser. I wanted to do it and it felt like the right thing to do. So, I jumped head first into cosmetology school and graduated with flying colors. After graduating, I decided to work for a lady named Rose Frazer, who owned two salons. She was a superb hairstylist and taught me well. She always pushed me to be better. After working for Rose at Hair Reflections for a year, I ventured out and purchased a hair salon, Salon Concepts by Bill Myers. Being an owner of a business was fun, creative, interesting, and stressful. I kept ownership for almost a year. It was a beautiful salon nestled in the heart of Hoover, Alabama where we offered many amenities for the clients. The salon employed several hairstylists and manicurists and for the most part, everyone worked in harmony. During my hair career tenure, I had the opportunity to work several hair shows and conventions. Poor Teri always seemed to be my guinea pig on new hair styles and ideas.

As spring 1994 approached, the Holy Spirit began speaking to my heart in that still small voice to sell the salon and return to ministry. Prior to the world of cosmetology, I had been teaching music at the Christian school, working with children, where I had directed the Christmas program the night before finding out that Teri was pregnant with Steffan. Whether serving at the church or the school, I was always in a place of ministry. Even though I had ministered to several clients at the salon, it wasn't the same as full–time ministry service.

On Friday of Memorial Day weekend, May 1994, I was finishing my work day at the salon, when a friend of mine, Sherry Holtzclaw, who had attended church with us a few years before, came into the salon for her hair appointment. She immediately shared how God wanted her to pray for me. Being a spiritual know–it–all, I began to share with her that God was leading me to sell the salon and return to ministry. Our chatting and hair cut continued on for a few more minutes. After the hair cut was complete, she stood up, thanked me for the cut, and said, "I don't think I can leave here without praying for you." I agreed, and she laid her hand on my chest and began praying safety over me. Safety? This wasn't what my mind thought she should have prayed since I wanted to sell the salon. After she prayed, I thanked her and she left. I really didn't think much about it. Since she was my last client for the day, I closed shop and met Teri and Steffan, who was four years old, at our favorite Chinese restaurant for dinner. When we finished eating, Teri mentioned that she needed to stop by WalMart on her way home for a few items.

Steffan always rode with me, especially since I was driving a new convertible. But that particular night, he decided to ride with Teri, not me. As we left the restaurant and turned onto a busy four–lane road, Teri and Steffan turned off at the WalMart and I kept going, headed home. I decided to leave the convertible top closed since Steffan wasn't riding with me. Approaching me in the opposite lanes were two teenagers racing another vehicle. Their speed was estimated by police at 103 mph. This wasn't a four–lane highway. This was a busy four–lane road that was heavily traveled. Their car clipped a van traveling their same direction, and came across the median airborne, crashing sideways into my car. The impact was so great that it actually split the teenagers' small red car completely in half. Part of their car flew over my car, scraping the top of my windshield, leaving red paint. The other part of the car went the opposite direction. Sadly, both teenagers were killed instantly. Thank God I was wearing my seatbelt and had an airbag that deployed. Much of this horrific wreck was a mental blur. I was in total shock. All I knew in my mind was that I was alive. Oh, thank God that Steffan was not riding with me. I know it was the hand of God leading him to ride with Teri.

Remember Sherry, the lady who had come into my salon and prayed protection over me that same afternoon? She had acted out of obedience to God. What if she had not obeyed? What if she had been too embarrassed to pray for me in my salon? I could have been killed also. But I was alive! What a miracle!! Thank God I had allowed her to pray for me. Needless to say, she was a blessed woman when she found out about the wreck and that I was alive! Sherry told me later that she had driven passed that exact spot on the road after leaving my salon. When she drove by there, she felt another sense of urgency to pray for me.

My new car was completely totaled, and my doctor found crushed vertebraes in my back and a broken sternum. The recovery was painful, long and drawn out. As I was recuperating, I kept mourning for the families of those two teenagers who died. Even though the wreck wasn't my fault, I felt such sympathy for the families. What a storm! Their parents would never be the same again. I had no idea that I would travel down the same road years later by losing my own son.

As I was slowly recovering physically, I began to seek the Lord with all my heart as to what He wanted me to do with my life. I was able to sell the salon just after the wreck. I was now free to do what God wanted me to do. But the days of praying turned into weeks and then months. Several months later, I caught myself sitting on my staircase, crying out to God in anguish. I cried and prayed, "Where are you God?" In desperation, I told Him that morning that I had to know something by the end of the day. I felt I was at the end of my rope (faith) and couldn't go on another day. It was such a discouraging time in my life. I had experienced a tragic car wreck, sold my salon and I began to feel everything was hopeless. Honestly, this was a major storm in my life. I felt useless and unwanted.

Can you relate with what I was going through? Sometimes we get desperate and feel God doesn't care and nothing will happen for us. What a lie of Satan! Of course, God cares. He's our Daddy! His plans are perfect. His timing is perfect.

At the close of that long day of waiting, praying, and crying, when all seemed to be lost, God led a pastor friend, Donny Acton, to call and ask me if I was available and willing to come to his church, New Hope Church, and play the piano for a few weeks. I was thrilled! God had answered my prayers in the eleventh hour of my waiting. My loving Father had come through. I now had an opportunity to be used by God! This was a miracle! It was reassurance that God cares about us and hears our prayers and cries of desperation. My Father had brought me through this depressing storm in my life. I felt victorious!

You might think to yourself that playing the piano for a few weeks isn't much of ministry. Listen, my friend, God knew what He was doing. I was so thankful to have anything. The piano job quickly turned into the church minister of music and education where I served for several years. God's plan, not mine was the key. It took getting my attention, interceding, and my yielding to God for Him to open a door for me to serve Him. I could have easily gotten a position in a church somewhere, but I wanted the God-anointed position. I knew from Bible teaching, that He would make a way where there seemed to be no way. I wanted Him to open the door and He did.

While I was working at New Hope, the Lord led Teri to quit work and homeschool with Steffan. The one–on–one schooling made a huge difference in his life. Teri had him tested each year, and he excelled far beyond his grade level every year. We joined a homeschool network which provided Steffan with more than enough field trips, friendships, and recreation with other homeschooled students. Teri absolutely loved staying home with him. Indeed, it was a wonderful decision we will never regret.

Questions:

1. Do I believe there is power in prayer?
2. When the Holy Spirit speaks for me to pray, am I obedient?

The eyes of the lord are on the righteous and his ears are attentive to their prayer. 1 Peter 3:12 NIV.

Let's pray:

Because your ways are best, O Lord, I trust you with my whole heart. I pray you will watch over and protect me in all I do. In Jesus's name, amen.

God Is Good

It was during that sweet time at New Hope Church that I was surprised again by my wife. It was Father's Day morning 1996, and I was downstairs shaving when Teri came into the bathroom and told me she had a Father's Day gift for me. I told her that we had agreed not to spend any money for this holiday. She just smiled and said, "It's just a little 'happy'." I sat down in the den waiting to be presented with my new bottle of cologne or shirt. Instead, there was that same doll house again with the same baby doll inside. I was so surprised! Of course, I cried buckets of tears again. What a Father's Day gift! Steffan's announcement had been my Christmas present eight years before.

I've always wanted a baby girl, and the Lord granted the desire of my heart. After Steffan was born, we prayed and tried for years to have another baby. Our precious baby girl, Lydia Noelle Myers, came into our lives February 13, 1997. On that particular night, our New Hope Church had a Valentine's banquet and Teri and I were the entertainment. We had worked together on several funny skits. It was an elegant banquet with steak as the main course. As we were mingling with the crowd just before the banquet, someone asked Teri when the baby was due. She replied, "Next week. But I'd be happy if she was born tomorrow." Guess what? Just as the words came out of her mouth, her water broke. So much for entertaining at the banquet! Ha! We headed to the hospital dressed in our banquet attire and Teri birthed our baby Lydia. We were so blessed to have a wonderful Christian doctor who delivered Lydia and immediately lifted her to God while still in his hands, praying and dedicating her to our loving and faithful Father. We now were the parents of a precious curly headed Steffan and a beautiful Lydia.

Lydia Noelle Myers was dedicated to God at New Hope Church by Pastor Donny Acton. It was a beautiful ceremony and I thank God for bringing such wonderful friends across our path.

My friend, can you see how the hand of God moves in our lives? He's a miracle–working God! Our loving Father cares so much about each of us. Maybe as you're reading this, you're relating as you are in the eleventh hour of needing a breakthrough in your storm. Hold fast! Our Father is faithful! Please don't give up! He'll bring you through your storm! Storms are never permanent! He is the God of breakthroughs! His plans are awesome! Trust!

After several years of ministry with Pastor Donny and Mindy Acton and the beautiful people of New Hope Church, I felt God leading me to move forward with Him. A church in Goodlettsville, Tennessee called me for a minister of music and education position. I was so honored and said yes! At the time we owned a beautiful new two–and–a–half story home in Alabaster, Alabama, just south of Birmingham. To me, it really was beautiful. It had four bedrooms, two full baths and two half baths. The large foyer had a winding staircase. We loved it. When I accepted the position at the Tennessee church, we quickly placed our home on the real estate market, expecting that this showcase house would sell in thirty minutes! But it didn't; so I had to leave my family behind and move on to Goodlettsville, with the expectations that the house would sell and they would move up very soon.

The weeks again turned into months of waiting for the house to sell. The church arranged for me to live with a sweet couple in Goodlettsville until we could get the family moved to Tennessee. Finally, a small rental house that the church owned became available, allowing my family to move to where I was. It was small, but we didn't care at all. After almost six months of waiting and being separated, we were finally together as a family. Even though our house was still on the market, we were allowed to live rent–free in this house.

Teri and I found a new home under construction in the Goodlettsville area and put a contract on it with the contingency that our Alabama home would sell first. But God's plans are much better than ours.

Within a couple of months, we realized that this church position wasn't what God wanted for us to do permanently. I wondered, *Had I missed God?* I didn't understand, but was flooded with peace. Through prayer and several husband–and–wife discussions, we resigned in late October but agreed to stay until after the Christmas program, which was already in rehearsal. I do have to say that God blessed my program. It was an awesome extravaganza with full orchestra, costumes, sets, lights, etc.

Just after Christmas, we left the church position and began seeking God about His will and direction for our lives. The church was very gracious and gave us two months' salary and the opportunity to live in the house rent–free for two more months. The house we had put a contract on sold quickly to someone else. We weren't able to keep the contract since our house in Alabama hadn't sold. That was another thing to praise God for–to be relieved from the pressure of paying two mortgages. God is good.

I began getting up very early in the mornings before anyone in the house would awake, and praying for God's will. I earnestly fasted often and prayed every day for God to open a door for us. Many days I had the opportunity to get discouraged, feel sorry for myself, and give up. But I wouldn't. I was responsible for my family. God had created me to be the spiritual leader in my household. I didn't have any answers except I knew I needed to seek God. I will admit that there was one moment when I got in the flesh and mailed a music resume to a church in Tennessee. I thought maybe I needed to help God. I mean, He is very busy. But, the very moment I placed the envelope in the mailbox, I realized I had disobeyed God. I quickly repented and kept pursuing my Father. Many people thought we were crazy for not getting out and knocking on doors for job opportunities. In the natural, it seemed to be the logical thing to do, but the Holy Spirit kept nudging me and speaking to me to hold fast and trust my God. The storm waves seemed high, but I made the decision to obey my loving Father, no matter what anyone thought. Sending out resumes and seeking employment isn't wrong at all. But for me, at this time in my life, I truly felt in my heart that God wanted me to wait on Him and allow Him to open the door.

As the two–month time limit came to a close and money was running out, I told Teri that all I knew to do was move back to Alabama into our house and look for a job. We arranged for a mover to move us.

As we made preparations to move back into our house in Alabama, our plans quickly came to a halt. Our real estate agent and friend, Randall Williams, called and informed us that our house had finally sold. While we needed a place to go and direction from God, we were relieved to be out from under the mortgage payments.

After the call from Randall, I clearly remember explaining to the mover, "I'm not sure where we're going, but I'll let you know when you get here to load the truck." He must have thought I was a crazy man! I felt at that point I needed the Red Sea to open for us as it did for Moses. Bill and Teri needed a miracle. This was a big storm in our lives. We seemed to be at the edge of a cliff ready to fall off. But I kept feeling in my heart that God loved me and He had a plan.

As we were packing our belongings, I received a phone call from a Birmingham pastor asking me whether I would be interested in a pastor's position in a church in the Northeast Birmingham area. Praise God! I said, "Yes! Yes!" The call was a miracle! Our dear friends in Birmingham, Don and Susan Casey, offered to store our furniture in their huge basement while decisions were being made. Another good Birmingham friend, Judy Goode, called and offered to let us live with her temporarily. It was another miracle! How precious is the body of Christ! God uses His people to bless others. God is good. His plan was coming about. He hadn't forgotten the Myers, as I was tempted to feel. I preached my trial sermon at Branchville Church and just knew in my heart that it was God's will to take the pastoral position. Now the whole scenario had come to light. God had taken me to the Nashville area for the third time to do some more work in my life. I love music, but my Heavenly Father had a different ministry for me in this new season. I would be shepherding His flock. It was in my heart to do so. Saints of God, when we just allow Him to take the reins of our lives, His will can be accomplished. Note: God is smarter than we are.

When Teri and I met with the church committee to look at the house the church provided for us to live in, we were surprised at the condition it was in. Teri was discouraged when she looked at it. We had owned this beautiful house in Alabaster, and this small church home was in deplorable condition. When I say it was in rough shape, trust me, it was. I encouraged her to pray and allow God to do His work. She reluctantly agreed and we sought God. Not only did the church extend a call to us to take the pastor position, but in their precious love, they decided to completely remodel the house! Another miracle! The house turned out so nice. I'm in awe how God's hand gently leads and guides us. He spiritually places an umbrella of protection over us as we walk through the storm together, and He leads us to sunshine. You too can make it through your storm. Trust God today and allow Him to place His umbrella of protection over you as you walk through to victory. Trust and obey, for there's no other way to be happy in Jesus.

The lord's unfailing love surrounds the man who trusts in Him. Psalm 32:10 NIV.

Questions:

1. Have there been times you felt you were on the cliff of life about to fall off?

2. Can you name times that God has rescued you from total failure?

The Lord is good, a refuge in times of trouble. He cares for those who trust in him. Nahum 1:7 NIV.

Let's pray:

God, our ways aren't always your ways, but you love us and desire to bless us. Help us to trust in you, not our own ways. You know what's best for us. We trust. In Jesus's name, amen.

Click! Click! Click!!

I just love my wife so much! Teri is so doting. She has always been one to take pictures and videos of everything. I mean everything! We have drawers, boxes, and closets full of videos and pictures. We used to tease her about always grabbing the camera when some occasion would arrive. I have laughingly rolled my eyes more than once over her wanting to get that momentous occasion of our kids, but now I praise her for doing so. We have so much to look back on and remember. So if you're not a big fan of getting your picture taken or videoed, get over it. You'll be thankful when your children are grown and you'll have great memories through pictures and videos.

Many of our pictures and videos ranging from infant to adulthood were usually of Steffan hugging someone with a big smile on his face. That seemed to be who he was. He genuinely loved people and was such an encourager to his friends. Now he wasn't born with these traits, we taught him the ways of God and His precious love.

My desire for Steffan was to grow up and just know what God's calling on his life would be. I truly believe that many times we confuse our children by telling them to be this or that in their adult careers. Every parent wants the best for their children and desires for them to be successful. That's understandable. But we should be instructing them to seek God with their whole heart and listen to the Holy Spirit. The Word states that the Holy Spirit will lead us into all truth. Don't you believe that includes our careers and marriages? Maybe if we taught our children at an early age to seek God about these, they would make wiser choices, experience fewer career changes and less divorce. I'll admit and confess to you that there were times that I got in the flesh and began thinking like the world system, throwing career ideas at him. I knew his gifting and his talents, but I had to keep reminding myself with the help of Teri, that we ultimately wanted what God wanted for him and really encouraged him to pray. Saints of God, to be in God's will is peace.

My children are taught of the Lord and great is their peace. Isaiah 54:13 NIV.

Most of Steffan's young life was centered around homeschooling with Teri. I have to admit, my wife is brilliant and taught him well. His test scores each year of homeschooling soared. There are so many wonderful memories of field trips and special lessons at home. When he approached seventh grade, he really began his staunch campaign to attend Odenville Middle School where most of our church youth were attending. My first reaction was "No way!" We are a homeschooling family. But God began tugging on my heart about putting him in school, so we decided on a compromise. I should've known that God isn't into compromise. We enrolled him in a nearby community Christian school where he could play sports and interact with other students. We honestly didn't pray about this. The Christian school just seemed the best choice, the right thing to do as Christians. Well, Steffan was miserable from the first day, but never complained. We just saw it in his face.

To this day, I regret that man–made decision. Why didn't I pray? I mean, I was pastoring a church, but I just went on my gut feelings of what I thought was best, instead of seeking God. After repenting, I decided to pray. With only a week or two of school under his belt, I was in the Odenville Middle School parking lot to attend an event, when I heard God's voice telling me to let Steffan go to school there. I knew it was God's voice because it was almost audible. This voice consumed me. I even looked around to see if anyone else heard His voice. As He spoke, a flood of peace covered me, which confirmed it was the right decision. I came home crying with joy that God had spoken to me and told Teri that God had spoken and we should obey. Needless to say, Steffan was thrilled, and I was relieved that I was finally listening to God's voice. We immediately withdrew him from the Christian school and enrolled him in the public school. He rode the bus the first day at his new school, and upon its arrival, he saw a large crowd of student friends waiting and cheering for him as he stepped off the bus.

Lesson learned by daddy. God knows best. You can't make wise decisions based on your feelings. They can be misleading. Jesus said the Holy Spirit would lead and guide us into all truth. God cares about all areas of our lives. Yes, He cares about where our children go to school. Please understand, there's absolutely nothing wrong with Christian schools. I even taught three years at Pelham Christian School, Pelham, Alabama, and loved every minute of it. My point is that God had a specific plan for Steffan and it was public school. I wish I could say that this was the last bad decision I made. I've been learning to follow God for many years, making many mistakes along the way. But my heart is to follow His will.

Questions:

1. Am I guilty of saying I trust God, but making my own decisions?
2. Do I have faith in God that he will answer my prayers?

The Lord is my strength and my shield; my heart trusts in him, and I am helped. My heart leaps for joy and I will give thanks to him in song. Psalm 28:7 NIV.

Let's pray:

Father, it's not my will that's important, but rather your will. Following your will and obeying brings me peace. I trust you, God, with my situations....Thank you for loving me. In Jesus's name, amen.

Home Once Again

As Steffan finished his eighth grade year, the Lord opened a door for us to move from Alabama to Laurel, MS, to be near my family. Unfortunately, we didn't get moved before my mother, who was stricken with cancer, went to Heaven. I still miss that wonderful lady with the beautiful smile called Mom.

It was this time in Steffan's life that a bit of teenage "attitude" began to kick in. He kept his grades up, but every now and then his attitude would crave independence. It really wasn't too bad. He would still hug and kiss us daily. I recall many times he would come and plop down in my lap for a big hug.

From the ninth grade through graduation, I was Steffan's show choir teacher at Northeast Jones High School in Laurel, so he got to see his dad every day. This was good for me, but sometimes a real pain for him. He knew that I knew everything he was doing. If he made a bad grade, I'd know. If he was tardy for a class, I'd know. But overall, we got along extremely well together. Of course as many of his close friends would testify, there were a few times that we did butt heads, especially in show choir. Yes, that's part of the "I'm grown now" stage. But God never left him nor forsook him. When Steffan would repent, God always forgave him. How do I know this? God's word is clear, "He forgives and remembers no more." Grace. Actually amazing grace. God has shown me time and time again that if He forgives, we should also forgive.

As Christians, we cry out to God to forgive us but will turn around and hold resentment toward another. Parents included. This sounds a bit contradictive doesn't it? Oh Lord, teach us Grace. It was especially hard for me to understand grace involving discipline with my children. Steffan came into this world a strong–willed child. Believe it or not, we noticed this trait while he was still an infant in the crib. We always believed the Bible in regard to discipline. David cried out, "They rod and thy staff, they comfort me." We always knew in our hearts that raising children correctly takes a balance of love and discipline. Some children are born easygoing, never requiring any sort of major discipline. With Steffan, it was quite different. We had to discipline him many times. We were always constructive and concise in our method. We made a policy to never discipline our children while we were still angry. Steffan would have to fully understand what he did wrong and that we loved him with all our heart. We always taught him to pray to create a sensitive heart toward repentance. It's our mission in life to raise our children to hear the voice of God, be obedient, and follow God's will.

With our daughter Lydia, we've hardly needed to use anything stronger than "don't do that again." She has always been extremely tenderhearted and obedient to our word.

As Steffan got older, I began to really learn about grace. This helped me in my forgiving and dealing with his on-and-off teenage attitude. He really was a good son. He was in Beta Club, student counsel, and Teenage Republicans, serving as officer in various clubs. He was the band drum major his tenth grade, our school tiger mascot his eleventh grade and show choir captain for two years. During Steffan's senior year, he had the opportunity to perform as the Cowardly Lion in the musical production of The Wizard of Oz. I have to admit he did a great job with his character and was hilarious in his costume.

During high school, Steffan dated Kate Presley who was in my show choir. They dated throughout part of their junior year and all through their senior year. Kate was also chosen as captain of show choir in their senior year and they were chosen "cutest couple" for the school's Who's Who awards. Everyone thought they would get married one day.

Knowing Steffan was God's child prompted me to daily lay him at the foot of the cross. There was a lot of interceding, praying scriptures over him and confessing the Word in faith.

Greater is He that is in me than he that is in the world. 1 John 4:4 NIV.

Thank God for His grace. God began to teach me that grace covers over a multitude of sins. I learned that God gave me grace when I sinned and I was learning to show grace to Steffan also. Through my prayers for my son, a deeper love for Steffan developed. My desire was for him to see the love of Jesus in my eyes and actions, and my heart always determined to love him unconditionally. Thank God for a Godly wife who daily encouraged me in this area. Understanding grace brought peace to my heart. Even when I felt Steffan had an "attitude," he still had such a loving attitude toward everyone. He was always a big hugger and encourager to his friends.

Raising a teenager caused me to pray more and more. I believe that my loving God is powerful and He can make a way where there seems to be no way. I believe in miracles. I've seen so many in my life. Prayer changes everything!

Questions:

1. Do I believe that prayer can truly move the biggest mountains in my life?

2. Have I been meditating on God's Word for strength during my storms?

In my distress I called to the Lord; I called out to my God. From his temple he heard my voice; my cry came to his ears. 2 Samuel 22:7 NIV.

Let's pray:

My heavenly Father, I surrender all to you and choose this day to trust you. I will pray, seek your face, study your word, and believe by faith you will answer my prayers. In Jesus's name, amen.

GRACE GREATER THAN ALL OUR SIN

That God was reconciling the world to himself in Christ, not counting men's sins against them. And He has committed to us the message of reconciliation. God made him (Jesus) who had no sin to be sin for us, so that in Him we might become the righteousness of God. 2 Corinthians 5:19 NIV.

One of the biggest lessons I've learned through the tragedy of losing my son, Steffan, is God's Grace. Many years ago, I worried and struggled with the thoughts that if I did anything wrong, I'd go straight to hell when I died. Sounds like fear, huh? You bet it was! I would keep repeating, "Oh God, please forgive me," over and over again. You know, God isn't deaf. Our loving Father hears us the first time we repent. I felt I wasn't good enough to receive forgiveness, therefore more begging and pleading for God to forgive me would be needed. How frustrating! How wrong! Listen, my friend, our loving Father forgives you the moment you ask.

I will forgive their wickedness and remember their sins no more. Jeremiah 31:34 NIV.

Unfortunately, some religions teach that you must keep begging and maybe, just maybe, He'll forgive. I'm not condemning them in anyway, but for me, it causes exhaustion and stress. Besides, God probably got tired of the hours of begging and pleading since He forgave me the moment I asked.

As I've grown in the Word, I have understood that God isn't keeping a scorecard like a ballgame. He's not sitting on some big throne in the heavenly clouds, eating grapes, just waiting for us to mess up so He can zap us. Listen, we're talking about Abba Father, our loving God who deeply loves and cares about us. Abba Father basically means Daddy. Let's close our eyes and imagine this for a moment. He's our Daddy. I know as a dad, I have always wanted the very best for my children. That's just the parental love inside me. Now here is the good news! He loves us so much more than we have capacity to love anyone. God has more love for us than I have for my children. He's God! He genuinely wants to bless us in every area of our life. Wow, that's love. Remember the old Christian song, "He looked beyond my fault and saw my every need." Let's get a mental picture of this. If you are a Christian, you are God's child. You are grafted into the tree of Life. You belong to Him. God doesn't divorce His children, nor does he write us off if we stumble. If that old feeling I had when I was young were true, no one would be in Heaven.

We've ALL sinned and come short of the glory of God. Romans 3:23 NIV.

We all have faults, but I did try to convince my precious wife, Teri, that I was an exception to the rule. Don't worry, she didn't buy it.

This is where grace kicks in, my friend. God loves us and gives us mercy and grace. Now this isn't a ticket to go out and rob a bank. God will forgive if we ask Him, but unfortunately our laws are not as forgiving. So please don't go crazy on me. Anyway, grace covers a multitude of sins. That's love. That's God, our God. We also need to remember that even though God forgives, there is the reaping and sowing factor to deal with. The Word says that "Whatever a man sows, he will reap." We need to think about this. I don't want my sowing and reaping to affect my family in a negative way, but we all sow life's seeds and we will reap the product of the sowing, whether good or bad. That's why it's important to sow a life for Jesus.

I'm the first to tell you that Steffan wasn't perfect. I led him to the Lord at an early age and baptized him. He was our firstborn gift from God. Teri and I spent his entire life teaching him about the Word and the beautiful love of God. During my pastorate at Branchville Cumberland Presbyterian Church in Alabama, there was a Sunday where our young son stood in front of the entire church and quoted from memory the eleventh chapter of Hebrews. To many it was impressive, but to Teri and me, it was instilling God's Word inside him. We saw the memorization as seed being planted inside of him that would grow into a spiritual harvest. Each day Teri and I would try to pray over our children and speak to them about Jesus. I recall him kneeling at the altar, praying for his friends during many Sunday services.

Unfortunately, the same mentality I had years before, crept into my upbringing of Steffan. I always worried about his spiritual life. If I thought he did something that wasn't Christlike, I would panic, pray, and talk to him like it was the end of the world! I guess my subconscious mind was filled with worry, doubt, and fear. Where was my faith in God? Where was my assurance that Steffan was His child? I can recall times after he became much older when he would tell me he had worked late the night before and decided to stay home from church and rest. I would immediately think he was backsliding and needed me to preach a sermon so he would have a life change. (I'm not kidding.) Many times those sermons led him into shaking his head in dismay. I can still remember him saying to me, "Dad, my spiritual life is fine! I'm just tired!" Let me clarify again that Steffan was a good boy. He was extremely loving, tenderhearted and affectionate. He would have made a great husband and daddy. I look back and think the biggest problem I had was I was trying to make him perfect for God. But God didn't need or want my help with making him perfect. He loved Steffan as he was. It was His job as Abba Father to change Steffan, not mine.

Sadly, it was after his death that God set me free from this mentality once and for all. Through my grieving, I cried out for answers and the Holy Spirit began speaking to me. Setting me free from "religious" thinking was high on His agenda. After the funeral, Steffan's girlfriend Megan, gave us a book that he had read just before his death and that he had given to her to read. It was called *The Shack* written by William P. Young and dealt with our relationship with God. It has been a bestseller and many have read it, but some have labeled it blasphemy. I will be honest. It changed my life and my "religious" thinking for the better. I began to see through this book how much God desired to have a deep personal relationship with me. What I received from this book was positive. I remember weeping as I read, thinking how I had tried to push God down Steffan's throat. Thankfully, God gave me assurance on more than one occasion that my intentions had been good and that Steffan was with Him, which gave me tremendous peace. Oh, the lessons I've learned.

Grace and mercy....what a beautiful gift from God.

Jesus said, My grace is sufficient for you, for my power is made perfect in weakness. Therefore I will boast all the more gladly about my weaknesses, so that Christ's power may rest on me. 2 Corinthians 12:9 NIV.

No matter what struggles we face or how hard the temptations seem to be, God provides grace for His children. His grace is sufficient for what we're going through. If you have sincerely asked Jesus to save you, then you have been adopted into His family. You are a child of the Most High! Sleep well tonight, my friend, knowing that if you don't wake, you will spend eternity with Jesus. Maybe you had a bad day at work and didn't live the Christian life as you should have. Maybe you have gone through a divorce or had an extra–marital affair. Remember grace, God's grace. His grace covers a multitude of sins. We don't have to start over with our Christian walk or feel like scum for blowing it. When we repent, we don't have to start over with our Christian walk or feel like a scum for blowing it. We don't have to get resaved. Once a son, always a son. It's called grace and mercy, dear friend. His Word tells us that He forgives and remembers no more. Since this is the case, we don't need to go around reminding God of our sins. It's all washed under the blood of Jesus! We don't have to live in condemnation any longer. We're free! He has set the captives free! The captives represent you and me. Grace.

Saints of God, you are forgiven and cleansed, so move forward and don't look back. The devil will tempt you by reminding you of your failures and sins. Don't listen to him any longer. Keep your eyes and heart on Jesus.

Questions:

1. Is the devil whispering in your ears that you aren't good enough?
2. Do you feel your past is too blemished to be used of God?

Grace and peace be yours in abundance through the knowledge of God and of Jesus our Lord. 2 Peter 1:2 NIV.

Let's pray:

I thank you, my loving Abba Father (Daddy) for forgiving me of my sins and remembering them no more. I thank you for your grace that covers my sins. I thank you for the blood of Jesus that washes over my sins. Thank you for cleansing me white as snow. Thank you for loving and accepting me as I am. I thank you that my salvation isn't based on what I do, but who I am in Christ. I love you, God, I do. In Jesus's name, amen.

"He Looked Beyond My Fault"

Amazing Grace, shall always be my song of praise.
For it was grace that brought me liberty,
I do not know, just why He came to love me so.
He looked beyond my fault and saw my need.

I shall forever lift mine eyes to Calvary,
To view the cross, where Jesus died for me
How marvelous, His grace that caught my falling soul
He Looked beyond my fault and saw my need.

COLLEGE BOUND

Finally Steffan's high school years came to an end. As Fine Arts Chairman, I chose him to sing the National Anthem for his graduation and I was proud of his performance. Then it was on to college. We chose our local community college, Jones County Junior College, as the basis to begin his college life. He had earned three full scholarships. Again, we were very proud of him. He auditioned in the spring of his senior year of high school for the college show choir, Jones onStage, and stayed involved in this group for the two years he was enrolled. He was also president of the College Republicans and a member of the college concert choir.

During college, he and Kate finally called it quits with their relationship. I believe they had outgrown each other. Their life's interests were going in different directions so they parted as friends, but always had a love that remained between them.

Steffan had chosen to major in accounting. He was great with numbers and basically eased through all his math courses in high school and in the first semester in college. Every few days I would talk with him and ask if he was happy with his career choices and he would always answer with a fervent, "yes". Near the end of his first semester, I asked him again, and this time he began to stammer. He said, "Dad, you know I love music with all my heart." I replied, "Well son, change your college major to Music and become a great show choir director." He just looked at me with those sad brown eyes and said, "Dad, It's too late. I've gone too far with Accounting." I chuckled and said, "Son, it's never too late. Change your major." Suddenly his eyes brightened and that happy, ecstatic look on his face still remains with me. He immediately changed his major to Music and became so content with his decision.

Near the end of his two years at Jones County Junior College, he and his high school buddy Curtis Holland drove to the University of Mississippi in Oxford, to audition for scholarships. Steffan got a decent scholarship and was happy. But I insisted he audition at University of Southern Mississippi, which was in Hattiesburg, less than an hour from home, to see if he could get more money. Indeed he did, almost twice as much. At that point we persuaded him to go to USM. He auditioned for the men's a cappella group, Spirit of Southern, which was led by my good friend Dr. John Flannery. He absolutely loved this group of performers and friends. They performed locally and were a hit with the audiences.

Just before school began at USM, Steffan was cast in the role of Coach Bolton in our community theatre's production of High School Musical. During those rehearsals he met Megan Ruffin, a beautiful dancer in the show. They talked, laughed, rehearsed, ate together, watched movies, and eventually became a couple. Megan was sweet, quiet, and easy going. They seemed to get along so well. I don't recall them even having a disagreement. Through the months, they fell in love and Steffan truly seemed happy. Their plans for education were taking them in different directions, but they seemed at peace. They knew they would always be there for each other.

Steffan began classes at the University of Southern Mississippi in August, 2009. I thought everything was great. But other that the Spirit of Southern, he didn't really get involved at USM. He never went to football games or other activities. He was commuting back and forth each day from home and continuing to work part time at Catfish One, a restaurant run by his good friend, Blake Smith.

One Sunday in late September, we were eating lunch at a local restaurant. Steffan was sitting across from me and said, "Dad, can I talk to you?"

I replied, "Sure, what's going on?"

He seemed to have a bit of trouble expressing what he wanted to say but finally looked at me with his big brown eyes and said, "You know I enjoy USM and really like my professors, but I'm just not happy there. I wondered if in a year or two, I could transfer to Ole Miss? My heart has always been there."

I looked at him with a fatherly love and replied, "Son, you don't have to wait a year or two. Make plans to transfer to Ole Miss at the end of this semester."

The look on his face was priceless! He was shocked at first, but quickly became elated! Yes, he was one happy son! He quickly called his best friend Curtis, who was at Ole Miss, and shared the news.

Looking back, I'm so thankful I listened to God and didn't argue the point. I knew in my heart that it was the right decision. He had gone to USM out of love for Teri and me, but wasn't happy. We could have avoided all this if I had tuned my ears to God. In my heart, I felt USM was the right place and believe me, the University of Southern Mississippi is a great university with an outstanding fine arts department. But I had to just listen to God's will for Steffan. Another lesson learned by me. His only regret about leaving the university was the men's group, Spirit of Southern. They had become like family. But after a personal visit with Dr. Flannery (Flan, as Steffan called him), he felt peace. John and the group understood and wished him well.

Doing what "looks right" may not be God's will for us. We can't be led by facts or frills, but we need to be led by the Holy Spirit. What is right for one, may not be right for another. Each of us must pray and seek God for our own personal plan.

From the moment we concluded the conversation in the restaurant on that Sunday, Steffan began making plans for the big move to Oxford and Ole Miss. His friend Curtis was already enrolled at the university and was living in an apartment with another friend. Their apartment had an extra bedroom for rent, so Steffan quickly grabbed it. Everything was falling into place. October, November, and December became planning months for Steffan. I'm thankful he was so happy during the ending months of his life.

As Thanksgiving arrived, Teri's entire family joined us and our house was full of laughter, joy and lots of food. For several years, this has been an annual event for the Braddy clan. Since we weren't able to get together at Christmas, Teri's parents, George and Mildred, would normally give everyone their Christmas presents at Thanksgiving. The gift was usually money for each to buy what they desired, which was a big blessing. When Steffan and the other grandkids got their Christmas money, he and the cousins, Michael, Joshua, Rachael Ann, Seth and his fiancé Whitney, all went shopping. Steffan came home with bed coverings and bath towels for his apartment. Even though he was headed to Oxford to become an Ole Miss Rebel (red and blue), he bought crimson and white colors in honor of his favorite team, the University of Alabama (Roll Tide). I jokingly told him it was a conflict of interest, but he didn't care. He loved Alabama but was happy and looking forward to being a student at Ole Miss. I even offered to send him to Alabama if he wanted to go, but he felt adamant about going to Ole Miss. So final plans were made for him to move to Ole Miss after Christmas.

Questions:

1. Have you been guilty of following what seems to be right or best in your life and not considering God's will?

2. Can you recall times you made life's plans for yourself and your family without seeking God?

Jesus said, I am the light of this world. Whoever follows me will never walk in darkness, but will have the light of life.
John 8:12 NIV.

Let's pray:

Dear God, please forgive me for being led by what I thought was right instead of listening to your voice. Holy Spirit, please lead and guide me each step of the way. I give you my life. I'm yours, oh God. In Jesus's name, amen.

The Nightmare

On Saturday January 9th, 2010, just days before Steffan was to leave for Ole Miss, it seemed like any normal Saturday. We had been forecast for snow in south Mississippi over the weekend. On that Thursday night, January 7, we watched as Steffan's beloved Bama beat the Texas Longhorns to win the BCS National Championship. The local schools had been canceled on that Friday. I had an all-day show choir rehearsal scheduled that day, but it, along with all other school activities, was canceled. I thought, "Oh well, let's play this weekend since school is canceled!"

Anyone who knew Steffan knew he loved to sleep late in the mornings. He could stay up half the night without any problems but would crash in the mornings. I have found that to be typical of many teenagers and college students. He definitely didn't inherit that trait from his dad. My boat docks around 9:00 p.m. I have never been one to stay up all night, but Steffan had no problem. He would just pay the price the next day.

As lunch rolled around that Saturday, Teri decided she better wake Steffan so he wouldn't be late for work. He realized upon waking that he actually was running late. He dashed into the shower, grabbed some clothes, and quickly headed out the door. Catfish One was in Hattiesburg, about a forty-five minute drive. After he left, Teri remarked, "He was in such a hurry, he forgot to hug and kiss me goodbye." We hardly ever left each other without a hug or kiss. This was almost mandatory for the Myers. After he arrived at work, tender–hearted Steffan called to apologize for not giving his mom that good–bye hug. It was very cold that Saturday and he texted us funny stories about how everything at work was frozen.

We planned to attend a Miss Mississippi preliminary pageant that evening in Hattiesburg, so Lydia could be recognized as Miss Northridge's Outstanding Teen 2010. She had won her teen preliminary pageant in October and was eligible to compete in the Miss Mississippi's Outstanding Teen Pageant to be held in Vicksburg in June, 2010. Each local preliminary pageant usually recognized girls who had already won their crowns and were present in the audience. Unfortunately, Steffan was still working and couldn't attend the pageant. That night his friend and ex–girlfriend, Kimberly Page, won the pageant and we texted him the news of her winning. It was a fun night of watching the pageant, texting back and forth pageant updates with Steffan, and watching Lydia get recognized on stage.

After the pageant, we headed to get a bite to eat. At the restaurant, Steffan and I continued texting back and forth several times. He was going to a friend's birthday party and mentioned spending the night there. I asked him to please come home after the party so we could go to church as a family, have lunch together, then do some shopping for school clothes. We wanted this to be our last family outing together before he moved away from home the following Friday, January 15, to Ole Miss.

After getting home very late from the pageant, I literally crashed in the bed.

Teri and Steffan continued to text each other until about midnight. He told her that they were having fun at the birthday party. Several of the Jones onStage kids were there playing music, singing, dancing, and playing cards. Steffan was also texting his girlfriend, Megan, who had gone to the pageant rather than the birthday party.

As usual, I got up early to pray Sunday morning, continuing my spiritual fast that I participated in each January. I desired direction from God. Jesus spoke of prayer and fasting in God's Word and on this particular day, I was on day nine of the fast. I got up and realized Steffan had not come home. I was discouraged at first because I thought he had chosen to stay with his friends at the birthday party instead of coming home and going to church with us. As I began to pray and intercede, God gave me an overwhelming peace that Steffan was fine. I had prayed many mornings for God to wrap His loving arms around my son. I just didn't know He was literally doing that at the time I was praying.

Teri had awakened again at 4:30 a.m., realized Steffan wasn't home, and texted him asking, "Are you OK?" When she awoke to get ready for church and realized he never answered, she thought that he had decided to spend the night at the birthday party. She was disappointed. Later, Teri read on the accident report that the officers had finished working the accident, towed his car and left the wrecker service location at about 4:30 a.m.

I lovingly told her how God had flooded me with His peace and His hand was on our son. Again, I was clueless during this time that my precious son was in the arms of Jesus. We both felt in our hearts that we'd see him at church.

Teri, Lydia and I dressed, went to church and enjoyed the service. Teri kept looking over her shoulder to the back corner of the auditorium to see if Steffan had slipped in, but he wasn't there.

After the close of the service, we decided to eat lunch at a favorite restaurant. Teri tried to call Steffan's cell to find out when he was coming home, but there was no answer. Nothing seemed to be out of the ordinary. Many times his cell phone battery would die, and he wouldn't be able to call. She decided to run a quick errand after lunch, then head home. About that time, his girlfriend Megan called and wanted to know where he was. He had talked to her the night before and made plans to pick her up so they could attend church with us. They normally spent each

Sunday afternoon with us at the house watching movies. She had been waiting for him all morning. She also had tried his cell, and had gotten no answer. We all decided he had stayed up late at the party and slept in on Sunday. We were all disappointed.

When Teri returned from her errand, she said, "Something's not right. Even if Steffan slept all morning and his phone was dead, he would have borrowed someone's phone and called by now." I called his friend who had hosted the birthday party and asked if Steffan was still asleep. His reply made me dizzy. "Steffan didn't stay here last night. He left about one a.m. headed home so he could go to church with you guys."

His answer brought the first lump in my throat. My heart began to race, but I still thought maybe he went to somebody else's house for the night. He usually notified us where he was or who he was staying with. He was twenty years old, and we tried to respect his growing adult independence; but he was still loving and respectful enough to stay in touch with us. This time, we had heard nothing. After trying two more friends to no avail, my heart began beating almost out of my chest. Where was our beloved son? Where was my little boy? I didn't care if he was 20 years old, he was still my little boy and I wanted him to come home.

Teri and I looked at each other in desperation and realized that we probably needed to check with authorities. I first called the local police station, and there was nothing. One of his friends called the hospital and another went looking for him. Again, nothing. The second call I made was to the Jones County Sheriff's Department which was in the area we lived. I told them we were missing our son, and we were put on hold for what seemed to be eternity. After waiting, the next voice on the phone was the assistant coroner who told me there had been a wreck the night before involving a black car and another car. I do believe my heart stopped beating at that point. His words began ripping my life away. Both drivers were killed in a head-on collision and the black car had burst into flames, completely burning the driver

SURVIVING THE STORMS OF LIFE

and everything in it. My mind, at this point, started fading. He went on to say that the car did not have a car tag and it looked like the driver had been wearing Levi's and tube socks. I immediately shouted, "No! No! No! It's not him! His car had a car tag and he didn't wear Levi brand jeans and never wore tube socks!" Later I realized that the coroner was simply speaking generically, and Levi's to him meant "jeans" and tube socks meant sock material, even footies. But I knew his black Camry had a tag. We found out later that the car tag probably melted.

I tried to stay in denial, but ended the call and quickly called my brother and sister-in-law, Buddy and Sonja, who lived down the hill from me. I could hardly breathe at that point and don't even remember what I said to them. They knew it was an emergency, raced to our home and began helping us put the pieces together and making calls. Before I knew it, our house began filling with friends and family. Teri and I went into our bedroom, closed the door, and just held one another. I looked into her pain-stricken eyes and told her that we must stick together through this potential horror. As a former minister and counselor, I had known of many couples who divorced as a result of tragedy. Their grief became too much to bear. We vowed at that moment, with our bodies shaking and our minds in a state of shock, to stick together for ourselves and for Lydia.

As the minutes rolled by, I was becoming an emotional wreck. I only wanted to wake up from the nightmare and find everything back to normal. I don't remember much about that terrible Sunday evening except that I began to worry whether Steffan was in Heaven if he died.

Don't you know that the devil loves to torment our minds? Why was I worried? We had just talked three days before his death about his relationship with Jesus and he assured me that everything was fine. He had worshiped our Father by my side on many occasions, prayed with his girlfriend and shared Jesus with several of his friends; but fear and panic began to creep in. Those old feelings began to emerge. Yep, we were back to the ballgame with me feeling that God was keeping score. But God is so sweet to us. He understands what we're going through. He was also patient with me and my panic. He knew my deep fears so He led our dear friend Pastor David Hagen, who had been right by our side the entire time of this nightmare, to kneel down, put his loving arms around Teri and me and gently told us, "Once sons of God, always sons of God." That small, simple statement brought us peace in the midst of the storm we were facing. I think back and truly believe it was Jesus speaking to us. When I looked into Pastor David's eyes, I felt like I was looking into the eyes of Jesus. God was speaking through him. Grace, God's grace. Thank you Jesus!

Within a very short time, our house was full of people offering comfort, bringing food, and praying for us. Still, part of us was in denial. It just couldn't be! No! This was our loving son, our firstborn! This is the little baby we had prayed so earnestly for! Pastor Jerry Bishop had lifted him to God at his baby dedication! He was only five days away from the University of Mississippi (Ole Miss)! He had his apartment and roommates. He was ready and excited about finishing his degree in music and becoming a high school show choir director like his dad! His plans! His dreams! My prayers and fasting! I thought I had been doing the right thing each morning by praying! I never let one single day go by that I wasn't praying and interceding for my family's safety and that the hand of God would be on each of them.

We were told his black burned car, or what was left of it, had been towed to a location. One of the sheriff's deputies met my niece and nephew, Sean and Misty, at the site to examine the car for any possible evidence or identification of Steffan. When they returned, they came into the bedroom with those painful eyes that said, "It was Steffan," and then, they both burst into tears. We just stood there holding each other in a family group hug crying. In my hysteria, I begged them to tell me it wasn't him.

Pastor David showed us a picture they had taken of a tennis shoe that had melted into the floorboard. When Steffan's girlfriend, Megan, looked at it, she burst into uncontrollable tears and her petite little body fell into a heap on the floor.

Reality was sinking in. Pastor David looked at us and gently and lovingly said, "Bill, Teri, we now believe that it was Steffan in the wreck." At that moment, every part of my being left me, and I don't recall much after that. Was I even breathing? My mind went into a blur. I do remember at one point I couldn't even remember my last name. Later we discovered that because of this horror, we were experiencing post–traumatic syndrome, the sudden shock that people experience from the death of a loved one causing memory lapse, depression, lack of concentration and much more.

I thank God for a true man of God, our pastor, Brother David, who along with the Life Church staff, took the reins and began helping us make decisions. We weren't emotionally able to do anything at that point but cry.

Poor Lydia was only twelve, almost thirteen, and her little emotions went awry. Her tears turned to anger. This is a normal reaction for children. They don't know how to channel their emotions in the proper direction. They can get distant and angry, even feeling abandoned by the one who died. Parents must understand these emotions and allow their grieving children to experience them. We have video and pictures of precious Lydia at the funeral. I don't recall her crying much at all during the service. Of course, the week after the funeral, as Steffan's death became more of a reality, her world completely crumbled. She went through a horrible mourning stage. I thank God for her school counselor, Ramona Doggett, who had lost a son of her own, and had so much compassion toward Lydia. She even came to our house to visit with Lydia. They talked, hugged and cried together. Even after Lydia returned to school, Ramona's office door was always open for her to visit and share her feelings. God takes care of His children by placing the right people in our path!

Never take for granted that children will be okay. They need help just like adults. Even if they seem fine, they probably aren't. Try to get them help through counseling. Children are fragile, and traumatic events can scar them for a long time.

Some people feel receiving counseling or taking medication for grief shows weakness or a lack of spirituality. I say, get over it! Do whatever is necessary to make it through your horrible journey. God understands! I personally don't like to take medicine of any sort, but after the funeral I could feel mounds of depression flooding into my life. I was losing sleep, appetite, concentration, and much more. Teri and I both decided to seek temporary professional medical treatment to survive. The medicine we received did numb us a bit, but we were at least able to concentrate better and slowly make it through each day. Post traumatic stress disorder can take six months to a year for the brain to heal. I have some people tell me that they wouldn't take medicine for grief. They would survive. Again, I say it's not unspiritual to seek medical help. Bill and Teri realized we needed help and I'm thankful we did what we did. No regrets over medicine. After several months, we were able to cease the medication with the feeling that we could make it.

The first morning after discovering Steffan's death, I got up as usual for my prayer time. Teri and Lydia were still in bed. For some strange reason, the house seemed quieter than ever before. I really don't think any of us slept much at all. My normal cup of coffee had very little taste to me. I went to the couch in our living room, lay in a fetal position, and literally wished to die. I began begging God to take me to Heaven so I could be with my son. It was the worst pain I had ever experienced. I've never had feelings of not wanting to live before, but the pain was completely overwhelming. As a minister, I had always been on the other side of family deaths. I was always the one praying, comforting, and counseling. Now, I was wearing the shoes of pain. I couldn't really pray. I just lay there begging to die. Feeling my life had no further meaning, I truly wanted to die and be with Steffan. I needed to put my arms around him and make sure he was okay. When I describe the horrible pain I felt from losing my son, I truly mean it's the worst pain imaginable. I felt as if I couldn't breathe. I would have felt less if someone had stabbed me in the chest with a knife. After a time of begging God to die, I heard God's audible voice speak.

Amid the stillness of the room and the storm raging in my heart, God lovingly spoke, "Teri. Lydia."

I knew it was God's voice even though it was softer and gentler sounding than I would have imagined. But I knew He was telling me to live for my wife and daughter, who needed me. Never again did I wish to die.

I never got very angry with God. I had been so close to Him and knew deep in my heart that He loved me. I knew He wasn't punishing me, but I just didn't understand how and why. How could Steffan die when I was praying and fasting for him? Why would He take my son? He was only twenty years old. What purpose was there? Why, God why? Let me share at this point that it's truly okay to question God. You're not unspiritual for doing so. Jesus himself questioned God.

My God, my God, why have you forsaken me?
Matthew 27:46 NIV.

Please don't feel guilty for asking questions. Don't we, as parents, allow our children to ask us questions? Aren't we God's children? He loves us so much. He understands our pain and suffering and desires to carry us through our storms. He has never left our side but He is there speaking to us, if we'll just listen. I remember the old hymn, "In the Garden." "And He walks with me and He talks with me, and tells me I am His own." This hymn says it all.

I encourage you—If you are going through a storm in your life, whether it's the death of a loved one, a divorce, or a job loss, run into the arms of God and allow Him to comfort you and get you through it. He will, I promise. And remember, storms are only temporary.

Through the pain and complete agony, we were forced to make funeral plans. Because his body was so badly burned, the local coroner sent his body and dental records to Jackson, MS, for identification. This delayed the funeral. He died early Sunday morning and his funeral was Friday. Because of the fire, we were forced to have a closed casket.

It was the most horrific experience I had ever gone through. Many years ago, I had lost my younger brother, Stevie to a gun accident and more recently, had lost my mom to cancer. But nothing, nothing, *nothing*, compared to losing my child. The ultimate plan of life is for our children to outlive us. As I began to think about the funeral service, I knew Teri, Lydia and I wouldn't be able to sit on the front row of the church staring at a closed silver casket that had our son's body in it. So I went to the local florists who were dear friends, and together we designed a large cascade of flowers to completely cover the entire casket. They covered the top of the casket with six dozen red roses and surrounded the roses with an array of white flowers that cascaded all the way to the floor. It was so beautiful and easier to look at. Steffan was such an Alabama (Roll Tide) fan. We thought the crimson and white would be fitting for him. A local photographer called and told us he had a beautiful picture of Steffan that he had taken in one of his college musical performances. He had it enlarged for us and brought it to our house. When we saw it, we wept. We displayed by the casket for the visitation and for the funeral.

The feeling of just having your child suddenly snatched away from you with no closure, not even a body to look at to say goodbye, is beyond description. One moment you're laughing, hugging, and loving, and the next moment your child is completely gone. Vanished. It was only through God that we survived the ordeal. Not only did we lose Steffan and his car, but we lost all his special belongings that were in his car. He was a typical college student who practically lived out of his car. All his new Ole Miss school clothes were in the back seat of the car. Gone. His cell phone, iPod, CD's, pictures, and even a new football trophy he had won playing fantasy football with his boss, Blake Smith, and several others, were now gone. He was so proud of that trophy. Steffan loved Blake and his wife Ashlee like family and they loved watching football together. But now all of his memorabilia was destroyed in the fire. Note: Shortly after the funeral, Blake had an identical fantasy football trophy made for us with Steffan's name engraved on it. We were blessed by his thoughtfulness and generosity.

In planning his funeral, we asked Steffan's best friend Curtis to sing the only song that would come to my mind, "You Raise Me Up." Even though it was an older song, I believe the Holy Spirit spoke to me that this was the song. The title kept reminding me that God had raised him to heaven.

"You Raise Me Up"
by Josh Groban

You raise me up, so I can stand on mountains;
You raise me up to walk on stormy seas;
I am strong when I am on your shoulders;
You raise me up to more than I can be.

Questions:

1. Do you feel alone or abandoned in your particular storm?

2. Have you felt guilty for questioning God?

I, even I, am he who comforts you, declares the Lord.
Isaiah 51:12 NIV.

Let's pray:

Oh Heavenly Father, thank you for always being with me when I am faced with storms. I thank you that you are my shepherd and you love your sheep. I thank you that I can run into your arms for comfort. I also thank you, God, that you will answer my questions. I know when I hurt, you hurt. There are things I don't understand, but I'm confident you will show me truth. In Jesus's name, amen.

God speaks

At the time of Steffan's death, we had a missionary friend from our church named Jim Buckman who was leading a pastors' conference in California made up of ministers from another nation. During a prayer session, Jim received a text from someone in our church stating that Steffan had been killed in an automobile accident. He shared the tragic news with the ministers, and they began to drop to their knees weeping and interceding for our family. Just after that, he received another text, but this time it was from Curtis, asking for prayer. He told Jim he wasn't sure he could emotionally handle standing in front of the church and singing at his best friend's funeral. He was so broken from Steffan's death. Steffan and Curtis were like brothers and were always hanging out together. They were so excited about sharing an apartment together in Oxford, MS, while attending Ole Miss. Their friendship had dated back to 2003 when they were both in high school.

Jim shared that when he received Curtis' text, he immediately heard the voice of God speak to him. He looked up in the room where he was and literally saw Heaven open. There he saw our son Steffan, standing before the throne of God, smiling with his hands raised, worshiping our most Holy Father. Jim said he couldn't see God, but he just knew in his spirit that was where Steffan was standing. The voice of God spoke, "Jim, tell Curtis to sing to me. Steffan is no longer there; he is with me." Then the opened view of Heaven closed. This, my friends, actually happened inside a conference room in California! It was almost three weeks later before Jim had the opportunity to return to our church in Laurel and share this awesome testimony with me. I stood there listening with tears running down my cheeks. It was beautiful. When he finished, I hugged and thanked him and began to walk away with tears still streaming down my face. But he put his hand onto my arm and stopped me. I turned around and looked him into his eyes as he said, "Dr. Myers, I *saw* Steffan. This wasn't a vision. I saw him."

At that point, I believe I wept from my head all the way to my feet. Dear God! Jim had actually seen my son! He really was alive! Steffan was in Heaven! He was happy! God had called him by name! Needless to say, I didn't sleep much that night, but just kept thanking God. Wow, what a miracle of love!

The funeral was beautiful, but excruciatingly painful. I never stopped crying from the moment I entered the sanctuary. Walking to the front row from the back of the auditorium seemed like eternity.

As I reached the front, I remember seeing my older brother Buddy, sitting on the second pew. It seemed he was waiting for me. I think I literally fell into his arms and wept uncontrollably. I will never forget how he and his precious wife Sonja cared for us during this nightmare time in our lives. Steffan loved them both. He loved to bring his friends over to their house for Aunt Sonja's cooking. They would eat until they were so stuffed that they could hardly breathe. We made some precious family memories at their home. A favorite photograph we have to cherish shows Steffan, Curtis and Buddy laughing hysterically at a Steffan's last Christmas gathering held at Buddy and Sonja's house.

Beside Curtis' solo, our church choir sang, "Cry Holy," which had featured Steffan as soloist several months before. Through technology, they were able to play the video with Steffan singing the solo while the Life Church Choir sang live. It was so beautiful to see him on the big screen worshipping God. From then on, that song took on a new meaning to the Myers family. On the back of Steffan's headstone are some of the words from the song "Cry Holy."

"Cry Holy" by Salvador

We come this far
by light of day,
through deserts of loneliness,
to the sacred place.
Well you know my life,
and all I've been through,
the sin in my heart,
has kept me from you.
But Father your grace
is greater than sin.

Your mercy rains down,
and heals me again.

All I can do is fall down on my knees and
cry, holy, holy, holy.
You are holy

When I'm on my face,
in my darkest night,
I cry for a way,
to your shining light.
And Father your grace,
is greater than sin.
It shines down on me,
and heals me again.

Most of the funeral service was a blur. I do remember the close of the service, when the pall bearers, who were very close friends of Steffan, stood and walked over to move the casket from the church to the hearse waiting outside. My emotions overcame me and I jumped to my feet and threw my arms around several of his buddies. These boys were like my adopted sons, and I loved each one of them. We embraced one another and cried. As I glanced over my shoulder, I noticed they were beginning to roll the casket. I wheeled around and in my uncontrollable grief, threw my arms over the casket, trying to hug my son one last time. All I could think was, "Steffan, don't leave me!" I desperately wanted our lives to go back to the way they were before!

Many family members and friends came to the house afterward to visit including Judy and Larry Brasher, the couple who had prayed for us to have this child. Judy was Steffan's godmother and she loved him so. She was fighting cancer at the time of his death, but made the trip from Birmingham, Alabama, to be with us to painfully say good–bye to Steffan. Only a year later, Judy went to Heaven to be with Jesus and Steffan.

I also recall looking at Steffan's cousins at our house that afternoon. They were in the kitchen quietly talking. I was sitting in the living room corner looking at each one– Michael, Joshua, Rachel Ann, Seth and some of Steffan's friends, Channing *and* Curtis, and I thought to myself, *They will all grow up, get married and have children. But Steffan will always be twenty years old. Even one day his baby sister, Lydia, will be older than him.* Those thoughts were so painful.

Questions:

1. Has there been a painful time in your life when you thought you were all alone and wouldn't make it another step?
2. Have you felt that your storm was more than you could bear?

The Lord is close to the brokenhearted and saves those who are crushed in spirit. Psalm 34:18 NIV.

Let's pray:

My Abba Father, I acknowledge that I need you. There are times when my storms are so rough, I feel I will sink. But you, loving Father, will sustain me, and hold me tight. Thank you for your protection, compassion, and love. Today, I give you my hurts and pain. I will walk with you, knowing there will be moments you will need to carry me. I'm comforted by your love. In Jesus's name, amen.

The Journey begins

The Lord is close to the brokenhearted and saves those who are crushed in spirit. Psalm 34:18 NIV.

If you've ever lost a loved one, you know the worst part isn't the funeral, but the journey that begins afterward. Many people meant well by telling us to cheer up or rejoice because he was in Heaven! They missed the point. We knew he was a Christian and was in Heaven. Our pain was we that were missing our son whom we normally saw on a daily basis. We missed the hugs, kisses, and the big grin on his face. He just had that sweet grin that everyone seemed to love. We missed that. Our house didn't seem the same. A dark emptiness hovered throughout the house. There were mornings after the funeral when I would wake in my grief and just want to burn the house down and move away, never returning. I know that sounds bad, but I'm being honest. The house was so full of Steffan. Those mornings would just be overwhelming and in desperation, I would think if I could only take Teri and Lydia away, the pain would cease. Of course, I knew that wouldn't solve anything and I would probably go to jail for burning the house down.

But there were also mornings when I would get up and seemingly feel and smell him. I wanted to bask in that beautiful feeling, not wanting to leave. The house would seem so warm and inviting. You can tell my emotions were running to and fro. Jim, my missionary friend, caught me just before the worship service one Sunday morning a couple of months after the funeral and took me by the hand. He made me promise him that I wouldn't make any major decisions regarding my life for one year. At the time, I thought, *Why is he making me promise this?* Puzzled, I reluctantly promised. As the days and months rolled on, I completely understood why he made me promise. My emotions were on a giant roller coaster, going up and down. I really wasn't emotionally stable to make good, Spirit–led decisions. I'm so glad I promised this brother in Christ. It was one of the best decisions I made. I encourage you to heed this advice if you are experiencing tragedy of some kind. You might be going through divorce, or have lost your job. You might be facing foreclosure on your home or broken relationships. Just sit tight, rest, trust God, and allow God to heal you before making any major decisions. Down the road of life, you'll be glad you waited.

The Lord is my shepherd.........He makes me lie down in green pastures, He leads me beside quiet waters, He restores my soul.... Psalm 23 NIV.

Rest and heal, my friend, under the shadow of the almighty.

Everyone has to deal with grief in their own way. Some people feel compelled to go to the grave often; but that's just not who we were. We haven't visited the grave much at all. We knew Steffan wasn't there and it was too painful to go. Every now and then, Teri would go into his bedroom and look at everything that belonged to him. We had left everything as it was. It was comfort for her. I would recommend not changing anything at first. Take your time. I believe you'll know when the time is right. Again, everyone deals with grief differently. There is no set– in–stone recipe for healing. We are all different. I do recommend that you take some time to heal and not jump back into the swing of life too soon. There is a grieving time that we must, and need, to face.

I remember many years ago there was a married couple in a church we attended who had lost a son in an automobile accident.

At the funeral, we were asked to join the parents in worship and praise. I recall them testifying with big smiles to those attending the funeral service that they were delivered from grief. I knew in my heart, they would have to go through it sooner or later. Unfortunately, it was later for them. A couple of weeks after the funeral, their world began crumbling. I believe the strength they were feeling at the service was more shock and denial. The day that we learned of Steffan's death, God reminded both Teri and me of this sweet couple. We knew that we were in shock and would have to go through a grieving process.

Some individuals who have lost someone in their lives and are hurting feel the need to be strong for other family members. That's okay, but I believe they are delaying the grieving process that is necessary to go through. Teri and I decided to just be real with Lydia. We desired for her to express what was churning inside of her. We agreed that if she was going to feel comfortable sharing her feelings, then we, as parents, would have to mentor her by taking off our masks and being real ourselves. Many times, she witnessed us crying. I believe it didn't convey to her that we were weak or unspiritual, but instead, were real. Our emotions showed how much love we had for both our children. We continuously reiterated our love for her and how thankful we were to have her. Our decision that all three of us would walk through this storm together was wise.

We must give ourselves ample time to heal. Our hearts are wounded and our focus can be blurred during the grieving process. God doesn't expect us to be 100 percent on top of our game immediately following a storm.

In the shadow of Your wings will I trust. Psalm 57:1 NIV.

This verse makes me think of a mother duck that cuddles her babies under her wings with protection from the storms. What an illustration of God's love. Rest and heal, my friend. Crawl into Abba Father's lap and be comforted. Teri has often said that she felt God protected us in a "grace bubble." Although the pain was, at times, excruciating, it wasn't constant. God protected us from total emotional annihilation.

Through all the trauma, pain, and grief, I tried my best to seek God. Honestly, because of the severity of my pain and hurt, there were days I couldn't muster much prayer. But God understood. I even recall days through my weeping, I could only mutter, "God, I love you" and nothing more. Again, God understood. But what I did hear from God was that He loved me, I was His child, and His desire was for me to slowly put one foot in front of the other. I began to take baby steps with my life. Yes, He was encouraging me to begin moving forward.

Mourning and grieving are necessary for healing, but God's Word says it's for a season, not a lifetime. He didn't expect me to go out and conquer a mountain, but just begin to walk. And that's what I did. One step at a time, one day at a time, one month at a time. Friend, please know I didn't walk alone. He was there all the way. Some days He walked with me and other days He carried me. He never left my side. He'll do the same for you. Part of the reason you may be reading this book is you're experiencing pain in your own life. Don't give up! He will walk with you, and if need be, He'll carry you because He loves you. But you must decide to move forward. The devil loves for us to stay down and depressed because when we are experiencing forms of sadness and depression, our attention focuses more on us and our problem, not God. That's why it's important at some point in your grieving, to begin to move forward, even if it's slow. I encourage you to not let the devil win this battle. His will is for you to stay down! Don't give in. You can do it! Remember, there's light (Jesus) at the end of the broken heart tunnel.

Looking back on it now, Teri believes that part of the grieving process that includes denial is an overwhelming desire to keep your loved one "alive"—

alive in your thoughts, alive in your memories, alive to those around you. You don't want others to forget him; to forget how special he was, what an impact he made. Because everything was frozen the day Steffan died, Teri wanted to world to stop, to stay frozen. The first day she noticed flowers blooming, she got angry. How dare the world go on without Steffan! As time goes on, and you realize that you have to let your loved one go, that you can't keep them "alive," but you can honor their memory, healing can begin to take place as you begin to let go and move forward.

I am established in righteousness, and oppression (depression and grief) is far from me. Isaiah 54:14 NIV.

This scripture is powerful and it works! After quoting that verse in faith, I would feel the pain lift and the "joy of the Lord" would return. As I've said throughout this book, storms are only temporary. Look for your rainbow.

Right after the funeral Lydia, who had been angry over losing her brother, had a spiritual dream/visitation from Steffan that came from God. It brought healing in her heart and helped her begin those difficult steps forward.

Lydia shared, "As I stood over Steffan's grave, I cried. My brother was gone. I just couldn't stop crying. I couldn't believe it, even though his car wreck had happened over two weeks before. I could understand that he was in Heaven, but I just wanted him here with me. Then suddenly, the setting around me changed. I was in Heaven! I saw Steffan! I ran to him and tackled him with a hug. His hair was perfect, his skin was perfect, just everything about him was perfect. We hugged with excitement and he kissed me on my cheek."

Wasn't God good to give her this visitation dream in her darkest hours? Her dream brought her healing.

Teri also experienced a dream that comforted her. She shared, "Right before I woke up, I dreamed I saw Steffan and gave him a kiss. I don't know if we spoke or not, or how long I was with him. I just remember seeing his face, looking into his eyes and giving him a kiss. It was what I needed."

He is truly the God of comfort.

One of the most touching spiritual dreams came from a dear friend of Steffan's, Samantha Ruffin. When she shared what God had given her, I cried with tears of joy and comfort. Samantha shared, "I looked around and noticed we were in a room that looked like the den or family room of a house where I saw Bill sitting in a chair with his eyes closed, and with a book on my stomach. Steffan walked over to where his dad was sitting and told me (Samantha) with a big smile, 'This man will never know how much I love him.' He then kissed his dad on the forehead. (That forehead kiss was so typical of Steffan.) He then walked over and looked at his mom and said, 'I love my mom so much.' He lovingly hugged his mom very tightly. Finally turned, looked at his sister, Lydia, and said with the biggest grin, 'This one I can't get over.' He seemed to be in awe how beautiful she was. Steffan could see his family but they couldn't see him."

As I began to seek God and question Him about why and how, He began revealing answers piece by piece. One of the mind–boggling questions I asked was, "Why did everything have to burn in the fire?" What He gave me was some scriptures that only related to me. You may interpret these verses differently, but He gave these to me and it helped.

You are the God that answers by fire. 1 Kings 18:24 NIV.

Deliver me with your fire. Psalm 18:13 NIV.

Purify my life with your fire. Malachi 3:2 NIV.

Let Your glory kindle a burning like the burning of a fire. Isaiah 10:16 NIV

The Holy Spirit reminded me of my prayers, asking God to purify and change Steffan into the image of Jesus more each day. This prayer was answered. Maybe not the way I had planned, but it was answered. The Holy Spirit also spoke to me on two separate occasions in church that God had received my offering of Steffan. In the Old Testament, the Levites would offer their sacrifices to God through offerings laid on the fire. For an offering to God, I gave up one of my most precious gifts, my child. You might think at this point that I'm crazy, but I'm being honest sharing what God revealed to me. These scriptures regarding the fire of God comforted me. Not having a body to look at during the funeral forced me to only look to my loving Father God for consolation, closure, and understanding.

There have been many unanswered questions that I would have liked to have answered, but I learned to trust God in a greater way. He absolutely knows what's best for me. I'm His child and the apple of His eye. He desires for me to experience "life and life more abundantly" (John 10: 10). I love the old hymn, "Tis so sweet to trust in Jesus."

The righteous perish, and no one ponders it in his heart; devout men are taken away, and no one understands that the righteous are taken away to be spared from evil. Isaiah 57:1 NIV. We had this verse inscribed on Steffan's headstone.

Having an interest in music, I often refer to song lyrics in order to express my emotions. All of us who have experienced a major storm are bombarded with questions. The song lyrics from the Broadway musical *Mame* expresses some of the questions that ran through my head after my loss. In this song, Mame questions herself about mistakes she made raising her little Patrick, who had now grown up.

"If He Walked Into My Life Today"

Where is that boy with the bugle?
My little love who was always my big romance;
Where's that boy with the bugle?
And why did I ever buy him those d___ long pants?
Did he need a stronger hand?
Did he need a lighter touch?
Was I soft or was I tough?
Did I give enough?
Did I give too much?

At the moment when he needed me,
Did I ever turn away?
Would I be there when he called,
If he walked into my life today?
Did I stress the man?
And forget the child.
And there must have been a million things.
that my heart forgot to say.
Would I think of one or two,
If he walked into my life today?

It's normal to have questions bombard you when you have suffered through a storm or a major setback in life. Only God can truly give us the answers we so desire. He has answered many of my questions, and He will do the same for you, I promise.

One month after his death, God gave me a dream about Steffan and answered many questions through this dream.

My dream: In my grieving mind, I had been worrying about Steffan's life. I found myself sitting in the passenger seat of our old van. Steffan was driving. Between him and the driver's door was an old friend that in my opinion, wasn't a good influence on him. The van ran off the road and got stuck in someone's yard. In my dream, I got out of the van and began pushing from behind. The van slowly made its way back on the road and the friend in the van vanished. The Lord spoke to me about the interpretation. The van represented Steffan's life. For a short time, He had veered off God's chosen path and become bogged down. God spoke truth in his life and he got back on the right path. The so-called friend in the dream represented a negative influence the devil had set up to pull him away from God. This dream was more assurance that Steffan was with Jesus.

Ask and it will be given to you; seek and you will find; knock and the door will be opened to you. For everyone who asks receives; he who seeks finds; and to him who knocks, the door will be opened. Matthew 7:7–8 NIV.

Friends, it's not wrong to ask questions. God is waiting to answer.

One night while I was rehearsing with the Life Church Choir on a Wednesday evening, we were seated, worshiping God from our hearts. Suddenly, I saw a vision in front of me. It was my mother sitting with Steffan in Heaven. She looked so beautiful. She had her arm around Steffan, singing praises to God. She had the biggest smile on her glowing face. I couldn't see Steffan's face but recognized his curly hair. It was a beautiful moment that my loving Father allowed me to see.

The most significant spiritual dream I experienced as of this writing regarding my son, was in 2012. I dreamed I was at the foot of a very large staircase. I looked to the top of the staircase and saw an image of Steffan. At first I thought it was a hologram, like we've all seen in movies. He walked down the staircase with that same big smile on his face. Thinking it was a hologram, I reached to touch the image and realized I was actually touching him. I felt his body! I immediately threw my arms around him with a big hug, and cried uncontrollably. As I was hugging him, I told him how much I loved him and how much that I was missing him. I remember him telling me as he was hugging me that he loved and missed me too. He looked so happy. In the next moment, I was standing on top of the large platform that the staircase had led to. In front of me was Steffan worshipping with his arms lifted to God. He looked so happy and peaceful. Then he turned around and walked back to where I was standing and hugged me again. In my tears of joy, I choked out the words, "I love you son." He lovingly looked into my eyes and replied, "I love you too, Dad."

The dream brought closure to my mind and heart. No, he wasn't ever coming back. But he looked peaceful and happy. It was exactly what I needed.

Questions:

1. Have you felt guilty for asking God questions?
2. Do you believe He will answer?

You understand, O Lord; remember me and care for me. Jeremiah 15:15 NIV.

Let's pray:
Thank you God for allowing me the opportunity to approach your throne and present my requests and questions. I thank you for understanding my thoughts and my questions. I thank you for answering my questions because you love me. In Jesus's name, amen.

It's A New Day

We are no longer survivors, but conquerors. We have experienced and overcome one of the worst storms a family could endure. If we hadn't relied on God each step, our ship would have sunk. Today, we feel victorious! God has beautiful plans for the three of us as we have chosen to keep moving forward. Do we wish things were different? Of course, we do. Not a day goes by that I don't wish Steffan was here with us; but he's not coming back. Yes. We'll see him again, and that's exciting, but he won't be coming home again.

As we have come through this storm, Teri and I have sensed God's anointing on Lydia. He has blessed her with many gifts and talents. Not only is she beautiful on the outside, but she radiates the love of God in her heart. Through her painful experience, she has taught two Bible study groups at her high school, offering hope and encouragement. She's an active member of our church music program and sings on the youth praise team. God has blessed her as she has competed in and won many pageants and talent shows. She also wrote a children's book to help children and young teens who are struggling with low self–esteem.

Yes, we have made our choice to keep moving forward. We have weathered this storm and will weather more in this life, but our ship will not sink! Friends, choose to be a conqueror through

Jesus! Choose life and life more abundantly! Choose to survive and remember storms are only temporary.

SURVIVAL TIPS WHEN EXPERIENCING A STORM.

Whether it's the loss of a loved one, divorce, job loss, loss of health, etc., I encourage you to read these 10 vital steps to recovery and allow them to help you during your time of grief, your storm. They aren't a magic pill, but simple steps that you can take to help you survive your storm nightmare.

1. Cry. Crying is not a sign of weakness. It's needed and part of the healing process. Trying to restrain your emotions to "be strong" can cause a multitude of problems, including physical problems. Just let it out. Cry, scream, or get angry. It's okay to feel these emotions. You are not unspiritual

for having these feelings. There are stages, such as anger, you will need to travel through in your grieving process. It's okay. Allow yourself ample time to experience what needs to come out. There are times even now that I still need to cry. It might be watching a movie or listening to a song that reminds me of my son, Steffan. One day I might smile thinking about him, but on another day I might feel the need to cry. I've learned through this process that it's part of my ongoing healing. Learn to express your feelings without shame or guilt. You can help others by being real.

If you're a parent, don't hide your emotions from your children. They need to see the real you, which will help them in dealing with their own grief.

Do not take your emotions and aggressions out on others. Don't cross the line by hurting others, especially those that love you. But it's okay to let it out. Remember Jesus wept over Lazarus. God created tears to not only express our feelings, but also as a healing. The good news is, your heart rate usually decreases after crying. Tears have salt and actually clean your eyes. Your body normally enters a calming state after a good cry. When I look at those individuals who refuse to cry, but instead hold their emotions in all in the name of being strong, I see an enormous time bomb getting ready to explode. Blood pressure and heart problems have been correlated with restraining emotions. Let it out and be real!

2. Don't make any major decisions during your time of grief that you will later regret. Your mind is probably not thinking clearly at the moment. Move slowly and allow yourself time to heal. I have known people who went through a particular crisis or storm and hastily sold their home feeling they needed a fresh start, only to regret the move later. With the death of a family member, take your time regarding their clothes and belongings. You'll know

when it's time to pack away these items. We've all watched movies where someone experiences a broken heart from a bad relationship. In their emotions, they destroy pictures and trash memorabilia, only to regret it later. Making rash decisions can bring harm and much regret. Friends, take your time making decisions, so you'll have no regrets. Don't allow others who mean well, convince you to make decisions that aren't agreeable with your heart. Remember the chapter where I promised not to make any major decisions for one year after losing my son? It was one of the best decisions I made. I had to keep my promise even though my emotions were screaming, "change." I'm so thankful I kept my promise. God will give you peace when it is time to clean a room of a loved one who has died, give away belongings, sell a house, or move locations. My old saying that I have used for years is, "When you don't know what to do, don't do." In other words, if you're in doubt or not sure about a particular matter, put the decision brakes on and wait on God's timing. His direction will bring peace in your heart that it's the right decision and timing. Take your time.

3. Counseling can be beneficial. If you need counseling or someone to talk with, don't hesitate to get it. It's not a sign of weakness. There are times we just need someone to talk to who will listen and not lecture. I recall visiting a pastor years before losing Steffan for counsel on a particular matter. Before I could even get half of the problem out of my mouth, he was already giving me advice along with scriptures. He never listened to what I needed to say. I left his office feeling worse instead of better. Professional counselors are trained to probe conversation from their clients. In other words, they are trained to listen and help get us to talk about and release our emotions. If someone who is hurting comes to you needing to talk, please listen

and don't do all the talking. They need to talk. Most of the time, they know the answers in their heart but they're longing for an understanding ear. (Note: I would not submit myself to a counselor unless they were a Christian and believed in Christian values.) If someone who is hurting comes to you needing to talk, please listen and don't do all the talking. They need to talk. Counseling isn't weakness, but rather wisdom. If you need it, get it.

4. If you need temporary medication to help you get through the rough time, see your doctor. Again, it's okay. Don't feel guilty. Medicine isn't a sign that you're weak or unspiritual. Teri and I both took a prescription to help us get through the first few months of our tragedy. If you've been diagnosed with post traumatic stress disorder, you very well may need medication to help you concentrate. During the first few months after losing my son, my brain had become like a fog due to the shock of his death. I couldn't think of simple answers, would get confused easily, couldn't remember names, and felt myself sinking deep into a well of depression. Now, I'm personally not in favor of long term medication, but each one of us has to deal with our pain differently. If you're emotionally hurting and don't think you can go on, please see your doctor and get the medical help you need. Do not feel guilty for doing so. I do encourage you to try to research the medication and make sure it's right for you.

5. Please understand that most people mean well with their comments during your tragedy. Many friends and relatives are clueless about what words to speak for comfort. Sometimes their words sting or aggravate us. I encourage you to ignore words that irritate and hurt you. Try not to lose your temper and say something you will later regret. Most of the time they truly mean well. Friends, the best

words to use when comforting others who are hurting are: "I'm sorry," "I'm praying for you," "I love you," and "I'm here for you if you need me." Try not get offended with others' comments. They're just trying to help. I remember hearing certain well–meant comments and wanted to scream, but each time someone would say an off-the-wall comment, God would remind me that they meant well. During our tragedy, I definitely learned patience.

Remember, for those of us giving comfort and advice, the fewer words we speak, the better. If someone is experiencing the death of a family member or any major storm, they don't need to hear your personal stories of loss. Just loving someone who is suffering and choosing to pray for them is the best and most positive steps to take in comforting others. Remember, the fewer words spoken, the better. Hurting people need love, not an earful of advice or your own personal stories of loss.

6. Don't beat yourself up with guilt or the "what if's". Many parents blame themselves or each other when a child is lost. Many broken hearted individuals who have come out of a broken-relationship such as divorce, tend to look in the mirror and blame themselves for the failed relationship. My advice is, let it go. The guilt and blame won't fix the grief; it only makes it worse. Many marriages dissolve over guilt and blame after experiencing a tragedy. Even though my wife, Teri, and I vowed to stick together during our tragedy, we still experienced small amounts of blame toward each other. There wasn't any legitimate reason to blame except our emotions were in an upheaval and we ended up taking it out on each other. Thankfully, we talked and realized blaming each other over what we did or didn't do, wouldn't bring our son back in our lives. We chose to walk through the fire of grief together. I'm thankful we did. I encourage you to vow to stick together

as a family through the storms you face. I wish I could tell you that it only lasts a certain number of months, but we're all different. Remember, we can't change the past but we can change the present; so bury the blame and keep your eyes on Jesus.

7. Give yourself time to adjust your thinking and don't feel guilty for mistakes. I remember after losing our son we went into a restaurant and my wife, out of habit, asked for a table for four instead of three. It happens. It takes time to adjust your thinking, so give yourself a break. You can't be expected to think differently overnight. Maybe for a while, you should avoid certain places or destinations that flood your mind with painful memories. This could be certain visitations to restaurants, or the cemetery. Maybe it's songs that bring a painful memory. There's nothing wrong with avoiding them temporarily. Later you will probably feel led to face these destinations as part of your healing. But while you are severely suffering, please avoid making your pain any worse. Don't feel guilty for doing so. I recall visiting our dear friends, Don and Susan Casey a year after Steffan's death, in Birmingham, Alabama where we had previously lived. We went to a restaurant where we had celebrated our children's birthdays for many years. As I sat down at our table and looked around at the surroundings, I was flooded with memories of Steffan's birthdays. Tears began to flow uncontrollably. At first, I felt guilty for possibly ruining the night. Don and Susan didn't try to change the subject or cheer me up, but instead comforted me and encouraged me to let it out. After crying for a minute or two, I felt better and went on to enjoy the evening. Experiences like these will happen, so try to work through them and not feel guilty.

8. Make a decision to eventually move forward. Begin by taking one step at a time. It takes time, but choosing

to move forward instead of living your life in pain and depression will eventually bring victory from a life of reclusiveness. As I mentioned in step 7, sometimes you might have to temporarily avoid pictures, videos, cemetery visits, restaurants, etc. until you can receive substantial healing. It's okay. You're not showing disrespect, but just trying to survive. Sometimes in a relationship breakup, it might be best to temporarily put away pictures and other memorabilia to help you get through the grieving. There are no set rules, so do what's in your heart that will help you. This step is a major challenge when you have suffered a loss. We have watched many movies where a certain character had their heart broken and ended up on the couch watching a sad movie, crying, and eating a gallon of ice cream for comfort. That might be okay for a short term comfort, but there has to come a time when we decide to take the step and begin to live again. It's step by step, day by day. Teri, Lydia, and I chose to spend our first Christmas after Steffan's death in New York City watching Broadway musicals instead of trying to survive at home with all the painful holiday memories. It was a wise decision for us. When the second Christmas season came around, we were a bit stronger and were able to face the holidays with an inner strength. You might have to make some changes in your traditions to help you to survive. But choose to move forward!

9. We must understand that life goes on. After your storm, there will be others who will experience heartache also. Because so many others are suffering, people may forget about your suffering, when you haven't forgotten a single moment. Don't allow bitterness or anger to creep in if people don't remember birthdays or special holidays that deal with your suffering. What's important to us may not be that important to others. It's okay. I knew a woman who

held bitterness toward her pastor because he quit visiting her a few months after her son died. He did visit the first few months, but as time went on, there were others who needed him. If she had called him, he probably would have visited her; but she allowed anger to build up because she felt he had forgotten her pain. Friends, life goes on. We mustn't take our grief out on others for not performing the way we believe they should. Each day the news media posts new headlines. Other events are happening all around us daily with others suffering also. We're not the only ones suffering through a storm.

10. Choose to stay close to God. He is love and He loves us. We won't be able to succeed without Him. He is the only true answer to victory from the storm. Don't blame or run from Him, but choose to run *to* Him. Many people were amazed at how Teri and I were able to move forward. I give total credit to God. We wouldn't have made it without Him. Even though we still hurt, our Father gives us strength to keep living. When you are experiencing or have gone through a storm, leaning on Jesus is a major key to survival. We must choose to lean on and trust God, knowing He is with us each step of the way. I encourage each of you to not allow your hurt to confine or imprison you away from others. Friends, don't run from church, but instead run to it. We need the feeding of God's Word and the love and support from others. The worst decision to make would be to alienate you from others. There are times when we need to be alone to pray and meditate, but the devil loves to alienate us from the body of Christ, which is our support. We need one another. Choose to stay close to God and to those you love.

The Love of God

Even in the midst of our storm, we must decide, whether parent or teenager, to lean on God. That means to love Him, even in the worse circumstances.

He (God) knows exactly what we need for comfort. I remember one morning just after Steffan's death, I had been praying, crying, and grieving in my prayer life, a combination of emotions as a result of missing him. I heard a noise outside my front door and got up to see what is was. It was nothing but a dog in the front yard barking. When I returned to my recliner to continue praying, I heard an audible male voice. Teri and Lydia were still asleep and there were no one else in the house. The voice gently spoke to me and said, "Steffan said thank you for loving him and thank you for teaching him about Jesus." Friends, I actually heard this voice! Immediately, my first reaction was to look around to see if anyone had come in! In the back of my mind, I knew no one else was in our house except Teri and Lydia. I quickly realized the voice came from God, because I was overwhelmed with peace. It didn't frighten or scare me, but instead gave me peace. My emotions were like a volcano that had erupted, and I burst into tears, ran into our bedroom and woke Teri. How comforting, how loving, and how needed. I had heard from Heaven about my son. Yes, Jesus loves me.

God is love. The first commandment of the Ten Commandments, Exodus 20:3, speaks of putting God first. That's a love for Him. God is love. When we read about love in his Word, we're reading about Him because He is love. This should be our sole resolution during a storm, choosing to love and trust God, even when we don't feel like it.

Love the Lord your God with all your heart, and with all your soul, and with all your mind. This is the first and greatest commandment. And the second is like it. Love your neighbor as much as you love yourself. All the law and the prophets hang onto these two commandments. Matthew 22:38 NIV.

You may ask, "What kind of love can I give others when I am hurting myself?"

Love (God) is patient, love (God) is kind. It does not envy, it does not boast, it is not proud. It does not dishonor others, it is not self-seeking, it is not easily angered, it keeps no record of wrongs. Love (God) does not delight in evil but rejoices with the truth. It always protects, always trusts, always hopes, always perseveres. Love (God) never fails. 1 Corinthians 13:4–8 NIV (emphasis added).

Loving your neighbors mean you are giving them God because He is love. The flow of God through you will affect others who are suffering. Grasping these truths will keep your head above water in your storm. You might not have answers at the moment, but you can choose to trust God, knowing He loves and cares for you deeply.

Here are three facts about love (God) we need to understand for those experiencing storms:

1. Love (God) is a gift.

    For the wages of sin is death, but the gift of God is eternal life in Christ Jesus our lord. Romans 6:23 NIV.

During storm times, we can't successfully lead our household to Jesus by commanding or demanding. The true way to reach their heart is through love. Yes, rules and advice are important, but ultimately it's God's gift of love through us to others that make a difference. The greatest gift you can give your family in a crisis is love, whether parent or teenager. Love (God) changes everything about us. You might say, "I'm just me. I speak my mind and that's who I am!" No, that's who you have chosen to become. Love causes us to become more aware and passionate about prayer which brings results. We become more patient and kind to others, and we become more Christ–minded, not demanding. It's a gift. It's free. Choose to give it to someone who is hurting. If you know of someone going through a major storm in their life, make every effort to love them unconditionally. Love (God) will sustain them in their darkest hours.

2.   Love (God) is truth.

Then you will know the truth, and the truth will set you free John 8:32 NIV.

Walking in the love of God puts a passion in us to walk in truth. Why? Jesus is truth. Love and truth go hand in hand and the more time we spend with God, the more His love cleanses us. The result is that we become more like Jesus. Jesus attracted thousands in His ministry. People yearned to be around Him. That love in us works the same way. People are hungry for truth, especially when they're hurting. They are hungry for someone to stand tall for Jesus and offer hope. People are always looking for answers during a crisis. Allowing God to heal and change us, we will become a magnet to others. They will be drawn to us. People will look to us for hope.

This has been my best healing recipe. Teri, Lydia, and I have chosen to help others in their storms. This mode of help has continually healed us each step.

3. Love (God) is an encourager.

My purpose is that they may be encouraged in heart and united in love. Colossians 2:2 NIV.

Encouragement in love during a storm goes a long way and will successfully change an individual much more than criticism or advice. A great portion of Jesus' ministry was encouragement. No one enjoys being around a complainer or lecturer, especially when you're hurting. It's negative and never accomplishes anything positive. We should ask God to allow us to see others and situations through the eyes of Jesus. Instead of judging based on the outside view, we would begin to see the heart of others and truth in their situations. No one needs lectures during a storm. They need love and encouragement. The more time we spend worshiping God, we'll notice that love will begin to flow from us to others. That love is encouraging. We can't make others follow Jesus during a crisis, but we can be like a navigator and lead them in the right direction through encouragement. Jesus encouraged his disciples to follow Him.

As for me and my house, we will serve the Lord. Joshua 24: 15 NIV.

This verse is not speaking about duty, but about serving God in love in the good times as well as the bad. It's a desire and a passion. It's a commitment of hope to the family experiencing tragedy and a commitment of peace during a storm. It's a commitment of Joy in your family when you feel engulfed in pain and a commitment of love (rescue) to make it through the storm.

I pray you will be encouraged with the knowledge that Jesus loves you so much. Because our Savior suffered and died on the cross, God lovingly pours out his mercy, grace, comfort and love to all who ask. Remember the hymn, "Jesus Paid It All." If you are living a defeated life thinking that God doesn't care, stop now! Know that He truly loves you! He is so awesome. Please take some time and just talk to Him. I promise He's waiting with open arms to love and comfort you. What a loving Father. When the storms hit, don't allow the devil an avenue into your mind. Just know God's Word and stand on it. His Abba Father. His our God, the God of grace.

Who shall separate us from the love of Christ? Will trouble or hardship or persecution or famine or nakedness or danger or sword? In all these things we are more than conquerors through him who loved us." Romans 8:35–37 NIV.

Let's pray:

Father, we surrender our pain and heartbreak. As we begin to take steps forward, we choose to spend more time with you, allowing you to heal and change us to be like Jesus. This change will create a love in us for others who are suffering. We declare that we love you and put you first in our lives. Use us, oh God, to help others with your love. In Jesus's name, amen.

Remember, storms are only temporary

Storm Daily Devotions

Part of the healing in our journey, is staying close to God, growing and maturing in Him. God yearns for us to spend time with Him each day. This communion time strengthens and equips us to face daily trials and storms. I have written 100 daily devotions to help you in your walk. I encourage you to read one per day, meditate on it and ask God to speak to your heart. Each devotion was written from my heart as I prayed and sought God. It will help you grow and mature in Jesus.

So, place this book on your coffee table for easy access and enjoy reading a daily devotion. A daily devotion and a good cup of coffee will jump start your day! Enjoy!

God Will Comfort You

God heals the brokenhearted and binds up their wounds. Psalm 147: 3 NIV.

All of us, at some point in our brokenness and hurt, have cried out, "Where are you God?" Our broken heart causes us to feel alone and alienated from the world. BUT, our Father NEVER leaves our side. Not for a moment...He lovingly tells us in this scripture that He WILL heal our wounds and hurts...not maybe. God is a God of restoration. He desires to take us under His wings, nourish us and heal us, and restore us better than before. When our children are hurting, we rush to their side to offer comfort. How much greater does our Abba Father (Daddy) do for us when we're hurting and needing to be comforted. God is LOVE.

Bless those that mourn, for they will be comforted. Matthew 5:4 NIV.

Today, if you are hurting, disappointed, broken, discouraged, etc., please know Jesus cares about EVERY detail of your life. Trust His word and promises....

I will restore you to health and heal your wounds. Jeremiah 30:17 NIV.

Begin_to thank Him for what He's going to do....Your faith will heal and make you whole! That's a promise to you from God!

I will turn their mourning into gladness; I will give them comfort and joy instead of sorrow, declares the Lord.Jeremiah 31:13 NIV.

Have You Lost All Hope?

Are you discouraged feeling you can't go on? Are you hurting today?

You will restore my life again, O Lord; from the depths of the earth you will again bring me up. You will increase my honor and comfort me once again. Psalm 71: 20–21 NIV.

O Lord my God, I called to you for help and you healed me. Psalm 30:2 NIV.

Our Heavenly Father's Word tells us He WILL heal our wounds if we ask. When our hearts are broken and we are hurting, it's hard to function, be productive, and difficult to smile and be happy. God understands our pain when we're hurting and desires for us to be comforted as He heals and restores us. I always vision Him wrapping His loving arms me like a daddy would his child.

God heals the brokenhearted and binds up their wounds. Psalm 147:3 NIV.

Friends, there are times when all of us get hurt or have our hearts broken. The disappointment is great and we feel like giving up. But our Abba Father (Daddy) cares so much about us and will not leave or abandon us. If we will lean on Him and allow Him to heal our wounds, we will be healed and stronger than before. He will even carry us if we can't walk another step. Jesus loves me this I know, for the Bible tells me so.

I will turn their mourning into gladness; I will give them comfort and joy instead of sorrow, declares the Lord. Jeremiah 31:13 NIV.

Yes, God desires to give us joy again, no matter what tragedy or brokenness we've been through. The "joy of the Lord is our strength" to continue living and helping others.

Whatever pain you're feeling today, please know you are loved and God WILL comfort and heal you.

Remember, it's okay to cry and mourn when you're hurting! God understands. We don't have to be "strong" for ourselves or others. Crying and releasing our emotions are part of our healing. Please don't feel guilty for your tears. BUT, our loving Father desires to see us whole and strong again. Let's trust that He will heal us. God is the god of restoration and I'm living proof that He will heal your broken heart!

YOU ARE NOT ALONE

In ALL things (everything) God works for the good of those who love Him, who have been called according to His purpose (that's us). Romans 8:28 NIV.

Sometimes it's difficult to understand this verse, especially when we're going through a storm. We wonder, *How can good come forth from this situation I have or am going through?* Many have asked me how I can see any good in losing my son. Friends, yes, it took my breath away when Steffan went to heaven. I didn't think I could live a single day without him, and at first, didn't want to live without him. But what I have witnessed in the past three years that is good is how my loving Father has given me compassion for those that are hurting, broken, and at a loss. I made a decision to not live in bitterness and anger, which would only suffocate my life, but to live for my family, and those hurting around me. I didn't want to lose the memory of my son or feel it was a total loss. I deeply wanted to feel that through all the traumatic pain and suffering, that maybe, just maybe something good could and would come from losing him.

Do you relate this devotion what you are going through in your life? By helping others, our lives can take on a new meaning and purpose. I remember the pain was so severe from Steffan's death. I have wanted to give others a ray of hope and encouragement so they will survive their storm. Choosing to help others when we have gone through a rough situation, helps in our healing. You see, I had a choice to make after Steffan left us for Heaven. I could give up or I could live. I chose to live.

When you have gone through a painful divorce, or maybe a death of someone in your life, fighting to survive a disease, or financial ruin, we must know that God truly loves us and is right beside us each small step we take. Has there been good in these past three years of my life? Yes, I have witnessed many lives touched and changed from Steffan's death. Many have been encouraged by the choice Teri, Lydia, and I made to move forward, and I have witnessed God's hand on my daughter Lydia with a greater anointing than I could imagine.

Today, be encouraged and know that in the midst of your storm, Jesus is walking on water toward you, because He cares..........

WE MUST MOVE FORWARD

Forget the former things; do not dwell on the past. See, I am doing a new thing! Now it springs up; do you not perceive it? I am making a way in the desert and streams in the wasteland, declares the Lord. Isaiah 43: 18–19 NIV.

God is speaking to us, His children, to focus on the now and what's ahead and not to look back at our past failures and mistakes (sins). God is not into branding an individual for life because of bad choices in the past. God is a restoration Father who loves us so much. Because Jesus paid the price on the cross, we are already forgiven. Our past sins are remembered no more. My dear friends, we should never live our lives dwelling on our past, but be excited about our future with God. He has special, unique plans just for us! Don't let the devil talk you out of your blessings and favor with God by making you feel unworthy. Remember, the devil is the accuser, not God!

Here's an FYI: There are no perfect Christians.

We have all sinned and come short of the glory of God. Romans 3:23 NIV.

We do not have the right to judge others over their past. If God says He remembers no more (Hebrews 8:12), do we have the right to remind people of their past or hold former sins over their head? I believe, as Christians, we know the answer. We are called to be loving, forgiving, and compassionate with a heart to see others restored by God. When God restores us, it's usually greater than before. Most successful individuals have learned more valued life's lessons from their failures than successes.

Let's look with excitement to the plans God has for us! By reading His Word and praying, we will understand our purpose and reason for living. God is a God of restoration. He is a God of hope. He is a God of compassion and forgiveness. He is a God of LOVE...........p.s. Don't look back.....

GOD WILL RESTORE

Return to the stronghold, you prisoners of hope. Even today I declare that I will restore double to you. Zechariah 9:12 NIV.

Do you feel that it just couldn't get any worse in your life? Do you feel like the 'bottom has just fallen out' and you could possibly drown in all your troubles?

God's Word tells us to NOT give up! He will restore (repay) what the locust has eaten. Joel 2:25 NIV. This scripture in Joel assures us that our loving Father will restore to us what we have lost or was stolen by the devil. We should DEMAND the devil to repay a double portion of what he has stolen from us in Jesus' name!

The thief (devil) comes only to steal, kill, and destroy.. John 10:10 NIV.

Friends, we should refuse to give the devil anything that is ours. We should demand and expect repayment on what he has stolen in the POWERFUL name of Jesus!

Therefore God exalted him (Jesus) to the highest place and gave him the name that is above every name that at the name of Jesus EVERY knee should bow in heaven and on earth and under the earth, and every tongue acknowledge that Jesus Christ is Lord, to the glory of God the Father. Philippians 2: 9:11 NIV. That's right! Praise God! The devil cowers down and trembles at the name of Jesus (Yeshua)! We should use the name of Jesus with power and authority because we're God's children.

When we attacked on all sides, we should begin to worship our Father. There is tremendous power in worship. When King David lost his child with Bathsheba, He began to worship God with his whole heart. God gave him restoration with a son, Solomon, who became a mighty king of Israel.

And we know that in all things God works for the good of those who love him, who have been called according to his purpose (that's us). Romans 8:28 NIV.

When we have experienced a major storm or tragedy, we honestly don't want to hear this particular verse at the time of our pain. It's not comforting at the moment, but, this verse is truth and if we will allow, God will bring forth good from our storm.

I meditated on this verse many times during the shock and aftermath of losing our son. I thought, *How can any good come from losing my precious child?* Over the past three years of recovery, I have seen a lot of good. Did I get my son back? No. Do I still miss him? Yes. But, many lives were spiritually changed through his death.

Today, let's look to God and know His Word is full of promises. He will restore what we have lost. Yes, He is a good God...

OUR FATHER WILL NOT ABANDON US

Look at the birds of the air, for they neither sow nor reap nor gather into barns; yet your heavenly Father feeds them. Are you not of more value than they? Can any one of you by worrying add a single hour to your life? And why do you worry about clothes? See how the flowers of the field grow. They do not labor or spin. Yet I tell you that not even Solomon in all his splendor was dressed like one of these. If that is how God clothes the grass of the field, which is here today and tomorrow is thrown into the fire, will he not much more clothe you—you of little faith? So do not worry, saying, 'What shall we eat?' or 'What shall we drink?' or 'What shall we wear?' For the pagans run after all these things, and your heavenly Father knows that you need them. Matthew 6: 26–32 NIV.

As Christians and believers of God's Word, we have to remind ourselves daily that God desires to take care of us and He WILL provide for us. So many times we are guilty of saying He will provide, but are filled with doubt and fear that He won't.

I'm not referring to a mentality of laziness, refusing to work, with expectations that God will give us what we need while we lie on the sofa at home playing video games 24/7. No, our Father expects us to work, but lovingly tells us that He will take care and provide for our needs and bless us beyond

imagination. Why? Because we are righteous! Jesus, our Savior, paid the price for us to be blessed!

And Abraham called the name of that place 'Jehovah–Jireh,' because it is said this day in the mount, **'Jehovah does provide'**. Genesis 22:14 NIV.

Friends, we call Him Jehovah–Jireh because He does provide for us. If He takes care of the birds in the air, He will surely provide for His children! We mustn't allow doubt and fear to creep in our minds and create a "worry session" which usually leads to a major headache or stomach pains. Let's decide to trust Him in ALL areas of our lives.

Seek first the kingdom of God and His righteousness, and ALL these things will be added unto you... Matthew 6:33 NIV.

No, He will NEVER abandon us! Yes, He WILL take care of our every need! Yes, He WILL provide! Trust and believe....

Don't Lose Hope..

Never will I leave you; never will I forsake you. Hebrews 13:5 NIV.

When we face the raging storms in our lives, the devil is the first to stand in line to tell us we are alone, God is too busy and doesn't care, or that we are lost with no hope. Yes, discouragement is his number one goal/fight against us. If he can get us discouraged, our focus will be removed off God and placed on ourselves. We will look into the mirror of our life and only see our problems, with no solutions, and begin to complain, "Poor me." Abandonment will creep into our minds and begin to torment us. But God lovingly tells us He is with us and will NEVER leave us!

I am the Lord, your God, who takes hold of your right hand and says to you, Do NOT fear; I WILL help you. Isaiah 41:13 NIV.

This verse can encourage us when we face uncertainties. He is with us and will NOT leave us, even for a moment. A shepherd tends to his sheep, leading, guiding, and protecting them and will not abandon them. Our loving Heavenly Father is our shepherd who will not leave us.

With your help, O Lord, I can advance against a troop, with my God I can scale a wall. 2 Samuel 22:30 NIV.

Yes! All things are possible "if" we will believe and trust Jesus!

Some Christians say, "I just don't have faith to believe." My friends, yes, we do have faith. God has given us faith.

God has dealt to each one a measure of faith. Romans 12:3 NIV.

When you get in your car, you have faith that it will crank and drive. When you pick up your TV remote, you have faith it will turn on when you press the on button. We really do have faith! To increase our faith, we must spend time with God through reading and meditating on His Word.

Faith comes from hearing the message, and the message is heard through the word about Christ. Romans 10:17 NIV.

We can do ALL things through Christ who strengthen us! Philippians 4:13 NIV.

Nothing is impossible! Today, we can have confidence that He (God) will help us be overcomers, we will be successful in what He leads us to do, and He will NEVER leave or forsake His children! He loves us!

Moving Forward
One Step At A Time

Are you experiencing disappointments? Discouraged? Are you feeling like a failure because of something in your past? Have you lost a race, failed a test, been turned down for a promotion, or just emerged from a broken relationship? If you have answered yes to any of these questions, then God is speaking to you to move forward, no longer focusing on the past and its failures. We must look ahead and continue striving to do our best.

Forgetting what is behind and straining toward what is ahead, I press on toward the goal to win the prize for which God has called me heavenward in Christ Jesus. Philippians 3:13–14 NIV.

Friends, we can't change the past. It's done. Once a sports event is over, it's over. One team wins, one team loses. If we experience a loss or a broken heart, we must continue moving forward with God, step by step. We can't allow the past to affect our future. Just because we failed in the past, doesn't mean we must fail in the future. If we will allow God to teach us valued lessons that derive from our failures and disappointments, we will gain strength AND wisdom. It's okay to be disappointed or hurt over a loss or broken heart. We shouldn't feel guilty for our emotions. The key is NOT to stay down when we are knocked down! We must pray, seek God with our whole heart, and continue moving forward with His leading. When we allow God to place us on the Potter's wheel, our lives will continuously be molded and developed into the image of Jesus.

Your attitude should be the same as that of Christ Jesus. Philippians 2:5 NIV.

Attitude? Yes, my friends, the attitude of Jesus is one of love. He loved everyone, even his enemies. He walked in peace, joy, AND love (God is love). He forgave those that despised him and plotted his death. He set an example of love for us to follow.

Walking with God is a journey. There will be days we will experience sunshine and days we experience storms.

Being confident of this, that He who began a good work in you will carry it on to completion until the day of Christ Jesus. Philippians 1: 6 NIV.

Our confidence is knowing that God has a specific plan for us. Let's rejoice in knowing that He loves us! It's a new day!

GOD MAKES THE IMPOSSIBLE POSSIBLE

Did you get up dreading this day? Are you "freaking" out over a situation that's facing you? Do you feel hopeless? Is your mind saying, "You're sunk?"

It's time to stop panicking and turn our eyes and hearts to Jesus, who tells us "All things are possible."

When the servant of the man of God got up and went out early the next morning, an army with horses and chariots had surrounded the city. "Oh no, my lord! What shall we do?" the servant asked. "Don't be afraid," the prophet answered. "Those who are with us are more than those who are with them." And Elisha prayed, "Open his eyes, LORD, so that he may see." Then the LORD opened the servant's eyes, and he looked and saw the hills full of horses and chariots of fire all around Elisha. 2 kings 6:15–17 NIV.

Friends, God is with us! No, He does NOT desire to see us fail or our ship sink. We must trust Him with our whole heart, knowing He WILL take care of us. When we see the enemy glaring at us, we should take heart/courage because our God is stronger and mightier than any enemy or giant trying to intimidate us and cause us to fear.

Because the hand of the Lord my God was on me, I took courage. Ezra 7:28 NIV. Nothing is impossible for us with God on our side!

God has said, "Never will I leave you; never will I forsake you." So we say with confidence. The Lord is my helper; I will NOT be afraid. What can man do to me? Hebrews 13:5–6 NIV.

Dear child of God, stand tall today in confidence, trusting your Father. Believe He WILL turn your situation around! He can and will, if you will trust Him! Remember, begin by worshiping Him with a thankful heart. Thanking Him in advance for what He's going to do (faith). To you, your mountain (situation) might seem impossible, but to God, it's a piece of cake. TRUST and believe for your miracle!

Lord, Take My Hand

Even though I walk through the valley of the shadow of death, I will fear no evil, for You are with me. Psalm 23:4 NIV.

As we read this verse, we understand that it's not a matter of IF but WHEN we will face "storms" in our lives. No one is exempt. As we understand that there are storms we will face, trusting God to lead us through to safety is the key to survival.

I have witnessed over the years several marriage partners who are faced with divorce (valley of the shadow of death) and can't seem to recover. Their ship begins to sink in the storm.

Also, losing a loved one can seem unbearable and the worst storm for someone to experience, but yet our loving Father promises in His Word that He is with us each step. No, we are NEVER alone in the valley. Storms can make us feel isolated and abandoned, but Abba Father (Daddy) PROMISES to be with us.

I, even I, am He who comforts you, declares the Lord. Isaiah 51:12 NIV.

When many broken hearts turn to "outside" sources for comfort like alcohol, drugs, etc., God promises to comfort and heal us if we will surrender our brokenness to Him. Yes, we must surrender/yield our hurts to Jesus and not be possessive with our emotions or feeling self–reliant that we can make it without anyone's help, including God's.

Friends, from my own tragedy experience, I encourage you to cling tightly to your Heavenly Father through the storm you are facing. "Storms are only temporary." He will hold your hand and comfort you each step you face.

You, O Lord, have helped me and comforted me. Psalm 86:1 NIV.

I remember, as a young boy, hearing Elvis sing this song..

"Precious Lord, take my hand lead me on, let me stand. I'm tired, I am weak I am worn. Through the storm, through the night lead me on to the light. Take my hand precious Lord, lead me home."

His Word tells us He will NOT abandon us. Today, reach out your hand to Him and let Him to walk with you through your valley of the shadow of death. You can and will make it.

OUR FATHER WILL SUPPLY ALL OUR NEEDS

This is the confidence we have in approaching God: that if we ask anything according to His will, He hears us. And if we know that he hears us (which He does)—whatever we ask—we know that we have what we asked of Him. 1 John 5:14–15 NIV.

We should understand that this verse is speaking about ALL areas of our lives, not just spiritual. Whatever we need in our lives, God is willing to supply.

Do you recall shopping for Christmas presents for small children in a toy store, when you had plenty of money to buy whatever you wanted? The excitement and joy would be great for us buying the gifts. On Christmas morning it was exciting to see the look in our children's eyes as they opened their gifts. This is a picture of our loving Heavenly Father. We are His children and He is thrilled to bless us.

And I will do whatever you ask in my name, so that the Father may be glorified in the Son. You may ask me for ANYTHING in my name, and I will do it. John 14: 13–14 NIV.

What a promise from God. ALL we have to do is ask and expect His loving blessings. If we're lacking in any area of our lives, we should come before our Father in Jesus' name and present our prayer requests. We have to change our thinking from not bothering God and I don't deserve to I am His child and He loves and wants me to have the very best.

If your marriage is suffering, then surrender it to God and believe He WILL restore what you have lost. Do you have someone in your family that has rejected God? Friends, nothing or no one is too big for our God! Begin thanking God in faith that this relative is saved and living for Him, even though you might not see it at the present.

Are you suffering financially?

God will supply ALL your needs… Philippians 4:19 niv. All means EVERYTHING.

If you are facing a big giant in your life or a mountain that seems impossible to move out of your way, trust God, the giant slayer and mountain mover. If you will trust Him, you will see victory! Nothing is impossible for Him!

The Lord hears the prayer of the righteous (that's us). Proverbs 15:29 niv.

IT BEGINS WITH LOVE

This is the message you have heard from the beginning: We should love one another. 1 John 3: 11 NIV.

I believe loving others is our biggest challenge as Christians. It seems easy to get along with and love our "best friends or buds," but it becomes difficult to love those that intentionally aggravate us, gossip about us, show jealous behavior, and etc. Our Heavenly Father commands us to love one another (no restrictions or boundaries). Jesus loved everyone. Yes, He even loved the Pharisees. We are called by God to love others no matter the circumstance or what church membership. When we begin to walk in true love for one another, small, petty issues diminish in our hearts and we have a much better tolerance and understanding for those whose personalities and actions can get on our nerves. When we choose to walk in God's love, we become more patient and kind toward those around us. Love (God) calms us and helps us see the true heart of others.

Beloved, let us love one another, for love is of God….. 1 John 4:7 NIV.

Yes friends, God is love and when we love someone, we are giving them God. Bottom line: Loving others is the best evangelism tool we can use to win the lost; a sincere love for one another. But before we can win the lost to Jesus with love, we must begin by loving other Christians around us. My heart breaks when I hear about church quarrels and fights. Isn't this the result of not walking in love and demanding that others do things "our" way?

Beloved Christian friends, it's time we walk the walk as followers of Christ and choose to love others, whether they are family members, co–workers, or even those at Wal–Mart.

Love is God, God is love. Today, let's give this gift to those we come in contact with.

GOD WILL SHOW US THE WAY

Worried about making a decision? Not sure if you're doing the right thing?

Jesus said, "I am the light of the world. Whoever follows me will never walk in darkness, but will have the light of life" John 8:12 NIV.

What a loving confirmation/promise that our Heavenly Father will lead and guide our every step. We are daily faced with decisions and need His guidance. His Word tells us the light of Jesus will show us the way down the dark path of life. No, we don't have to be afraid or worry. His light shines bright.

Your Word, O Lord, is a lamp to my feet and a light for my path. Psalm 119:105 NIV.

God is not the author of confusion and doubt. His voice speaks truth and will show us the way. If we won't rush through making a decision but wait on God's voice, we will save ourselves much headache and stress. When you don't know what to do, don't do! Begin to worship and thank God for His guidance as you wait on His direction. He WILL show you the path to follow.

O Lord, You have made known to me the path of life. Psalm 16:11 NIV.

This scripture is a promise from Abba Father (Daddy). No parent would leave their small child out in the woods alone in the dark to find their way home. Because of our love for our child, we would take a light and show them the way home to safety. This is an illustration of our Father and His love for us, His children.

God's loving promise: "I will guide you in the way of wisdom and lead you along straight paths. When you walk, your steps will NOT be hampered; when you run, you will NOT stumble" Proverbs 4: 11–12 NIV.

Whether it's buying a car, choosing a mate, looking for a job, or health decisions, please know that God cares about EVERY part of our lives. You are NOT bothering Him when you talk/pray to Him about "small" issues. There are NO small issues with God, He cares about EVERYTHING! He desires to be part of your life in EVERY area.

I will instruct you and teach you in the way you should go, says the Lord. Psalm 32:8 NIV.

Wait on God, listen to His voice, surrender every part of your life to Him, and He will lead you through every decision. God is good.......He is FULL of love for us.

God Won't Give Up On Us

O Lord, you will keep in perfect peace him whose mind is steadfast, because he trusts in You. Isaiah 26:3 NIV.

I often write about trust because it seems to be an important issue regarding our walk with God. We easily say we trust Him, but when it comes to walking in faith day to day, we can get attacked with worry, doubt, and fear which actually mean, "I don't trust you, God." The way to strengthen our faith is meditating on His Word and worshiping Him with a heart of thanksgiving.

The Lord is faithful to ALL His promises and loving toward ALL He has made. Psalm 145:13 NIV.

When we worship and meditate on His Word, knowing in our heart He doesn't lie or "forget" us, we can walk with assurance that He WILL keep His promises and answer at the proper time.

Trust and obey, for there's no other way to be happy in Jesus....

Friends, I encourage you to NOT be moved by situations and circumstances that will try to crush your faith in God. The way to stand strong is worship, thankfulness, and reading and meditating on His Word. The Bible is our sword to fight the attacks of worry, doubt and fear.

The Lord is my strength and my shield; my heart trusts in Him, and I AM HELPED. My heart leaps for joy and I will give thanks to Him in song.

Don't give up on trusting Him. He hasn't and won't give up on you!

Are We Listening?

Teach me, O Lord, to follow your decrees; then I will keep them to the end. Give me understanding, and I will keep your law and obey it with all my heart. Direct me in the path of your commands, for there I find delight. Psalm 119: 33–35 NIV.

With God on our side, we can't go wrong. He teaches us to listen and follow His voice. It's a wonderful, peaceful feeling to be in God's will. Our Heavenly Father WILL teach, lead and guide us if we'll give Him our lives in a trusting surrender. Unfortunately, our human will can be stubborn and self–focused. And there are times when we feel the need to make our own decisions since God gave us a brain.

Trust in the Lord with ALL your heart and lean not on your "own" understanding; in ALL your ways acknowledge Him (thank Him), and He will make your path straight. Proverbs 3: 5–6 NIV.

His Word encourages us to trust Him. He WILL lead us down the right path of decisions. When we choose to listen to His voice and follow His will, our stress level will diminish. Yes, stress and worry are very much related. Following God's voice brings peace to our lives, plus a good night's rest.

Your word is a lamp for my feet, a light on my path. Psalm 115:105 NIV.

Many of us have underestimated the POweR of God's Word. Friends, the Bible is a manual to live by, not just a history book. Some say that the Bible doesn't help them since we live in the now. I completely disagree. No matter what we're facing, His Word will bring life to us, and as we read and meditate on His scriptures, the Holy Spirit will speak to our heart. God does NOT want any of us to be in the dark regarding decision making. If we'll listen, He will speak. Jesus is the "light" in this dark world.

When it comes to decisions regarding changing jobs, relationships, housing, etc. we should use wisdom and seek God with ALL our hearts. Our faith and trust in Him will bring the answers we need. Today, let's not make any decisions without praying, seeking, and trusting God. He WILL speak to us, I promise. Let's listen to His voice.......

I AM A GIFT FROM GOD

For He made Him (Jesus) who knew no sin to be sin for us, that we might become the righteousness of God in Him. 2 Corinthians 5:21 NIV.

I receive abundance of grace AND the 'gift' (not earned) of righteousness, and (therefore) I reign in life through Christ Jesus. Romans 5:17 NIV.

I admit for many years I was constantly working on changing my mentality about righteousness. I grew up believing that I had to "earn" righteousness by living a good life. I don't think it was a particular church or religion that convinced me of this wrong teaching, but more my own thinking. For years I stayed frustrated at myself (most of the time) because "we have ALL sinned and come short of the glory of God" Romans 3:23. I lived by the law in regards to being good. Of course, when I sinned I would mentally beat myself up thinking I was a "bad" person. I lived in a cycle of repenting over and over, never matching up. When I would read scriptures about righteousness, I would think, "That's not about me because I'm not good enough to be righteous." I was also guilty of judging others for their mistakes and sins. I think I was trying to earn my position as a Pharisee!

It really hasn't been that long ago since my loving Father set me free of this wrong thinking and beliefs. I FINALLY realized through His Word that the moment I had asked Jesus to save me, I was given the 'free gift' of righteousness, permanently. It covered me from head to toe and wasn't based on being good or reaching some level of perfection. I realized that God didn't look upon me as something bad, but instead His precious child, a gift. Yes, God set me free!

After losing my son four years ago, God opened my eyes to TRUTH and taught me more and more about righteousness. I learned a great deal about the gift of GRACE and who I was in Christ Jesus. Nothing earned by being good, but a free gift. I have realized that I will never live in the dirty pig pen like the prodigal son again. I am a child of God, my Father (Daddy), and I AM righteous because Jesus paid the price for me on the cross.

Jesus paid it ALL, all to Him I owe. Sin had left a crimson stain (BUT) He washed it white as snow.

There is a name I love to hear.....Oh, how I love Jesus, because He first loved me.

God Is MY Comfort

Do not fear (worry), for I am with you; do not be dismayed (stressed), for I am your God. I will strengthen you and help you; I will uphold you with my righteous right hand. Isaiah 41:10 NIV.

Abba Father says He WILL strengthen and help us (answer our prayers). When we choose to trust God with our life, we can be assured that He will not throw us to the side and ignore us. He will lead and guide our every step. We praise and thank Him for making a way for us when there seems to be no way at all. He makes the impossible, possible! Yes friends, He still parts the "Red Sea" for us when there seems to be no way through a crisis we're facing. He makes a way through the impossible. Nothing is too difficult for Him.

In the midst of the biggest storm you are facing in your life, don't fear for Jesus is walking on the water toward you. He isn't afraid of the big waves (problems) that surround you. We must be like Peter and not look at the storm (mess) around us, but focus on Jesus, our rescuer.

God will give relief to you who are troubled. 2 Thessalonians 1:7 NIV.

This scripture reminds me of the Christian song, "Sheltered in the arms of God." It's a wonderful feeling to know that God desires to wrap His loving arms around us with comfort and protection. Many times when my children were afraid or upset,

I would let them crawl into my lap where I would hold them tightly so they would feel safe. That's a picture of our loving Abba Father (Daddy) and how He desires to comfort us.

No matter what you are facing today, know that Jesus is near you. God WILL rescue you in your storm, and remember storms are only temporary.

May the Lord answer you when you are in distress; may the name of the God of Jacob protect you. May He send you help from the sanctuary and grant you support from Zion…May he give you the desire of your heart and make ALL your plans succeed. Psalm 20: 1–2,4 NIV.

Our Heavenly Father Will Take Care of Us

Fear (love and respect) the Lord, you His saints, for those who fear Him lack nothing. The lions may grow weak and hungry, but those who seek the Lord lack no good thing. Psalm 34: 9–10 NIV.

What revelation from God's Word! His Word is truth! When we turn our attention to our Father in love through worship and thanksgiving, we can be assured that He WILL take care of us. Yes, EVERY need supplied!

He who did not spare His own Son, but gave Him up for us all—how will He not also, along with Him, graciously give us all things? Romans 8:32 NIV.

Nothing is too big for God. And we're not bothering Him when we ask, believe, and expect from Him. He loves for us to rely on Him for all our needs.

Have you been praying for a family member? Is someone you love sick? Is your heart broken? Do you need a job or better job?

God will meet ALL your needs according to His glorious riches in Christ Jesus. Philippians 4:19 NIV. All means EVERYTHING. God doesn't want His children living a life of lack in any area. If you have been praying for a lost family member or friend, you mustn't give up. Friends, we must visualize this person saved (that's faith). As we pray in faith, we must believe

He WILL answer our prayers, no matter our needs, big or small. Our loving Abba Father cares for His children.

The eyes of all look to you, O Lord, and you give them their food at the proper time. You open your hand and satisfy the desires of every living thing. Psalm 145:15–16 NIV.

Jesus said, "Ask and you will receive, and your joy will be complete." John 16:24 NIV.

Why do we feel guilty for asking? Many Christians believe it is wrong to ask God for material items. I personally believe His Word and choose to walk in faith that He will take care of me in every area. He has provided for me so many times throughout my life and answered my prayers. He has NEVER failed or abandoned me. I am a walking testimony of God's love and goodness. The blessings He has given me, He will give to each of His children. Why? It's because our Father is LOVE.

Today, trust and do NOT doubt His Word.

WE CAN'T CHANGE THE PAST

Forget the former things; do not dwell on the past. See, I am doing a new thing! Now it springs up; do you not perceive it? I am making a way in the wilderness and streams in the wasteland. Isaiah 43:18–19 NIV.

As you are reading this, you might be thinking, "I have committed so many sins. I'm a terrible person." But your loving Heavenly Father is a forgiving God and loves to restore us. He doesn't see what we see. We might see ourselves as a total mess but He sees us as pliable clay with much potential to mold into a beautiful piece of art. He doesn't throw our mistakes of the past in our face or constantly reminding us of our failures, but covers us in His love and grace.

You are the Potter, we are the clay. Isaiah 64:8 NIV.

He tells us to not look back at our past but know that today, this day, is a "new beginning." No matter what we've said or done, it's a new day with Jesus. He doesn't want us to look back, but to look forward at what He is doing in our lives.

Even with the hurts and disappointments that we have encountered, God is telling us to not look back and dwell 24/7 on those hurts, but to look ahead, taking one step at a time. Healing comes when we look to Jesus.

If anyone is in Christ, he is a new creation; the old has gone, the new has come. 2 Corinthians 5:17 NIV.

I love the old children's song, "Every day with Jesus, is sweeter than the day before…"

Friends, it's a new day with Jesus! He cares so much about us! He has fresh, new plans for us, and a beautiful future.

He desires for us to spend time with Him daily. His word for us will be fresh each day. Today, pray in love and faith and see your relationship grow..

It's a new day, "New Beginnings.."

WHO AM I?

Have you recently met someone that declared, "I need to discover who I am; I need to find ME" ??

Over the years I have come across many young people who have stated this. They don't feel they know who they really who. They may have lived many years to please others.

God's Word tells us, "When God created man, He made him in the likeness of God." Genesis 5:1.

Who am I? I'm God's creation, made in the likeness of God. God doesn't create "junk" or "mistakes."

You yourselves are God's temple and…God's Spirit lives in you. 1 Corinthians 3:16 NIV.

Who am I? I'm God's personal temple. His spirit lives in ME! This means I can't be as bad as the devil tells me I am! "I am the righteousness of God in Christ Jesus!" 2 Corinthians 5:21. I AM righteous and His spirit lives in me!

Who am I? Jesus calls us His friend. When we realize this, it won't matter who likes us and who doesn't.

Jesus said, "I no longer call you servants, because a servant does not know his master's business. Instead, I have called you friends, for everything that I learned from my Father I have made known to you."

He calls us His friends and reveals His plans to us.

Friends, God isn't the author of confusion. The devil will try to confuse us so we don't know who we are, but we must fight against these lies by thanking our Heavenly Father who created us for a reason/purpose.

He lovingly tells us, "You are a chosen people, a royal priesthood, a holy nation, a people belonging to God, that you may declare the praises of Him who called you out of darkness into His wonderful light." 1 Peter 2:9.

Who am I? That's an easy question to answer....I am God's child...

Nothing Is Impossible For God

God is able to do immeasurably more than all we ask or imagine. Ephesians 3:20 NIV.

Our Father is able AND willing to answer our prayers. He's the God of miracles and answers. What He does for others, He will do for us. We must EXPECT. Some people say they don't want to bother God, or He is too busy to be concerned about small issues. Friends, He cares about EVERY part of our lives.

Many times God is waiting for us to take our hands off the situation so He can answer or provide a miracle. Trust means we choose let go of the situation and give it totally to God. Our human nature tells us we need/should "fix" the problem, but trusting God means letting go, removing our hands/grips from the problem and having faith He will answer.

I lift up my eyes to the hills—where does my help come from? My help comes from the Lord, the Maker of Heaven and earth. Psalm 121:1–2 NIV.

I'm so thankful for the stories in the Bible that encourage us to trust our Father. Our God is a rescuer! When we focus our heart on Him with thankfulness, He will answer our prayers. Nothing, absolutely nothing, is too big for Him to handle for us. We may look at someone and say, "There is no way they will ever get saved." But ALL things are possible with God! Yes, ALL things!

Nothing is impossible with God. Luke 1:37 NIV.

We should pray this scripture all through our day to encourage our faith in God when all seems impossible.

A righteous man may have many troubles, but the Lord delivers him from them all. Psalm 34:19 NIV.

Who is righteous? We are! We are the "righteousness of God in Christ Jesus." Our Father gives us permission to approach His throne with confidence that He cares. We are NOT bothering Him! He welcomes His children with open arms.

I am the Lord, your God, who takes hold of your right hand and says to you, Do NOT fear; I WILL help you. Isaiah 41:13 NIV.

Have you been praying for an answer to your prayers and are still waiting? Don't give up! Remember, His timing is perfect. Trusting God matures and strengthens us to be strong.

In the day of my trouble I will call to you, O Lord, for you WILL answer me. Psalm 86:7 NIV.

He has NEVER forsaken His children. Your needs are important to Him. Trust and believe ……..

WE ARE THE RIGHTEOUSNESS OF GOD

The lord…hears the prayer of the righteous (that's us). Proverbs 15:29 NIV.

Because of the price Jesus paid on the cross for our sins, we ARE the "righteousness of God in Christ Jesus." It doesn't seem that long ago when I believed I wasn't as spiritual as someone who was righteous. I felt in my heart it was place of achievement, an upper level of Christianity and "if" I would try harder to be a good Christian, then maybe, just maybe God would see me as righteous and my prayers would be answered.

It's just like the devil to try and convince us that we're not good enough for God's standards and we should try harder. This defeated mentality of performance causes many Christians to throw their hands up in the air and walk away from their church and their faith.

Friends, we must read God's Word and understand that we were bought with a price that Jesus paid for on the cross. If we have been set free, why would we want to go back and put the chains of bondage back on?

Bottom line: We ARE righteous! Our Heavenly Father loves us and we ARE His children. His love is unconditional. And he hears our every prayer!

The prayer of a righteous man is POweRFUL and effective. James 5:16 NIV. Amen!

This scripture is talking about OUR prayers! Powerful and effective! When we pray, we must believe in our hearts that God hears every prayer we pray. He listens and will answer.

This is the confidence we have in approaching God: that if we ask ANYTHING according to His will, He hears us. And "if" we know that He hears us—whatever we ask—we KNOW that we have what we asked of Him. 1 John 5:14–15 NIV.

Let's erase the old "I don't deserve" mentality and realize who we really are, righteous children of God!

The eyes of the Lord are on the righteous and His ears are attentive to their prayers. 1 Peter 3:12 NIV.

Thank you Jesus for paying for my sins on the cross… …….I'm free…. I'm righteous….. I'm God's child…….

It's a New Day

If anyone is in Christ, he is a NEW creation; the old has gone, the new has come! 2 Corinthians 5:17 NIV.

God tells us that our past is behind us, gone forever; so therefore we shouldn't focus on or live in the past but instead live for today. We cannot change our past but we can make a difference today!

If God tells us that the old has gone and the new has come, why then do we hold on to others' past, holding their sins and mistakes over their head as a reminder of their past? It's almost as if we become judges or gods. Friends, we should NEVER judge someone for their past but instead rejoice when someone turns their life around and serves God. No matter what we have done, good or bad, God looks at our hearts in the NOW, not the past.

Forget the former things; do not dwell on the past. See, I am doing a NEW thing! Now, it springs up; do you not perceive it? I am making a way in the desert and streams in the wasteland, declares the Lord. Isaiah 43: 18–19 NIV.

For I will forgive their wickedness and will remember their sins no more. Hebrews 8:12 NIV.

If God forgives and refuses to remember our past sins, then we should do the same for others. The position of Christians and the church should be one of forgiveness and restoration. We should be known to the world as people of love (God). If we truly love others, we will forgive. Judging others for their past sins is pride. Yes, pride says we believe we are better than others and we are sinless or our sins aren't as bad as others. Unfortunately, the devil has convinced many Christians that it's their job to judge and police others. Do we really think we are helping God by judging? We should welcome everyone into our churches with humility and open arms, loving them unconditionally.

Father, please forgive us for judging others for their past. Help us to be a people of love and restoration. In Jesus's name, amen..

God Will Restore Our Hope

Have you lost all hope? Are you discouraged feeling you can't go on? Are you hurting today?

You will restore my life again, O Lord; from the depths of the earth you will again bring me up. You will increase my honor and comfort me once again. Psalm 71: 20–21 NIV.

O Lord my God, I called to you for help and you healed me. Psalm 30:2 NIV.

Our Heavenly Father's Word tells us He WILL heal our wounds if we ask. When our hearts are broken and we are hurting, it's hard to function, be productive, and difficult to smile and be happy. God understands our pain when we're hurting and desires for us to be comforted as He heals and restores us. I always vision Him wrapping His loving arms me like a daddy would his child.

God heals the brokenhearted and binds up their wounds. Psalm 147:3 NIV.

Friends, there are times when all of us get hurt or have our hearts broken. The disappointment is great and we feel like giving up. But our Abba Father (Daddy) cares so much about us and will not leave or abandon us. If we will lean on Him and allow Him to heal our wounds, we will be healed and stronger than before. He will even carry us if we can't walk another step. "Jesus loves me this I know, for the Bible tells me so…"

I will turn their mourning into gladness; I will give them comfort and joy instead of sorrow, declares the Lord. Jeremiah 31:13 NIV.

Yes, God desires to give us joy again, no matter what tragedy or brokenness we've been through. The "joy of the Lord is our strength" to continue living and helping others.

Whatever pain you're feeling today, please know you are loved and God WILL comfort and heal you.

Remember, it's okay to cry and mourn when you're hurting! God understands. We don't have to be "strong" for ourselves or others. Crying and releasing our emotions are part of our healing. Please don't feel guilty for your tears. BUT, our loving Father desires to see us whole and strong again. Let's trust that He will heal us. God is the god of restoration and I'm living proof that He will heal your broken heart!

Worship Gives Us Victory

A thief (devil) is only there to steal and kill and destroy. I (Jesus) came so they can have real and eternal life, more and better life than they ever dreamed of. John 10:10 Message Bible.

Looking at this particular translation of John 10:10, we can see that salvation encompasses not just eternal life in Heaven, but victory while we live on earth. Some Christians believe that life on this earth is meaningless and we should hope and wait for Heaven. I remember the old hymn, "When we all (finally) get to Heaven, what a day of rejoicing that will be.." It will truly be a day of rejoicing when we get to be with Jesus in Heaven, but His Word instructs us to live abundantly and victoriously while we are still living in our present bodies. God's will is for us, His children, to live an abundant/victorious life, not a defeated one.

How do we fight the devil? By choosing to worship our Heavenly Father and love Him with ALL our heart. We have to know in our heart that we ARE righteous! This was established on the cross. Living a victorious life is about "knowing who we are" not a life of doing and performing to be good.

Worship isn't just about a song we sing on Sunday mornings, but a daily mindset. We worship when we express our love to Him; we worship when we help and love others; and we worship when we give of ourselves. I love the chorus, "I'll give you (God) more than a song.."

When we worship and meditate on His Word, our faith is strengthened. Remember that His Word has instructed us to put on the whole armor of God, which includes the "shield of faith." The shield PROTECTS us from the attacks of the enemy. Yes, we are protected by the shield of faith!

Take up the shield of faith, with which you can extinguish all the flaming arrows of the evil one. Ephesians 6:16 NIV.

It's time that we, as Christians, cease living a defeated, "woe is me" life and begin experiencing life more abundantly in Jesus. We mustn't allow any mountain/obstacle to stand in our way of God's blessings! Friends, let's use our shield of faith to protect ourselves. Our shield is powerful when we pray, worship, and meditate on His Word! Remember, because of Jesus, the battle has already been won!

Today, rejoice that no mountain can stand in your way! FAITH=Believing in His promises.

Do We Really Believe?

Very truly I tell you, whoever believes in me will do the works I have been doing, and they will do even GREATER things than these, because I am going to the Father. And I will do WHATEVER you ask in my name, so that the Father may be glorified in the Son. You may ask me for ANYTHING in my name, and I WILL do it. John 14:12–14 NIV.

We have a loving Father who wants to give us the desires of our heart. He is Jehovah–Jireh, who supplies ALL our needs. Our problem is that we talk ourselves out of our gifts and blessings with feelings of unworthiness. We are His children! I'm continually amazed at the prosperity and blessings on Israel and the Jewish people. Everything they put their hands to, prospers. Yes, they are God's children, but friends, we are His children also. Jesus paid the price on the cross. We aren't step or foster children but true bloodline children of God. Many of the God loving Jewish people KNOW the power of blessings. They don't doubt God's blessings and favor.

You are ALL sons of God through faith in Christ Jesus, for ALL of you who were baptized into Christ have clothed yourselves with Christ. Galatians 3: 26–27 NIV.

Yes, we are children of God! Jesus said that we would greater things than Him. Why isn't this happening today? It's from a lack of faith in His Word. We tend to doubt that God would bless us today or what we read in the Bible is more of a history book than for now.

Friends, we must believe that the Holy Spirit dwells with in us and Jesus sits at the right hand of God praying for us. Praise God!

I encourage you who read this to begin speaking blessings over your family. If there is someone in your family who isn't saved, begin thanking God in faith that this family member will give their heart to Jesus. Let's speak health and healing over those who are sick. "The prayer offered in FAITH will make the sick person well….." James 5:15 NIV.

Let's speak blessings and God's favor over our family and friends. "Those who have faith are blessed." Galatians 3:9 NIV.

I believe in God's promises! The Lord is faithful to ALL His promises….. Psalm 145:13 NIV.

FORGIVENESS...

But Jesus was saying, 'Father, forgive them; for they do not know what they are doing.' And they cast lots, dividing up His garments among themselves. Luke 23:34 NIV.

What love and forgiveness! I'm amazed how Jesus chose to forgive even when He knew all along He would have to suffer and die. He knew at the Lord's Supper as he comforted his disciples that Judas would betray Him and Peter would even deny knowing Him......but, still He forgave......

If you forgive men when they sin against you, your heavenly Father will also forgive you. Matthew 5:7 NIV.

None of us have ever suffered and been betrayed like Jesus. Through it all, He forgave. How silly of us to get so upset at those who say an unkind word about us. We can get so "worked up" and angry, wanting to retaliate and get even. We should stop, look in the mirror and question ourselves, "Is it really worth it?" "Does this even compare to what Jesus experienced?" "He chose to forgive, shouldn't I?"

Forgiveness soothes and calms our soul and allows us to move forward in victory and freedom. Forgiveness breaks the chains that try to bind and hold us in the "unforgiveness prison." Friends, wherever we go and whatever we do, we will always experience some verbal attacks and personality clashes, only because people think differently than we do. We must recognize that the enemy,

Satan, enjoys getting us upset over what someone said or did against us. Today, let's be like Jesus and rise above the attacks, choosing to walk in forgiveness and love. Choosing to forgive makes us stronger, not weaker.

When we choose to make forgiveness a lifestyle, we will experience more joy in our daily lives and sleep better at night. We will be able to get along with co–workers, family members and friends much better. Peace will reign in our lives.

But I tell you who hear me: Love your enemies, do good to those who hate you, bless those who curse you, pray for those who mistreat you. Luke 6: 27–28 NIV.

Forgiveness……a life of LOVE (God).

BELIEVE IN HIS PROMISES

Delight yourself in the Lord and He will give you the desires of your heart. Psalm 37:4 NIV.

Blessed are those who hunger and thirst for righteousness, for they will be filled. Matthew 5:6 NIV.

When I am lacking in my life or praying about a particular matter, which seems impossible, I hang on to these two verses of God's promises. Knowing that my Father will NOT break His promises, I receive comfort, assurance, and excitement, knowing my promises and prayers will be answered. Amen! (So be it!)

Because of my past Pharisee thinking, full of limiting God or feeling I have to be "good" enough to receive anything from Him, I have to renew my mind daily by meditating on His Word so I can understand His heart, which is full of love for me. I tell myself every day that I have an Abba Father (Daddy) who cares for and loves me UNCONDIONTALLY. My past isn't important, washed away by the blood of Jesus, and I'm not required to perform in order to receive a blessing or answers to my prayers. My Heavenly Father "Looks beyond my faults and sees my every need." He chooses to bless me because He loves me and I am His child. ALL I have to do is believe He will do what His Word says He will do.

The Lord blesses the home of the righteous. Proverbs 3:33 NIV.

Yes! My household is blessed! My family is blessed! I stand firm on His promises and will not doubt His Word! I love to sing the chorus, "ALL His promises are true.."

Friends, do you relate with this devotion? Have you been worried and attacked with fear and doubt, feeling you aren't worthy or good enough to receive God's blessings and answers to your prayers? If yes, it's time to change your thinking and look to Jesus who paid the price on the cross so that you can receive ALL He in store for you!

"Oh, how he loves you and me.....He gave His life, what more could He give; oh, how He loves you and me..."

Today, rejoice and be thankful for what He has done, is doing, and will do FOR YOU!!!!!

ARE WE LISTENING TO GOD?

Let the wise listen and add to their learning. Proverbs 1:5 NIV.

Several years ago recording artist Beyonce recorded a hit song titled "Listen" dealing with listening to the heart of those around us. It seems to be a major problem in society today. The number one problem in marriage and relationships today is communication or the lack of. Over the years of counseling young couples I have heard time and time again, "He/she doesn't listen.." Yes, especially with technology i.e. cell phones and computers engulfing our attention, listening is becoming more of a problem. Sadly we can go into restaurants and see couples texting, etc. and ignoring each other.

Christian friends, we must take the time to listen to one another. How will we know the heart of someone if we don't listen to them? How will we know what they feel or think if we don't listen?

Unfortunately, listening is also a problem in our relationship with our Heavenly Father. We either don't have time to spend in prayer, or we jump into prayer doing all the talking. How can we hear God's plans if we don't listen? Our Father has so much to share that will benefit us for the day, if we will just listen.

My sheep listen to my voice; I know them and they follow me. John 10:27 NIV

This is why it's important to get alone with God without distractions. As we worship with a thankful heart, He will begin to speak to us. Following His will is the greatest feeling. The only way we can follow His plan and will is to listen. Even when we are reading His Word (Bible), we must listen. He will speak to our hearts through His Word, even scriptures that we have read over and over. Each time we read a verse, we should listen as He speaks in that still, small voice.

Speak, Lord, for your servant is listening.. 1 Samuel 3:9 NIV.

Today, let's choose to listen to the heart of those around us and also listen to our Heavenly Father as he speaks.

"I come to the garden alone........He walks with me and He talks with me...."

Lord, I Want More of You

Jesus replied, Anyone who loves me will obey my teaching. My Father will love them, and we will come to them and make our home with them. John 14:23 NIV.

I have to be honest. In the past I have intentionally stayed away from verses about obedience because I always felt it would put me into a religious thinking about rules and regulations. I thought I would end up like the Pharisees. But as I am growing in my Father, I understand the first step to obeying God is to fall in love with Him, desiring more of Him, desiring to be like Him, and desiring to spend more and more time with Him. When we begin walking in love with our Heavenly Father, our heart yearns to obey His Word. Yes, we desire to obey His Word and please Him because we love Him and He loves us.

When you fall in love with someone, you truly want to make them happy. That is a small example of the love between God and us. The more time we spend in worship with a thankful heart, the more we fall in love with Him, and that deeper desire develops within us to please Him, obeying His Word. No, it's not about being "good" but rather living a life of love with a desire to please.

If anyone obeys His Word, God's love is truly made complete in Him. 1 John 2:5 NIV.

I desire more of Him. This desire comes from spending time with Him through prayer and worship. As my love grows for Him, my desire to please and obey Him grows.......

As the deer pants for streams of water, so my soul pants for you, my God. Psalm 42..NIV

Ready For Change?

The prayer of a righteous man (that's us) is powerful and effective. James 5:16 NIV.

The Lord…..hears the prayers of the righteous. Proverbs 15:29 NIV.

Prayer changes EVERYTHING, no exceptions! Whatever needs we have, God is ready to meet those needs. When we seek Him, we WILL find Him. When we knock, He WILL answer. Friends, He WILL answer! He will not let us down or abandon us. He hears EVERY prayer that we pray!

Jesus said, And I will do whatever you ask in my name, so that the Father may be glorified in the Son. You may ask me for anything in my name, and I will do it. John 14: 13–14 NIV.

His Word says we can ask Him for ANYTHING. Nothing is too big or small for our Father. We are His children and He LOVES to bless us.

When churches, families, businesses, relationships are covered in prayer, blessings are flowing and problems minimized. The devil is afraid of a praying Christian. He knows there is power involved in their prayers which is greater than him.

If you're ready to see change in your life, change in your church, change in your relationships, change in your health, and change in your career/business, then begin to seek God in prayer and don't let up! Come before Him in confidence that He is hearing your prayers/cries. If you pray and diligently seek Him, change will come, I promise!

This is the CONFIDENCE we have in approaching God: that if we ask ANYTHING according to his will, he hears us. And if we know that he hears us—WHATEVER we ask—we know that we have what we asked of Him. 1 John 5: 14–15 NIV.

Prayer, a powerful conversation with God!

Love One Another

Anyone who claims to be in the light but hates a brother or sister is still in the darkness. Anyone who loves their brother and sister lives in the light, and there is nothing in them to make them stumble. 1 John 2:9–10 NIV.

When we get angry and hold unforgiveness toward someone, it's like we are living our life with a ball and chain tied to our ankle. We're dragging the heavy weight wherever we go, which results in exhaustion and frustration. God's Word tells us that when we choose to forgive others for the hurt they have caused us, we will experience a freedom and the weight that was tied around our ankle will be removed. We will feel lighter, not weighted down. Forgiveness =freedom.

Do not judge, and you will not be judged. Do not condemn, and you will not be condemned. Forgive, and you will be forgiven. Luke 6:37 NIV.

God desires for us to rise above hurts and offences. We must choose to forgive others when they make hurtful comments, attack our character, gossip about us, or become jealous of our accomplishments. If we focus on what they have done to us, we waste our energy and time and allow unforgiveness to build up a negative wall. Then we become prisoners of unforgiveness, bitterness, and hatred. But when we choose to "rise above" the attacks and forgive (even when we don't feel like it) we become free from the darkness and heavy weights.

Beloved, let us love one another for love is of God…. 1 John 4:7 NIV.

We have a choice. Forgive and walk in love, or live our life with the heavy weight of unforgiveness tied around our ankle. Let's choose to forgive and live a life of freedom.

GOD IS FAITHFUL

The Lord is faithful to ALL His promises and loving toward all He has made. Psalm 145:13 NIV.

God's Word doesn't lie or fail. We don't have to hope that He'll bless and answer our prayers, nor do we have to hope that He might decide to favor us. His Word says He WILL bless His children (that's us). We have to walk in the confidence of the Lord. God says we are righteous, but he devil says we're not. So, who are we going to believe? I choose to believe God and His Word.

Very truly I tell you, whoever believes in me will do the works I have been doing, and they will do even GREATER things than these, because I am going to the Father. And I will do WHATEVER you ask in my name, so that the Father may be glorified in the Son. You may ask me for ANYTHING in my name, and I will do it. John 14: 12 NIV.

Friends, there is tremendous power in the name of Jesus. When we realize this, we can pray with confidence knowing that we can seal our prayers by using the name of Jesus. His Word tells us that mountains (obstacles) will be removed when we pray in faith "in the name of Jesus." We must know that we know there is power in His name that even makes the demons tremble. JESUS.....

Let's believe His Word and not doubt.. Remember, He is faithful to ALL His promises....

Be Strong In God

...take up the shield of faith, with which you can extinguish all the flaming arrows of the evil one. Ephesians 6:16 NIV.

When we watch sword movies, which I love dearly, we notice that in one hand the soldier carries his sword (God's Word, the scriptures), and in the other hand he carries his shield (faith) to protect him from the enemy trying to harm him.

Friends, we are in constant battle against the enemy. God tells us in Ephesians 6 to get up in the morning and put on the FULL armor of God, not partial.

Finally, be strong in the Lord and in his mighty power. Put on the FULL armor of God, so that you can take your stand against the devil's schemes. For our struggle is not against flesh and blood (people), but against the rulers, against the authorities, against the powers of this dark world and against the spiritual forces of evil in the heavenly realms. Therefore put on the FULL armor of God, so that when the day of evil comes, you may be able to stand your ground (don't allow the devil to bully you with fear), and after you have done everything, to stand. Stand firm then (don't back up in fear), with the belt of TRUTH buckled around your waist, with the breastplate of Righteousness in place (God says we are already righteous), and with your feet fitted with the readiness that comes from the gospel of PEACE. In addition to all this, take up the shield of FAITH, with which you can extinguish all the flaming arrows of the evil one. Take the helmet of SALVATION (completeness) and the SWORD of the Spirit, which is the word of God (the Bible).

I hate it when I realize that the devil has stolen from me. Yes, I get angry. We should all get angry and take a firm stand saying, "Enough is enough, devil! No more will you steal what I have in Jesus' name!"

Here is the antidote to win the battle: Let's understand that each part of the armor of God is built on LOVE. We should dress each day in the full armor of God (love) ready to protect what is ours. God tells us that the devil is sneaky and a schemer. But, we don't to need to concentrate on the devil, but rather turn ALL our attention in a heart of love (God) toward our Heavenly Father in worship with a thankful heart. Worship WILL defeat the enemy and chase him away. Love (God) conquers EVERYTHING!

Are you ready to win and receive what is yours? Fight back dressed in the armor of God with a heart of worship. I promise you will see victory!

JESUS WILL RESCUE US

Are you in need today? Have you felt all is lost? Do you feel like God has forgotten you?

Jesus said, I will do whatever you ask in my name, so that the Son may bring glory to the Father. You may ask me for anything in my name, and I WILL do it. Amen!

This is truth, God's Word. We shouldn't limit God in our minds. Many feel they aren't "good" enough to receive blessings and answers to prayers. Well, who is? We have "all sinned and come short of the glory of God." Romans 3:23. But, we are covered in God's grace and can approach the throne of grace with boldness and confidence (Hebrew 4; 14–16). God hears the cries of His children and Will answer. If you believe, you will receive WHATEVER you ask for in prayer. Matthew 21:22 NIV.

His Word says "whatever we ask for." The more time we spend with our Father, the more He molds us into the image of Jesus. As we grow closer to Him our desires will align more with God's will for us. We begin to desire His will for us in every decision we need to make. But friends, God cares about every need and desire we have, whether it's financial, physical healing, restoration of a loved one, friendships, careers, school, etc. Nothing is too little for God! If it's important to us, it's important to Him.

This is the confidence we have in approaching God: that if we ask anything according to His will, He hears us. And if we know that He hears us–whatever we ask–we know that we have what we asked of Him. 1 John 5: 14–15 NIV.

Yes, prayer changes EVERYTHING! Do you need a change/miracle in your life today? Do NOT lose hope! Your loving Father is ready to answer your requests. You don't have to earn God's attention. He's always with us.

In the day of trouble I will call to you, O Lord, for you WILL answer me. Psalm 86:7 NIV.

So, what are we waiting for? Let's begin talking to our Holy Father in love, presenting our requests with a thankful heart, and knowing He WILL answer! Believe in prayer! Believe in miracles! Believe in God!

LORD, HELP ME WATCH WHAT I SAY.

What causes fights and quarrels among you? Don't they come from your desires that battle within you? You want something but don't get it... James 4:1–2 NIV.

Jealously, envy, and criticism = strife. Most negative, critical remarks are produced from a jealous heart. Someone achieves an honor and we find fault because deep inside our heart we want what they have. Friends, we must recognize this ungodly trait and "nip it in the bud." We should look for the good in others and be happy when someone achieves an honor, promotion, new relationship, or new job. If someone beats us in a race, we should be happy for them, work harder for the next race, and rest knowing that God is in charge of our lives. When we submit our lives to Him, He will lead and direct our path. We shouldn't get jealous or angry when someone else gets an award or honor.

Have you ever been around people that enjoy criticizing others? Maybe it's because of someone's actions or even their clothing. When we tear others down, we're only masking our own insecurities about ourselves. If we can get the subject matter on others, then no one will focus on us and our situation.

Don't grumble against each other, brothers, or you will be judged. James 5:9 NIV.

We've all heard through our years, "If you can't say something nice about someone, then don't say anything at all." There's truth in this statement! Christian friends, let's not waste any more energy talking negative about God's children. And yes, God loves ALL His children.

Our Heavenly Father's Word reminds us to treat others as Jesus would. We need to love the unlovable, have patience with those who grind on our nerves, forgive those that hurt us, and pray for those that aren't walking with God.

Let us love one another for Love is of God.. 1 John 4:7 NIV.

Today, let's be conscience of what comes out of our mouth. Sometimes, silence is truly golden....

Choose to walk With God

Commit to the Lord whatever you do, and your plans WILL succeed. Proverbs 16:3 NIV.

This is a short but VERY powerful verse about believing in the power of God. It's simple, but life–changing. We should just believe what it says and not try to twist its words or make something philosophical out of it. God's Word is Rhema (fresh word) and is for us as we live each day. This scripture in Proverbs tells us to step back and put God in charge and follow His leading. I don't know about you, but I've made enough mistakes along the way, that I'm thrilled to commit my life and what I'm doing to the Lord. I'd rather He take control and bless what I'm doing than me trying to remain in control and trying to make it work.

I am always with you, O Lord; you hold me by my right hand. You guide me with your counsel, and afterward you will take me into glory. Psalm 73: 23–24 NIV.

Choosing to walk with God in everything we do, will bring blessings, success, joy and peace. Our pride says we know what's best, but when we humble ourselves and rely on His wisdom, we realize He knows best. I choose to follow God's ways. What about you?

Jesus Paid it All For Us

Which of you, if your son asks for bread, will give him a stone? Or if he asks for a fish, will give him a snake? If you, then, though you are evil (we're sinners), know how to give good gifts to your children, how much MORE will your Father in heaven give good gifts to those who ask him! Matthew 7:9–11 NIV.

God desires to meet ALL our needs. We don't have to worry if we're good enough to receive blessings from God. Thankfully, He doesn't base blessing us on our behavior or attitude. If this was true, no one would receive anything. God doesn't swell on our past. He's a NOW Heavenly Father, interested in the present in regards to our heart. He deeply cares about every single issue that we face. Nothing important to us is trivial to Him. We ARE a priority to our Abba Father (Daddy).

Now to him who is able to do immeasurably MORE than all we ask or imagine, according to his power that is at work within us, to him be glory in the church and in Christ Jesus throughout all generations, for ever and ever! Amen. Ephesians 3:20–21 NIV.

Today, don't allow the enemy to convince you that you aren't important to God or that your needs aren't worth bothering Him. God doesn't get too busy, He's almighty God! Nothing is too small or large for Him! He cares about YOU! He doesn't want you to carry your burden in life like some heavy backpack, but instead He desires for you to give it to Him so you can experience freedom.

God who did not spare His own Son, but gave him up for us all–how will He also, along with Him, graciously give us ALL things? Romans 8:32 NIV.

Friends, you haven't been forgotten or abandoned! Trust God and don't give up! Your miracle is coming!

God WILL meet ALL your needs according to His glorious riches in Christ Jesus. Philippians 4:19 NIV.

"Oh how He loves you and me…"

Complaining Or Thankful?

I know what it is to be in need, and I know what it is to have plenty. I have learned the secret of being content in any and every situation, whether well fed or hungry, whether living in plenty or in want. Philippians 4:12 NIV.

Many Christians misinterpret this verse by thinking the Apostle Paul meant to not ask for anything from God, and just be content. But this isn't what God is saying through this verse. We should present our requests to God in faith, believing that He has heard our prayers and will answer. But in the process of waiting, we should be content, not murmuring and complaining about our situation or the people we are around.

Having a thankful heart opens the door for God's blessings and also gives us a calming peace. Waiting on God (He is usually waiting on us) to open doors of opportunity or heal a situation, etc. can "try" our patience. But "if" we will TRUST Him with our whole heart and not take things into our own hands by "helping" God, we will see our miracles come forth. God doesn't desire to withhold any good thing from us. He loves us!

Let the peace of Christ rule in your hearts, since as members of one body you were called to peace. And be thankful. Colossians 3:15 NIV.

Friends, we know that walking/living in the peace of God is the opposite of complaining all the time. Do you know of someone around you that complains constantly? We all do. Complaining gives us a negative attitude that causes others to want to "get away from." Complaining all the time is poison to a church, work environment, or a relationship.

We must "choose" to be content/peaceful whether we're facing a storm or receiving a blessing. Thankfulness to God is an antidote for a complaining heart.

Give thanks in ALL circumstances; for this is the will of God in Christ Jesus for you. 1 Thessalonians 5:18 NIV.

Today, let's "look on the bright side of things" and be thankful. When the opportunity arises to complain about someone or a situation, let's choose to give God thanks instead. If someone around us receives a blessing, let's choose to be happy for them knowing our blessings are coming our way.

"Give thanks with a grateful heart......"

TROUBLES DO COME

Jesus said, In this world you will have trouble. But take heart! I have overcome the world. John 16:33 NIV.

There's no one that hasn't been attacked in some area of their life. It could be a personal attack on their character, financial, health, relationship, career, etc. An attack doesn't declare defeat in our lives! We must continually be on guard against the enemy (devil) who comes to "steal, kill, and destroy" (John 10:10) who we are, what we're doing, where we're going (plans). He knows he can't take Jesus away from us, so he tries us divert our attention from God to focus on our problems with discouragement, thinking, "Woe is me." When we get discouraged, we tend to focus on ourselves and what we're facing instead of worshiping God with confidence that He WILL take care of us.

The Lord WILL rescue me from EVERY evil attack and will bring me safely to his heavenly kingdom. 2 Timothy 4:18 NIV.

Isn't that exciting? Our Father God is watching over us to protect us from the evil one. We must learn to trust Him with ALL of our heart. Did you know that God sends His angels to protect us? Wow, that's exciting AND comforting to know that He loves us and sends His angels to watch over us.

For he will command his angels concerning you to guard you in all your ways. Psalm 91:11 NIV.

Friends, we are loved! Our Abba Father (Daddy) truly loves us! He desires for us to be overcomers to the things of this world.

Everyone born of God (that's us) overcomes the world. This is the victory that has overcome the world, even our faith. Who is it that overcomes the world? Only he (that's us) who believes that Jesus is the Son of God. 1 John 5:4–5 NIV.

Today is the day (our day) that our eyes are being opened to His Word that we ARE overcomers to the trials facing us! Victory!!

WE ARE CALLED TO BE LIKE JESUS

Be imitators of God...and live a life of love, just as Christ loved us and gave himself for us.... Ephesians 5:1 NIV.

I'm always amazed to have the opportunity to watch an artist work with clay. Much work goes into the mixing of the clay, etc. It doesn't happen instantly, but requires a process (patience). But after the molding and shaping have taken place, the clay object is placed in the potter's oven to bake. The end result is a beautiful piece of art.

God, our Potter, lovingly invites each of us to climb on his "potter's wheel" with a surrendered heart to be molded into the image of Jesus Christ. It doesn't feel comfortable to be molded and shaped, then placed in the fire, but the end result is beautiful. We become more like Jesus in the way we treat others. Our loving Father gives each of us a choice whether to stay on the potter's wheel or selfishly climb off to do and say what WE want. Yes, when the heat gets intense, some will quit and begin to handle their own life's situations and problems. Our pride and selfishness can get in the way, causing us to live our lives the way we want, not as God has planned. Doing things OUR way can also get us involved in unnecessary drama and strife. Our lack of time on the potter's wheel can cause our words to be negative and hurtful, piercing like a knife and leaving a wounded hole in others.

God truly desires for us to be like Jesus in the way we live and treat others. Patience is a gift from God that develops through spending time with Him on the Potter's wheel. Let's allow ourselves to be molded into the image of Jesus. God, our Potter, knows what He is doing. Let's trust Him.

I have always loved the old hymn, "Have thine own way Lord, have thine own way. Thou are the Potter, I am the clay. Mold me and make me after thine own will, while I am waiting 'yielded' and still."

We are the clay, you are the potter; we are all the work of your hand. Isaiah 64:8 NIV.

GIVE THANKS TO GOD DURING YOUR STORM

Rejoice always, pray continually, give thanks in all circumstances; for this is God's will for you in Christ Jesus. 1 Thessalonians 5:16–18 NIV.

When everything seems to be going our way, it's easy to lift our hands and thank God for His blessings. But our challenge comes when the clouds become dark over our head, the wind is blowing hard and the storm facing us is fierce. This comes down to a decision we must make. The above scripture tells us to give thanks in ALL circumstances, good or bad. When we choose to thank Him, even when we don't feel like giving thanks, His heart is moved. His love for us is a deep, unconditional love full of compassion, and He knows it's difficult for us to have a thankful attitude when we feel our world is falling apart. But His Word tells us to give thanks in ALL circumstances. ALL means EVERYTHING.

The morning after hearing the horrific news that we had lost our son in a car crash, I remember lying on the couch wishing to die so I could go to Heaven and be with Steffan. But in the midst of this terrible storm, God lovingly and gently spoke to me the names "Teri, Lydia." Upon hearing the names of my wife and daughter, I knew He wanted me to live for them. I somehow, in my excruciating pain, mumbled the words from my lips, "Thank you for loving me." I knew that even though He wasn't shocked over the news, His heart was broken for me experiencing so much pain. I attribute much of our healing to the fact we decided to give God thanks for His love during our storm.

Let us come before Him with thanksgiving and extol Him with music and song. Psalm 95:2 NIV.

Worship with a heart of thanksgiving moves the heart of God. When we're facing trials, let's look to God and give Him thanks that our lives are in His hands.

Let's be comforted by this chorus, "He knows my name; He knows my every thought. He sees each tear that falls and hears me when I call.."

WE ARE THE RIGHTEOUSNESS OF GOD

God made him (Jesus) who had no sin to be sin for us, so that in him we might become the righteousness of God. 2 Corinthians 5: 21 NIV.

Friends, I wasted so many years believing that I had to earn my righteousness by being good. When I would read about how God would bless the righteous, I felt I wouldn't qualify because I had sinned, etc. This wrong thinking caused me to live a defeated life with not much hope. I knew I was a Christian, but I felt unrighteous. I thank God He opened my eyes to TRUTH (Jesus).

Now I KNOW that I'm righteous because the price was paid at Calvary. Jesus' blood gave me the gift of righteousness, nothing earned, just a beautiful gift. I have had to change my old way of thinking, and to be honest, if I'm not careful, the old "earning my way by being good" thinking will creep back into my mind.

We must renew our minds daily with God's Word. The old thinking is gone. It's a new day with our Father. He loves us and desires to bless us. He gives us a choice whether we want to walk in His blessings or not. I choose to receive ALL that my Father desires to give me!

Let's thank Him for the gift of righteousness (right standing/ favor). Nothing earned, just a gift. I receive my gifts....

Looking Into the Hearts of Others

Do not judge, or you too will be judged. For in the same way you judge others, you will be judged, and with the measure you use, it will be measured to you.

Why do you look at the speck of sawdust in your brother's eye and pay no attention to the plank in your own eye? How can you say to your brother, 'Let me take the speck out of your eye,' when all the time there is a plank in your own eye? You hypocrite, first take the plank out of your own eye, and then you will see clearly to remove the speck from your brother's eye. Matthew 7:1–5 NIV.

Ouch! This scripture hits us over the head with truth. As Christians, we tend to categorize sin by thinking, "This particular sin is bigger than that one." Or, "Gossiping about someone or what they did is no big deal." Friends, we know that sin is sin. We might rank sin in regards to importance, but God doesn't. Romans states, "We've ALL sinned and fallen short of the glory of God." No one is perfect, but for some reason, we think it's okay to talk about others in a negative manner, because it's not as bad as a sexual sin. Sorry, but again, sin is sin. It could be someone's actions or even what they're wearing. There's an old saying, "We talk about others so we won't get talked about." Gossip, rumors, mocking, etc. is poison and hurts the victims as well as gives us a negative attitude.

But thank God we are redeemed by the blood of Jesus. The price has been paid. The slate wiped clean and we are covered like a snuggly blanket with GRACE. Praise God! God's desire is for us to look into the heart of others and see what He sees, a beautiful heart that He created.

Let's be conscience of our tongue and what we say or think. Let's make a habit of saying uplifting, positive words about others. It goes along with another old saying, "If we can't say something nice, then we should just close our mouth."

Today, let's look for the good in others and use our tongue to worship and praise God, thanking Him for ALL He has and is doing, instead of tearing others down.

IT'S TIME TO GET OUR FEET WET...

Lord, if it's you, Peter replied, "tell me to come to you on the water." "Come," He said. Then Peter got down out of the boat, walked on the water and came toward Jesus. But when he saw the wind, he was afraid and, beginning to sink, cried out, "Lord, save me!" Immediately Jesus reached out his hand and caught him. "You of little faith," He said, "why did you doubt? Matthew 14: 28 NIV.

Most of us have read this scripture and wrongly judged Peter for sinking in the water. Haven't we all been guilty of doubting God at times? I so admire Peter for having the faith in Jesus and the courage to step out of the boat and walk on water toward Him. We have to remember, the other disciples stayed in the boat where it seemed safe, but Peter, in his boldness and hunger for more of God, stepped out of the boat with his eyes on Jesus.

This scripture is a wonderful lesson. Many times as we look to Jesus for a miracle, He'll tell us to step out of our boat in faith, believing in Him and walk on water (the impossible). Dear friends, what storm or raging sea is facing you today? Is it financial, relationship problems, dead–end job/career, health issues, etc.? Whatever is facing you with its big waves crashing all around your boat, look into the midst of your storm and you'll see Jesus. No, He won't be on the banks of the sea waiting for you to come ashore, He'll be right there with you telling you to not be afraid. In love and encouragement, you'll hear Him gently saying, "Come, step out of your boat in faith, believe and follow me." As you begin to walk in faith, believing, "I can do all things through Christ who strengthens me." (Philippians 4:13), you will be attacked by the devil on all sides trying to get you to take your eyes off Jesus and instead focus on your problems. But, be reassured, Jesus WILL NOT leave you! If you begin sinking, His gentle hand will reach for you and save you from drowning in your problems. What a loving Savior!

God has said, "Never will I leave you; never will I forsake you." So we say with confidence, "The Lord is my helper; I will not be afraid. What can man do to me?" Hebrews 13: 5–6 NIV.

Do you hear God's gentle voice calling you to believe in His Word for your miracle? Today, dear friends, trust in Jesus who will save you from the raging storm. Don't give up and remember, He loves you!

ANCHOR YOUR SHIP

When peace, like a river, attendeth my way, when sorrows like sea billows roll; whatever my lot, Thou has taught me to say, it is well, it is well, with my soul.

Are you going through a big storm in your life at the present and feel as if you're ship is going to sink and all will be lost? Most of us have felt that way at times. It's a storm so big that it literally takes your breath away and you can't breathe and your mind becomes almost fuzzy where you can't think straight.

Many times the storms come as a shock or surprise, catching off guard. This can make us feel helpless.

Friends, this is actually a good place to be with God. When we feel lost and helpless, we should let go of our way of doing things and look to Jesus. Jesus will give us peace in the middle of the storm because our faith and trust is in Him, not in ourselves. We don't have to fear the outcome because we have surrendered our ship to God. He will comfort and take care of us when we feel alone and abandoned. He NEVER leaves our side, not even for a moment. What He will do is direct our ship to safety. It might mean that we are to take a different route with our ship. When we surrender to our Father, we can trust that He knows all and will do a better job at steering our ship.

No matter what you're going through at the present, turn your eyes to Jesus. God knew before you were born that you would be facing this storm. "He will make a way where there seems to be no way..".

Allow this storm, as painful as it is, to strengthen you and make you wiser. "And we know that in ALL things God works for the good of those who love him, who have been called according to his purpose (that's us)." With your eyes on Jesus, allow His peace to comfort you.......

HAVE FAITH IN GOD!

Now FAITH is confidence in what we hope for and assurance about what we do not see. Hebrew 11:1 NIV.

It would be much easier for us to have faith in what we can see with our eyes, but faith is choosing to believe in God's promises no matter what we feel or see. We can't be moved by what's happening around us. We must focus our attention on God's Word. Faith means believing that God doesn't lie or break promises and that He has not forgotten us. Faith says, "I believe."

The Lord is faithful to ALL His promises and loving toward ALL He has made. Psalm 145:13 NIV.

When we don't get an immediate answer to our prayers, doubts can seep into our minds like flood waters under a doorway. It's enters slowly but can cause much damage. We must pick up our shield of faith and quench the fiery darts (attacks of doubt) from the devil. Satan knows that faith in God makes us whole (brings answers and miracles) so he works hard to discourage and distract us from believing in God's promises. God isn't requiring us to be super heroes of faith. And we're not failures because our faith wavers.

Jesus said, "If you have faith as small as a mustard seed, you can say to this mountain, 'Move from here to there' and it WILL move. NOTHING will be impossible for you" Matthew 17:20.

We should begin by confessing with our lips that we believe God's Word and believe He will answer our prayers. Reading and meditating on His Word will strengthen our hearts to believe and not doubt. Reading scriptures about faith will help us become strong.

Friends, if you don't receive your answer today, just keep rejoicing and standing in faith. God's Word is truth and tells us that our miracles are coming! Faith says, "I won't give up!" Faith can and will remove any mountain blocking our way.

The Joy of the Lord is our strength (to stand strong in faith) Nehemiah 8:10 NIV.

When doubts begin to creep in, fight back with joy, worship, a thankful heart, and God's Word, which is more powerful than a two–edged sword.

NOTHING is impossible with God. Luke 1:37 NIV.

ALL things are possible to him who believes. Mark 9:23 NIV.

Let's believe in God's promises!

WE MUSTN'T LOOK BACK

Forget the former things; do not dwell on the past. Isaiah 43:18 NIV.

Each one of us has faced some regrets over decisions we have made in our past. Bad choices/decisions have caused us to shake our heads in regret wishing things could have been different.

We can't change the past, its history, but we CAN change the now and future decisions. Learning to walk with God and seeking Him before any decisions are made can save us much heartache. His Word tells us that "if" we will trust Him, He will "lead and guide" our every step.

I guide you in the way of wisdom and lead you along straight paths. When you walk, your steps will not be hampered; when you run, you will not stumble. Proverbs 4: 11–12 NIV.

Praise God for His promises to lead us. The Holy Spirit will lead us into ALL truth.

Truth + trust = right decisions. Whether it's a relationship decision, job offers, new purchases, etc., He WILL protect and lead us. When we are confused about what to do, DON'T DO! Stop! Wait on God to speak to your heart. When God speaks, there will be peace in your heart. God is NOT the author of turmoil and worry.

I will instruct you and teach you in the way you should go says the Lord. Psalm 32:8 NIV.

This scripture is a promise! We must seek Him with our whole heart and listen to His voice that speaks to our heart.

What decisions are you facing today? Are you discouraged about wrong choices of the past? Friends, it's a new day. Thank God for His GRACE that covers over our sins, bad choices, mistakes, etc. Today is a new day! New beginnings! Let's choose to listen to God's voice and His Word and not look back at our past mistakes. God is the God of "restoration" and if we will trust Him, He will restore us greater than before! That's His promise, and His promises are TRUE!

I Choose to Follow Jesus

Teach me, LORD, the way of your decrees, that I may follow it to the end. Give me understanding, so that I may keep your law and obey it with all my heart. Direct me in the path of your commands, for there I find delight. Psalm 119:33–35 NIV.

There is such joy when we hear God's voice and follow His plan for our lives. Putting away selfish motives and walking with a humble heart like Jesus opens the door for blessings. Doing what God asks of us, whether it's in our job, relationships, ministry, etc., gives us joy and peace. Life becomes more pleasant for us. We get up in the mornings with excitement (even tho we are sleepy), knowing we're in His will.

God desires to use each of us to bless others. He blesses us so we can bless others. But it comes down to choice. Yes, He gives us a choice to make. I can testify personally that when I'm serving God and following His will, I'm the most happy. When I get up in the mornings and spend time with Him, my day begins with joy.

Let's choose to follow Him. When He speaks to us in that still small voice, let's answer, "Here am I, Lord." Being where he wants us to be with our lives, is a great peaceful feeling.

Serving God has no age limits or restrictions. You don't have to be educated or wealthy. Our Father is looking for open hearts that love Him and desire to bless and help others.

Let's thank Him and give Him our all. That feeling of peace and joy that comes from obeying God, is the best!

Commit to the Lord whatever you do, and your plans will succeed. Proverbs 16:3 NIV.

Thank You God for the Gift of Peace

Have you been verbally attacked? Feel like fighting back?

Whoever of you loves life and desires to see many good days, keep your tongue from evil and your lips from speaking lies. Turn from evil and do good; seek peace and pursue it. Psalm 34: 12–14 NIV.

God's heart is for us to be like Jesus. It's not always easy holding our tongue from saying what's on our mind, or wanting to retaliate against someone who has hurt us, but we are reminded how Jesus walked in love, not fighting back. "He could have called 10,000 angels....." He was obedient throughout His earthly life, even on the cross, saying, "Father, forgive them for they don't know what they're doing." He died on the cross with a heart of forgiveness and love.

To be like Jesus is to let negative and hurtful remarks about us roll off our shoulders. It's not easy, but we are called to rise above in love. When we are attacked by someone's comments or actions, we should try to look into the heart of that person. Most of the time we will see hurts of their own, etc. They usually lash out from hurts and etc. If we will listen to our Heavenly Father, He will reveal truth and an understanding of the situation. Personally, I would rather rise above my attacks/storms than succumb to the negativity and fight back. When we lash back at someone or "get it off our chest," we usually feel good for only a brief moment. Fighting back puts us on the same sad level as our attackers. God tells us to keep our eyes focused on Jesus, not looking to the left or right at our situations, but to rise above by choosing to walk in love (God).

Blessed are the peacemakers, for they will be called children of God. Matthew 5:9 NIV. We receive blessings when we choose to walk in peace instead of strife.

Most problems in relationships arise from wanting our own way, or thinking our way is better. This usually stems from our lack of time with God. Our time with Him strengthens our fruit of the Spirit i.e. love, joy, peace, and etc.

To be like Jesus is to love and forgive those who persecute us. No, we don't have to be a door mat to be treated with disrespect over and over, but we can move on in love and forgiveness, which leads to freedom, peace, and a good night's sleep. Love and forgive....

Our Heavenly Father Has Plans For Us

God who began a good work in your will carry it on to completion until the day of Christ Jesus. Philippians 1:6 NIV.

Friends, this verse in Philippians reassures us that our loving Father will continue to work in our lives and not stop "mid-stream" because He's angry or aggravated with us. God doesn't throw the towel in the ring desiring to quit working in our lives because of our attitudes or lack of faith.

I'm sure there are times when we have felt forgotten or abandoned by God. When storms hit our lives, isolation will try to creep in making us feel we are alone on a deserted island with no hope. Biblically, we know this isn't true. His Word declares that He will never leave nor forsake us.

The Lord is close to the brokenhearted and saves those who are crushed in spirit. Psalm 34:18 NIV.

"He looked beyond my faults and saw my every need.."

God looks past the sins and "stupid decisions" we have made, and sees our hearts. Because He created each of us individually, He knows the great potential that He has placed inside each of us.

For I know the plans I have for you, declares the Lord, plans to prosper you and not to harm you, plans to give you hope and a future. Jeremiah 29:11 NIV.

Yes, each plan for us is unique and He will continue working in our lives. He's the Potter and we are the clay. Let's thank Him that He is working in our lives and will continue until the day we are home with Him.

I used to love singing the old gospel song, "Jesus got ahold of my life and He won't let me go.." True! He loves us and is ALWAYS working in our lives. Remember, His love for us isn't based on what we do or how much we pray....His love is unconditional..

What Are We Focused On?

Shortly before dawn Jesus went out to them, walking on the lake. When the disciples saw him walking on the lake, they were terrified. "It's a ghost," they said, and cried out in fear. But Jesus immediately said to them: "Take courage! It is I. Don't be afraid." "Lord, if it's you," Peter replied, "tell me to come to you on the water." "Come," He said. Then Peter got down out of the boat, walked on the water and came toward Jesus. Matthew 14: 25–30 NIV.

I love this story from God's Word as it teaches us to keep our eyes on Jesus in all our situations and circumstances. We tend to focus on our problems and crisis as we're going through the storms, when we need to turn our eyes on Jesus, knowing He can and will take care of us.

He is our Shepherd who leads us as a shepherd would lead his flock. Jesus tells us, "Come, follow me." He leads the way and protects us each step we take.

But seek first his kingdom and his righteousness, and all these things will be given to you as well. Matthew 6:33 NIV.

This verse lovingly tells us to focus on Him, not on our problems. As Peter focused on Jesus, he walked on water toward Him. It was only when he looked around at his situation (big waves) that he began to fear and started sinking. Thank God

Jesus was right there with Peter as He is with us today. The key is keeping our eyes on Jesus, and He will take care of our needs.

The devil loves for us to take things in our own hands, and make our own decisions. But God tells us to follow Him and He will in return give us rest. I personally like God's ways much better!

Whatever you are facing today, please know that your Shepherd (Jesus) will not leave or forsake you. He is showing you the way. "Trust and obey, for there's no other way to be happy in Jesus." Let's focus our minds and hearts on Him as we thank Him for taking care of us. He won't let us down, I promise!

Are we a Martha or a Mary?

As Jesus and his disciples were on their way, he came to a village where a woman named Martha opened her home to him. She had a sister called Mary, who sat at the Lord's feet listening to what he said. But Martha was distracted by all the preparations that had to be made. She came to him and asked, "Lord, don't you care that my sister has left me to do the work by myself? Tell her to help me!" "Martha, Martha," the Lord answered, "you are worried and upset about many things, but few things are needed—or indeed only one. Mary has chosen what is better, and it will not be taken away from her. Luke 10: 38–42 NIV.

Do we often find ourselves like Martha wanting to "do" instead of communing with God like Mary? Many of us have been taught through the years that if we want to be "good Christians," we have to serve Him 24/7 by "doing." To some this means serving on multiple church committees, singing in the choir, baking for the needy, door to door witnessing, and etc. Now wait! All of these items listed are good and helpful, BUT they can't and shouldn't take the place of our relationship with God. That valued time we have praying, worshiping, reading and meditating on His Word, can't be substituted for works. I love the old hymn, "I come to the garden alone...And he walks with me and He talks with me.."

Friends, the opposite of faith isn't fear, but works (doing). Again, serving God is good but we shouldn't' put it above our relationship with Him. Remember, the greatest commandment given was "Love the Lord your God with all your heart.."

Because of Jesus' death on the cross, the price was paid for us (His children) to be righteous. Righteousness is not earned by doing, but a gift from God to believe in. When Jesus spoke His final words on the cross, "It is finished," He was saying that the price had been paid in full. We just need to believe in who we are, heirs of God, and joint–heirs with Jesus covered in grace.

I encourage you to spend time with the Father who loves you. Remember, "doing/serving" is good, but our "time" with Him is more important and should be a priority in our lives. Let's choose to be like Mary with a heart to listen and receive… He is speaking, are we listening?

EVERY DAY WITH JESUS IS SWEETER THAN THE DAY BEFORE

All the days ordained for me were written in your book, O Lord, before one of them came to be. Psalm 139: 16 NIV.

I have written this statement many times in the past, but need to share it again: "NOTHING surprises God!" Sometimes we feel He gets shocked over our sins and bad choices. Friends, He knew before we were born what choices we would make. Our loving Father is NEVER surprised, caught off guard, or shocked over our decisions. He's the Alpha and Omega, beginning and the end, and He has beautiful plans for us!

I know the plans I have for you, declares the Lord, plans to prosper you and not to harm you, plans to give you hope and a future. Jeremiah 29:11 NIV.

God's plans for us are always beautiful, full of prosperity and hope. We have to "choose" to follow His direction or ours. Sometimes our minds can get very independent when it comes to choices and decisions, feeling we know what's best. That independence will cause us to avoid seeking God's guidance through prayer and His Word. We've all heard the old saying, "God gave us a brain and we should use it." Yes, He did give us a brain, but he desires for us to follow Him. Personally, there were times in my past when I would get weary and exhausted from making my own choices, trying to open a closed door. If I had only taken time to seek God with a listening ear and heart, I would have avoided many bad decisions which gave me much heartache. Through the years, I have learned to rely on my Father, trusting His will for my life. He definitely knows more than me and His ways are much better than mine.

The Lord is good to those whose hope is in Him, to the one who seeks Him; it is good to wait quietly for the salvation (wholeness) of the Lord. Lamentations 3: 25–26 NIV.

Waiting/relying on God is worth it. He truly desires to direct us down the right path that will bless us. Today, let's begin by seeking His will for our lives. Because He has a special plan for us daily, let's not waste a single day by ignoring Him.

Dear Christians, His plans for us can also be fun! Yes, following God's will can give us joy, peace and a good time!

SERVE THE LORD WITH GLADNESS

What does it mean to "serve" God?

We serve God through worship and thanksgiving. We should express our love to our Heavenly Father as often as possible throughout the day, not just on Sundays. God loves and desires our expressions of love toward Him, and the more we express our love, the more love we feel. This is called "relationship." We should spend time with Him with a heart of thanksgiving. We have much to be thankful for, no matter what trial we have faced or facing.

We serve God by being loving and kind toward others. I'm humbled when I read how Jesus chose to wash His disciples' feet just before his arrest and crucifixion. Knowing all this was going to happen to Him, He still took time to love and serve them through the washing of their feet. It was a loving lesson that needed to be taught. There have been times in my life when I got verbally attacked by someone and instead of choosing to love and forgive, I lashed back or threw myself a pity party. By choosing to love instead of retaliation, God can use our actions to touch the other person's life. Yes, it's a challenge, but necessary in our growing to be like Jesus.

Serving God is forgiveness. We are called to forgive others as we desire to be forgiven. I remember the old gospel song, "But Still He Loved Me." Yes, in spite of my sins, goofiness, attitude, selfishness, etc, He (God) still loves me! He is a forgiving Father. We are called to forgive as Jesus forgave those who persecuted Him.

Friends, Let's rejoice today as we live our lives in JOY with a heart to serve our Heavenly Father. Remember, you can't truly serve our Father when you choose to be isolated from others 24/7. Our Christian walk involves us being around others. Yes, we need our alone prayer time and communion with God, but He desires for us to serve Him by loving others as we go through our day.....

Some days it can be a challenge, but we can do it through grace....

Beloved, let us love one another. 1 John 4:7 NIV.

God Desires to Bless Us

The LORD bless you and keep you; the LORD make his face shine on you and be gracious to you; the LORD turn his face toward you and give you peace. Numbers 6:24–26 NIV.

The Hebrew word for "bless" is barok, and the Greek word is eulogeo. Both words mean to endue with power for success, prosperity, fruitfulness in childbearing and longevity. It's a package deal that God desires to give to us. But like any gift we receive, we have the choice to open it or not. I choose to receive every blessing/gift that God desires to give me.

Even the word salvation, which comes from the Greek word soteria, means deliverance, preservation, safety and health. Yes, it does mean eternal living with God, but it gives us blessings while we're still on this earth. Again, I desire to receive every gift from God!

If we, as Christians, are called to be paupers, how can we help anyone who needs help? God desires to bless us so we can help others in return. This is encompasses "love thy neighbor." Through God's blessings we have the ability to help those in need. God blessed many churches when Hurricane Katrina hit the gulf coast/New Orleans area with the finances to help those in need. It's not God's will that we hoard our wealth, but instead have the freedom to bless and help others as God directs.

Let's believe our Father who tells us in His Word that we are "the seed and blessing of Abraham." Genesis 13:2 tells us Abraham was wealthy in livestock, silver and gold.

This devotion is not about getting rich quick, but about believing and trusting God for our blessings so we can bless others.........Thank you God that You "supply ALL our needs..." In Jesus's name, amen.

Truth Always Sets Us Free

Then you will know the truth, and the truth will set you free. John 8:32 NIV.

This scripture explains that the truth is Jesus. There is no other way to be saved except through Jesus, no matter how good we are or what we do for others. Jesus is the only way!

Jesus answered, I am the way and the truth and the life. No one comes to the Father except through me. John 14:6 NIV.

There are many religions in the world today declaring various means and ways to enter heaven, but we, as God's children, know the ONLY way for us is through Jesus Christ, our Savior.

Not only is Jesus the truth to understanding eternity but He's truth in how we should live our lives each day. God's Word describes to us the life of Jesus as a model to live by. By reading the scriptures, we understand how Jesus handled daily living. He walked in love and spoke truth. He encountered rejection and strife just like we do today. Yes, there were those who hated and despised him. Sometimes we feel we are the only ones going through a situation, but Jesus faced almost the same and conquered each situation with love.

Jesus is truth. He never lied even under pressure. He never fell prey to "white lies" (those little lies that we think aren't important). Friends, a lie is a lie and truth is truth. There's nothing in between and no justification for not telling the truth to smooth a situation over. We are called to live a life of truth (Jesus). When we walk in truth in what we say and do, we feel free and burdens are lifted off our shoulders. Lying usually lead to others lies, getting deeper and more difficult. I grew up hearing this old saying, "Oh the tangled web we weave."

I stand in the evil day having my loins girded about with truth….Ephesians 6:14 NIV. Today, I encourage you to choose truth, (Jesus). He is the way, truth, and life. Truth sets us free!

Are You Living in Freedom or Guilt?

If anyone is in Christ, he is a NEW creation; the old has gone, the new has come. 2 Corinthians 5:17NIV.

If we are a new creation (and we ARE), then there is no room for old junk to permanently return to our lives. We can't go backwards with Jesus. Just because we stumble in sin or think about the "old" life, doesn't mean we are scum, terrible, or need to get saved again, etc.

We have ALL sinned and come short of the glory of God. Romans 3:23 NIV.

Thank God we are RIGHTEOUS because Jesus, our Savior, paid the price on the cross for us. Yes, the price has already been paid! We mustn't listen to the devil, the accuser, as he whispers in our ears how terrible we are, that we will sin again, or that God is angry with us for letting Him down. Garbage, lies!!!

Jesus paid it ALL, all to Him I owe. Sin hath left a crimson stain, but He washed it white as snow!

What can wash away my sins? Nothing but the blood of Jesus. What can make me whole again? Nothing but the blood of Jesus.

Amen to these two great hymns that describe freedom! It's already done! The price has been paid! This is summed up in one loving word, "GRACE." Grace is greater than all our sins.

Nothing surprises our Heavenly Father, nothing. When we sin (mess up), we somehow feel that God is shocked and heavily disappointed. Sorry, my friends, that is not the case. He knew before we were even born that we would sin. But we are forgiven because of righteousness. He has and will always love us.

You are a chosen people, a royal priesthood, a holy nation, a people 'belonging to God,' that you may declare the praises of Him who called you out of darkness into His wonderful light (Jesus).

Let's memorize the following scripture and get it deep within our heart so when the accuser (devil) starts trying to make us feel guilty over our lives, we can fight back with God's Word that is sharper than any two–edged sword!

I am the righteousness of God in Christ Jesus. 2 Corinthians 5:21 NIV.

Nothing earned, but a free gift (righteousness) for being God's child. I love free gifts and I love being God's child!

Peace Like A River...

I will grant peace in the land, and you will lie down and no one will make you afraid, says the Lord. Leviticus 26:6 NIV.

Resting at night knowing that God has it all under control gives us peace. No one likes a sleepless night. Our minds begin to think of all the things we need to do or make better, then worry sets in and we find ourselves tossing and turning throughout the night. God's desire is to give us peace (security) that He alone can take care of our situations.

I will lie down and sleep in peace, for you alone, O Lord, make me dwell in safety. Psalm 4:8 NIV.

He truly loves us and will handle our problems if we'll allow. Peace says we will listen to His voice and do what He says do BECAUSE His ways are better than ours. Our human nature desires to "fix" everything in our lives and those around us when we should be trusting God, our Father, to handle our problems we're facing.

God's Word is peace. The more time we read and confess His Word, worship His almighty name, and pray with faith, the more peace we'll receive. There will be a calmness that surrounds us knowing that God is in control.

Great peace have they who love your law, O Lord, and nothing can make them stumble. Psalm 119:165 NIV.

Today, let's take a deep breath and relax knowing that we have surrendered our problems to our Heavenly Father and He will take care of us. Peace isn't just a onetime feeling. It's like a river that continuously flows peacefully. God desires to give us peace 24/7 so we can walk in confidence that He is in control and will not abandon us.

I Have Decided To Follow Jesus

Come, follow me, Jesus said, and I will send you out to fish for people. At once they left their nets and followed him. Matthew 4:19–20 NIV.

Many of us would have a difficult time in following God's direction, especially if it was out of our comfort zone. We say we will follow His call but most of the time, that means His call has to remain nestled in our comfort zone. I wonder if we would be willing to let go of our careers, homes, etc to follow God's call like the disciples. Now I'm not saying that God is calling all of us to leave everything behind, BUT, would we be willing to follow Him at all cost? God IS calling us to surrender our all to Him and that means putting Him first in our lives above our careers, marriage, relationships, etc. He will not forsake us, His children. He took care of the disciples as they followed Jesus and He will take care of us.

Learning to hear His voice isn't difficult. As we worship in prayer and spend quiet time with Him, our ears become sensitive to His voice.

I remember an old hymn that we used to sing, "Take up thy cross and follow me, I heard my Master say.....Wherever He leads, I'll go.."

Following Jesus is all about doing things His way instead of ours. It doesn't necessarily mean that He will call us to a foreign country, but it possibly could mean that He would speak to us about giving someone a loving hug that is hurting, inviting someone who is lonely and without family to eat with us, teaching a class in church, etc. When we do what our Heavenly Father asks of us, our hearts receive peace.

Is God speaking to you today about a particular situation? Maybe our reply should be, "I will follow you…"

UNITY

How good and pleasant it is when God's people live together in unity!..............For there the LORD bestows his blessing, even life forevermore. Psalm 133:1,3 NIV.

I believe it grieves God when His children quarrel and fight among themselves. He has called us to unity. This means we should be able to get along with each other. Unfortunately, many Christians have quit their jobs due to strife among employees, church members have changed churches over discord among members, and many families can't get together for family gatherings due to hatred among themselves.

I have learned through my years of walking with God that not everybody will like you. This was a particular difficult lesson for me to learn as a young man in the ministry because my personality was to be a people pleaser. I felt it was necessary as a Christian for everyone to like me, and I had to do what was necessary to make it happen. Obviously, that didn't work and I stayed frustrated for much of my youth.

I have learned in my walk with God to live with "clean hands and a pure heart" in regards to getting along with others. I realize there will always be that someone in my life that doesn't like me, and that's ok. God has called me to walk in love, not bitterness or a desire to pay back ill feelings. Walking in love doesn't mean

I am called to be a door mat to be trampled upon regularly, but I am called to forgive and love.

As God's children, we must realize that there are those who don't see our heart's motives and do not like our personalities. Again, that's ok. What's important is that WE walk in love. If someone hates us, we do not have the right to hate back! We must rise above the negative feelings and move on. Life on this earth is too short to hate those who hate us. We are called to walk in the love of Jesus toward all God's children. We don't have to be best friends with everyone, but we must daily guard our hearts that we don't pay back with ill feelings. Friends, we should rise above! Let's not waste valuable time worrying about those who don't like us. Jesus said "dust your sandals" and move on. God wants to use us to touch lives, but if someone won't receive from us, then we need to move on to someone who will....We should turn it over to God and rest in peace that our hearts are pure.

We can't change hearts. Only our Heavenly Father can. He is the Potter. Today, walk in LOVE (God), keep your eyes on Jesus and don't be concerned how others feel about you. Worrying is a waste of time.......

Prayer Changes EVERYTHING!!!

And I will do WHATEVER you ask in my name, so that the Father may be glorified in the Son. You may ask me for ANYTHING in my name, and I will do it. John 14: 13–14 NIV.

Have we put limits on God? It seems we can believe for certain areas of our lives, but when it comes to other matters, we don't believe it can or will happen. Friends, God is not a God of limitations! The only limitations to receiving answered prayers, is the limitations and restrictions that WE place on our faith.

If you believe, you will receive WHATEVER you ask for in prayer. Matthew 21:23 NIV.

What is it we are lacking faith for? Is it a relationship in need of repair, better job and promotion, our country and leaders, financial, health issues, etc.? ALL things are possible with God! Yes, ALL things! I have spoken to many who worry about their family members. They spend most of their time wringing their hands in fret and worry about their lifestyle or the problems they have. Is there anyone too big for God? We know the answer. Nothing or no one is too big for our loving Heavenly Father. He can turn any situation around for the better! We must believe He can and will. How do we believe in the impossible? The simple answer is by meditating (meditating means confessing with our lips) on God's powerful Word because the more we confess the

Word, the deeper it gets into our heart. His Word and our prayers create a faith in us that is strong and unshakable.

Therefore I tell you, WHATEVER you ask for in prayer, BELIEVE that you have received it, and it will be yours. Mark 11:24 NIV.

The more time we spend with Him and His Word, we begin to know/understand His will for our lives and our prayers take on purpose and power.

Many Christians are discouraged because their prayers seem unanswered. God will NOT ignore you or your request! He hears every prayer! Don't give up!

This is the confidence we have in approaching God: that if we ask ANYTHING according to His will, He hears us. And if we know that He hears us—WHATEVER we ask—we know that we have what we asked of Him. 1 John 5:14–15 NIV.

I pray these scriptures will help you today as you fight worry and discouragement. Let's rejoice and have faith that our loving Father will answer our prayers. Remember, ALL things are possible with God! Amen!

There Is Victory With God

David said to the Philistine, 'You come against me with sword and spear and javelin, but I come against you in the name of the Lord Almighty, the God of the armies of Israel, whom you have defied. This day the Lord will deliver you into my hands, and I'll strike you down and cut off your head. This very day I will give the carcasses of the Philistine army to the birds and the wild animals, and the whole world will know that there is a God in Israel. All those gathered here will know that it is not by sword or spear that the Lord saves; for the battle is the Lord's, and he will give all of you into our hands.' As the Philistine moved closer to attack him, David ran quickly toward the battle line to meet him. 1 Samuel 17:45–48 NIV.

David makes it plain that he was relying on God to give him the victory. It wasn't based on his experience or knowledge, but his devotion and faith in almighty God. He knew in his heart that "Nothing was impossible for God."

The last part of the verse clearly states that David didn't run and hide from his enemy but ran toward him with the confidence in God that he would kill the giant.

Today, God's Word is speaking to many of us. In days past, we've tried to handle, negotiate, run from, and etc. our giants that are facing us. We have looked at our situation as impossible, when God is lovingly telling us, with Him we will win/succeed. There's no ocean too wide that He can't separate, or a giant too big that He can't slay. There's no mountain too tall that He can't remove. We do not need to fear what is facing us, but instead stand firm in love and confidence in the power of our Heavenly Father. The size of the problem is not important. We have God's strength and power inside us. Let's determine we will trust Him to give us the victory in our situation! Our faith and trust is much stronger than any situation/crisis staring at us, trying to intimidate us into not believing! We are children of the Most High God! It's time to rejoice in the love of God that our victory has already been won, whether we see it or not! In the name of Jesus, it's done/over! Victory!!

LOVE IS GIVING

My prayer is not for them alone. I pray also for those who will believe in me through their message, that all of them may be one, Father, just as you are in me and I am in you. May they also be in us so that the world may believe that you have sent me. I have given them the glory that you gave me, that they may be one as we are one—I in them and you in me—so that they may be brought to complete unity. Then the world will know that you sent me and have loved them even as you have loved me. John 17:20–23 NIV.

To be like Jesus is making the decision to get along with others. God's will for us is to be in unity, which takes a lot of give and take and a willingness to not demand our own way in matters. Our unity is a witness to the world. We are daily faced with opportunities to get along or argue and stay in strife with others whether at work, school, or in relationships. Friends, there's no one on earth that we'll agree with 100% of the time. Everyone has different opinions and thoughts to how matters should be handled, etc. Demanding our own way, expecting others to feel the same as we do is selfish and will cause division quickly.

I'm not speaking about compromising the Word of God, but compromising our emotions and demands with others. Harmony and unity among believers creates an interest in those who aren't saved. There seems to be so much strife among those who work together, as well as marriages and relationships. We should look to the interest of others with a heart of Jesus, desiring to live in unity. This means we have to let much of our frustrations and anger roll off our shoulders and choose to rise above.

Unity says, "You're more important than me having my own way 24/7."

Is it someone at work? Your marriage partner? Your close friend? Today, let's walk in love for others and learn to let go of demanding our own selfish ways. Many of you have heard the old expression, "We might as well learn to live in harmony on earth, because we'll spend eternity living with one another."

Ask God to show you how to reach out to others in love, desiring unity.......It's God's heart.....It's God's will..

GOD IS OUR SUPPLIER

Now to him who is able to do immeasurably MORE than all we ask or imagine, according to his power that is at work within us….. Ephesians 3:20 NIV.

There are many times that we just need to reread scriptures such as this one over and over to get it in our heart. In this generation of "seeing is believing," it's difficult for many to trust God's Word and truly believe that He can perform miracles in our lives. Some will pray over a certain matter but when they don't see instant results, they give up and announce, "It (prayer) doesn't work." What they are missing is the POwER that God instills within us to pray, trust, believe, and see miracles happen. Yes, God equips us with His power to see our situations turn around, reverse, remove, etc.

Do we "feel" that power? Do we see it? Friends, it doesn't matter how we "feel." We should never live our lives or be moved by our emotions. Instead, we must stand on His promises (His Word) because it NEVER lies! We must make up our minds and hearts that we will NOT give up believing for our miracles! Trusting our Father each step of our journey gives us peace that He's got our crisis under control and will resolve our problems.

Today, let's be reminded to pray without ceasing and NOT give up! Let's trust God with all our heart, stand firm on His promises, and not be moved by our emotions and feelings. Remember, we have power inside us to pray, believe, and see miracles in our lives. His Word is powerful!

Fighting with Faith

The Lord will cause your enemies who rise against you to be defeated before your face; they shall come out against you one way and flee before you seven ways. Deuteronomy 28:7 NIV.

If this verse is true (and we know it is), then why are we so afraid of the actions of others or feel the need to fight back defending ourselves as if God isn't able?

We have to remind ourselves we are children of the Most High God! Yes, His Word says we are literally His children (heirs of God and joint heirs with Jesus). A parent's nature is to protect their children when danger arises, so how much more will our loving Heavenly Father take care of us?

When we open our hearts and minds to visualize how much He loves us and will protect us if we'll lean on Him and trust Him. We must allow His Word to strengthen us so we can confess His Word and see the devil flee from us. Friends, nowhere in the bible do we read that Jesus had to struggle and fight with the devil and his demons. He spoke the word and they fled.

Therefore God exalted him to the highest place and gave him the name that is above every name, that at the name of Jesus every knee should bow, in heaven and on earth and under the earth, and every tongue acknowledge that Jesus Christ is Lord, to the glory of God the Father. Philippians 2: 9–11 NIV.

Friends, enough is enough! Let's quit getting beat up by the enemy.

Greater is He that is in me than he that is in the world! 1 John 4:4 NIV.

If God be for us, who can be against us. Romans 8:31 NIV.

The next time we are attacked (and it will happen), let's draw our sword (the Word) and fight/win our battle! Amen!

God Is Our Shepherd

Because the LORD is my Shepherd, I lack for nothing (He supplies ALL my needs). He makes me lie down in green pastures (for rest), He leads me beside quiet waters, He "refreshes" my soul. He guides me along the "right" paths for His name's sake. Psalm 23:1–3 NIV.

As we read this scripture, we notice as our Shepherd, He leads AND guides us along the "right" paths in Jesus' name. He won't mislead us. He also refreshes us (like stopping at an oasis in the desert) as we follow His will so we won't be exhausted and weary!

"Every day with Jesus is sweeter than the day before."

God is our God for ever and ever; He will be our guide to the end. Psalm 48:14 NIV.

He will lead us down our path of life, showing us the way. Sometimes we don't understand His plan, especially when it's different from ours. And during the wait for His perfect timing, He is growing and maturing us to be like Jesus. Time with God is NEVER wasted. Every day He desires to teach us His will through His Word. When I don't understand what He's doing, or His timing, it causes me to seek Him with all my heart because I know in my heart, He doesn't desire to keep us in the dark. If I have questions about what He's doing, I ask. He does NOT get offended with our asking. He truly loves us!

Your Word, O Lord, is a lamp to my feet and a light for my path. Psalm 119:105 NIV.

God's will doesn't keep us in the dark in regards to answers. He is the light of the world. If we will trust Him and seek Him, He will show us the way and reveal to us His plan.

Jesus said, "I am the light of the world. Whoever follows me will NEVER walk in darkness, but will have the light of life" John 8:12 NIV.

Friends, don't allow confusion or worry to enter your minds. Trust God and walk in peace. His plans and timing are the best.

I will praise the Lord, who counsels me; even at night my heart instructs me. Psalm 16:7 NIV.

Whatever you are praying and seeking God about, rejoice and thank Him because He will be your guide. Yes, He will lead you down the road of blessings and He WILL reveal His plan at the right timing.

Remember, God answers prayer and prayer changes everything!

Forgiving Others

If you forgive men when they sin against you, your Heavenly Father will also forgive you. Matthew 6:14 NIV.

All of us at times get our feelings hurt by someone. They could be an acquaintance or someone very close to us. Maybe it's something they did or said, but it happens and we either get angry or wounded. Forgiving others (whether they apologize for not) isn't a onetime step we take, but it's an ongoing lifestyle as a Christian. We might spend our day in worship, but get our feelings hurt tomorrow. Maybe someone spread lies about us or lambasted us for something we are innocent about. Yes, it happens to all of us. Sometimes, it only takes a single word from someone to hurt us. Many families suffer with discourse because someone in the family feels they have the "right" to say what they want. Many people will hurt us without even knowing what they did. That also works vice versa. We might offend and hurt others and we are clueless to what we have done.

Friends, we MUST forgive those that wound or offend us. Retaliation isn't from God! Arguments and getting defensive usually make it worse. If we have a problem with someone, we should go to that person with a heart to reconcile, not argue or defend ourselves. Purposely ignoring others is wrong. We are called to love one another (in spite of...). When we are walking in the love of Christ, we can take that step to speak or reach out to someone who won't speak.

Blessed are the merciful (forgiving), for they will be shown mercy. Matthew 5:7 NIV.

Thank God for forgiving us with mercy and grace. Shouldn't we follow Jesus by showing mercy and grace to those who hurt us?

When we are hurt, lied about, ignored, wounded, or angry, we must first surrender our feelings to Jesus at the foot of the cross. We should then ask God to help us forgive those that hurt us and ask Him to bless them. By doing so, we begin to receive healing in our heart.

Today, listen to the voice of the Holy Spirit as he speaks to our hearts. When He reveals a name to us, choose to forgive and bless them. Jesus set the example for us to walk in love and forgiveness. As we spend time with our Father, forgiving others becomes much easier.

The Lord is compassionate and gracious; slow to anger, abounding in love. He will not always accuse, nor will He harbor His anger forever; He does not treat us as our sins deserve or repay us according to our iniquities. Psalm 103:8–10 NIV.

In Times Of Trouble, God Is With Us

In ALL things (everything) God works for the good of those who love Him, who have been called according to His purpose (that's us). Romans 8:28 NIV.

Sometimes it's difficult to understand this verse, especially when we're going through a storm. We wonder, "How can good come forth from this situation I have or am going through?" Many have asked me how I can see any good in losing my son. Friends, yes, it took my breath away when Steffan went to heaven. I didn't think I could live a single day without him, and at first, didn't want to live without him. But what I have witnessed in the past 3 years that is "good" is how my loving Father has given me compassion for those that are hurting, broken, and at a loss. I made a decision/chose to not live in bitterness and anger that would only suffocate my life, but to live for Teri, Lydia, and those hurting around me. I didn't want to lose the memory of my son or feel it was a total loss. I deeply wanted to feel that through all the traumatic pain and suffering, that maybe, just maybe something good could and would come from losing him.

Do you relate with what you have gone through in your life? By helping others, our lives can take on a new meaning and purpose. Choosing to help others when we have gone through a rough situation, helps in our healing.

When you have gone through a painful divorce, or maybe a death of someone in your life, fighting to survive a disease, or financial ruin, we must know that God truly loves us and is right beside us each small step we take.

Today, be encouraged and know that in the midst of your storm, Jesus is walking on water toward you, because He cares..........

Trusting God Strengthens And Changes Us

"Tis' so sweet to trust in Jesus, just to take Him at His Word. Just to rest upon His promise (His Word), just to know thus saith the Lord (His Word is final). Jesus, Jesus how I trust You, how I've proved You over and over. Jesus, Jesus, precious Jesus, oh for grace to trust You more...." Paraphrased...

None of us are perfect and obviously we don't always have the big faith to believe in the miracles we so want. That's why we are covered in God's grace. We are favored by Him and don't have to "earn" His love by doing. Rather it's recognizing who we are, children of God.

Trusting God means to rely upon Him to lead and guide us each step. Taking our hands off the situation and allowing Him full reign, gives us peace and quicker answers to our prayers. I have written on this subject quite often because we tend to be a self-reliant generation, wanting to do things ourselves, making our own decisions and handling our own crisis, instead of giving it to God. Friends, we must trust Him that He knows best (because He does). We don't always know why situations turn out the way they do, but if we will stay close to our Father, He will reveal answers and give us an understanding of the "whys."

"Change my heart, oh God, make it ever new. Change my heart, oh God, may I be like You. You are the Potter, I am the clay, mold me and make me, this is what I pray……."

Trust in the Lord with all your heart and lean not on your own understanding; in all your ways acknowledge Him, and he will make your paths straight. Proverbs 3:5–6 NIV.

"Your Attitude Should Be The Same As That of Christ Jesus" Philippians 2:5.

How many of us have heard the old cliché, "I am who I am and that's just the way it is, and people can get over it?" Being a teacher, I've heard this statement often from students who make excuses for what they say or do. As a Christian, we should be conscience of what we say and do. When we allow ourselves to be molded by God into the image of Jesus, we take on the same characteristics and nature of Jesus. We learn to refrain from being negative and a gossiper. We begin to look for the best in others instead of tearing them down.

God also "encourages us in Ephesians 5:1 to be "imitators of Christ as dearly beloved children." As children love to imitate what they see and repeat what they hear, we also are charged to imitate and model Christ's behavior and to be clear reflections of the Lord (Matthew 5:16).

To be Christ–like is freedom. To desire to be like Jesus is to feel as if the heavy weights of the world have been removed from our shoulders. Freedom!

How we choose to treat others is a witness to the world, good or bad. Yes, each of us represent a fruit bearing tree. We either bear good fruit like love, joy, peace, kindness, gentleness, etc., or our tree bears bad fruit which is the opposite of good fruit. Friends, we are known by our fruit. Do we really have to "tell and convince" people that we are Christians or can they see it in our lives in the way we treat others and handle life's problems. Facing problems and storms doesn't make us strong. But rather, how we handle the problems and storms and the attitude we display can make us strong and a witness to the world for God.

Do nothing out of selfish ambition or vain conceit. Rather, in humility value others above yourselves, not looking to your own interests but each of you to the interests of the others. Philippians 2: 3–4 NIV.

How does this work? No, we can't make it happen. But as we spend time daily with our Heavenly Father, our attitudes will change for the better. The time in worship and prayer we spend with God will cover us with love for Him which will flow from us to others. You can't give to others what you don't have. Just as a car can run out of gas and need to be refueled, we need to refresh ourselves with God daily.

The steadfast love of the Lord never ceases, his mercies never come to an end; they are new EVERY MORNING; great is your faithfulness. Lamentations 2:2–3 NIV.

Let's not run on yesterday's fuel, but instead spend time with God each day and allow Jesus to shine through us to others!

LET'S DESIRE MORE OF GOD

As the deer pants for streams of water, so my soul pants for you, my God. Psalm 42:1 NIV.

I'm always spiritually attracted to someone who is "desperate" for more of God. You can see the longing for more of the Father in their face, especially in their eyes.

Friends, this longing for more of God is the "best" evangelism tool to use in witnessing to the lost. People in today's generation are looking for hope and answers. But they want "real" not mere words thrown in their face. Bottom line: We can scream, holler, and push salvation in people's face all day long without very much result, but if we choose to fall in love with our Savior, allowing His love to flow through us to others, we will see many, many more souls come to Jesus. In other words, "talk is cheap." Living a life of God's love is a magnet to the lost.

If someone wants to share with me how to be successful in a certain area, the first thing I do is look at their life. Are they successful or are they just speaking words? I desire "real." This is the same for those who aren't saved. They want to see hope for their lives. They will look at the way we live, treat others, and handle life's challenges. If they see Jesus (Hope) in us as we live our lives, they will hunger for what we have. People are always seeking true answers to life.

If we share Jesus with the lost and invite them to church, but when they come they witness arguing, gossiping, complaining or members demanding their own selfish ways, why would they want to stay? Their response would probably be, "I see enough of this behavior every day without going to church."

We're not perfect. "We have all sinned and come short of the glory of God." Romans 3:23. But if the lost see us walking with Jesus with a hunger for more of Him, even when we stumble, they will want and desire what we have. In this crazy world, Jesus is peace and the lost souls in this world are desperately longing for that peace. The answer is Jesus!

Today. let's live a life of love (God) and allow that love to spread to others. "Let others see Jesus in you..." Great, successful evangelism......the way we live..

WHAT'S GOD LIKE?

Many ask what God's personality is like. They tend to view our Heavenly Father as a gruff king sitting on His throne, angry most of the time and ready to punish us for our sins. Friends, nothing could be further from the truth. God's Word reveals who God is and what His personality is like.

Remember, 1 John 4 tells us "God is Love."

Love (God) is patient, love (God) is kind. It (He) does not envy, it (He) does not boast, it (He) is not proud. It (He) does not dishonor others, it (He) is not self-seeking, it (He) is not easily angered, it (He) keeps no record of wrongs (grace). Love (God) does not delight in evil but rejoices with the truth. It (He) always protects, always trusts, always hopes, always perseveres. Love (God) never fails. 1 Corinthians 13:4–8 NIV.

These scriptures describe God's personality. So when the devil whispers in our ear that God is angry with us because we aren't "good enough," we should turn away from his lies and believe in our hearts that God is love and full of grace and mercy. We are His children!

When we choose to love others, we are actually giving them God because He is love. What a beautiful, evangelical gift (Love) to give the lost. If we don't love those around us, our words become useless.

Dear friends, let us love one another, for love comes from God. Everyone who loves has been born of God and knows God. Whoever does not love does not know God, because God is love. 1 John 4:7–8 NIV.

If you are seeking God's will for your life, begin with loving others. We can't pick and choose who we desire to love.

God so loved the world that He gave…. John 3:16 NIV.

This scripture in John 3:16 tells us who we should give love to…. The world (everyone).

SHOW US THE WAY, O LORD.

O Lord, you have made known to me the path of life. Psalm 16:11 NIV.

Choosing to follow God's will instead of our own is wisdom and peace. Because of His great love for us, God ALWAYS does what's best in our lives. There have been times when He has closed doors that we wanted open, only for us to be thankful down the road that He did close the door which saved us from much heartache. Yes, He sees what we cannot see regarding what lies ahead for us.

Heavenly Father, we thank You for leading and guiding us to victory. We worship and thank You for closing doors that needed to be closed and opening doors that need to be open, in Jesus' name, amen.

Your Word, O Lord, is a lamp unto my feet and a light for my path. Psalm 119:105 NIV.

When we're walking with God, He will keep us from stumbling and making wrong decisions. Like a bright beaming lighthouse overlooking the ocean, His light (Jesus) will show us the way. His Word is powerful and truth. If we will trust Him completely, we will not be deceived by the devil.

"Open the eyes of my heart, Lord."

When you don't know what to do regarding a decision you're facing, look to Jesus for your answer.

He Will show you the way!

How Do I Obey God? What Should I Do?

Jesus replied: 'Love the Lord your God with all your heart and with all your soul and with all your mind.' This is the first and greatest commandment. And the second is like it: 'Love your neighbor as yourself.' All the Law and the Prophets hang on these two commandments. Matthew 22: 37–40 NIV.

Many seek God for His will and purpose for their lives. They desire to obey but aren't sure what to do. Our loving Father makes it easy for us as he tells us to love Him with all our heart. As we spend time with Him through prayer and the Word, we begin to develop a deep love for Him. The more time we spend with Him, the more love we will have in our heart. Friends, it's difficult to love someone you don't know and it's almost impossible to give what we don't have. God will daily fill us with His love if we'll spend time with Him and receive all He has for us. The love He gives us is what we give to others. We are called to love unconditionally. Yes, even the unlovable are to be loved, but we must first love Jesus in order to give love to the world.

Do we have to love those that irritate us? What about the ones who hate us?

Jesus said, "If anyone loves me, he will obey my teaching. My Father will love him, and we will come to him and make our home with him" John 14:23 NIV.

Loving others is God's will for our lives. Sometimes, we'd rather just get a list of do's and don'ts to follow instead of loving those that don't reciprocate. But God's will for obedience is to live a life of love (God).

We might not be someone's "BFF", but we can still love them with the love of Jesus. Following the example of Jesus in everything we do, is God's will. Jesus loved.

Remember, the Pharisees put rules and regulations on the people of Israel, but Jesus came to set them free from "religious" thinking that included rules and regulations.

Jesus said, "..........I have come that they may have life, and have it to the full" John 10:10 NIV.

Friends, if we will try to learn to love others the way Jesus loved, we will rest at night knowing we are obeying His will. No, we're not perfect. We will "blow it" at times. But as we focus on Jesus and meditate on God's Word, we will find it much easier to love and forgive others.....

ARE YOU READY FOR SOME JOY?

Jesus said, "Ask and you will receive, and your joy will be complete" John 16:24.

The joy of the Lord is your strength. Nehemiah 8:10 NIV.

When we praise and worship God with a thankful heart, joy flows from our heart to others. Joy also strengthens us to fight the devil's attacks. With joy, we are overcomers. Living in joy isn't just about putting a smile on our face, but truly living a life of love (God). As we spend more time with our Heavenly Father, the joy will increase and strengthen us. Joy comes from love.

In the midst of our darkest trials and storms, we can be reassured that storms are only temporary and trusting God gives us peace. We may not know what the future holds for us but trusting our lives in His hands calms our fears and worries and gives us peace.

You turned my wailing into dancing, O Lord; you removed my sackcloth and clothed me with joy, that my heart may sing to you and not be silent. O Lord my God, I will give you thanks forever. Psalm 30: 11–12 NIV.

Friends, let's give thanks to God for His goodness. No matter what you are going through, reach out to Jesus who will calm your storm with peace. Thank Him for His joy that strengthens you to succeed through the darkest nights/storms. We have victory! We have Joy!

What Are You Trusting God For?

Those who know your name will trust in You, for You, Lord, have NEVER forsaken those who seek You. Psalm 9:10 NIV.

Our prayer life should be a combination of many aspects. We are called to worship our Heavenly Father with a heart of thanksgiving. Worship is expressing our love for God with a grateful and humble heart for the many blessings He has given us. Worship is surrendering our will to God and desiring His will for our lives.

We should ask.

Jesus said, "I will do whatever you ASK in my name, so that the Son may bring glory to the Father. You may ASK for "anything" in my name and I WILL do it" John 14: 13–14 NIV.

Why do we feel ashamed for asking or criticize others who ask? God is our Abba Father (Daddy). He desires for us to approach his throne and present our request.

We must believe.

This is the confidence we have in approaching God: that if we ask anything according to His will, He hears us. And if we know that He hears us–whatever we ask–we know that we have what we asked of Him. 1 John 5: 14–15 NIV.

Confidence in God answering our prayers is faith. When we ask, we must believe in faith that He will answer according to His will. Our faith is strengthened by reading and meditating on His Word. Whether we are praying and believing for a family member to get saved or even asking God for a vehicle to drive or a new job, He answers prayers. Some feel we should only ask God for spiritual things. His Word says, He will supply ALL our needs according to His riches in glory. Philippians 4:19 NIV.

He is Jehovah Jireh, our supplier.

Friends, let's choose to love Him with our whole heart and not be afraid or ashamed to present our request to Him. He cares about every aspect of our lives. God answers prayer!

You Are Not Forgotten!

Praise the LORD, my soul; all my inmost being, praise His holy name. Praise the LORD, my soul, and forget not all His benefits— who forgives ALL your sins and heals ALL your diseases, who redeems your life from the pit and crowns you with love and compassion, who satisfies your desires with good things so that your youth is renewed like the eagle's. Psalm 103:1–5 NIV.

This is a beautiful promise to us from God's Word. It's a reminder that He hasn't or never will forget us and the needs in our lives. Many times we feel as if we've been overlooked by God, but He ALWAYS has us on His mind. His heart is to bless us with the desires of our heart. Need a place to live? Looking for a better job? Has your car died? Is your relationship over? Are you deep into debt?

Our Father cares and WILL supply ALL our needs! Why? Because He loves us!

O Lord my God, I called to You for help and You healed me (answered my prayers). Psalm 30:2 NIV.

We must understand that this scripture is a promise that God won't break! He has NEVER broken a promise and He surely won't start breaking them with us! God is truth and His truth (Jesus) will set us free (from the yuk/crud in our lives).

Do we have to "do" or earn something in order to get blessed? No! We just need to believe His promises and that He loves and understands what we're going through. Friends, we aren't forgotten! Our Father is so full of compassion for His children. We can understand His heart when we read and meditate on the gospels of Jesus' life. He lived His earthly life full of love, forgiveness, and compassion.

When our Savior was crucified on the cross, He was crucified with all our sins, sicknesses, job losses, divorces, debt, broken relationships, etc. He died for it all so that we may have "life, and life more abundantly."

"Jesus paid it ALL, all to Him I owe (my heart)."

Christ himself bore our sins in His body on the tree, so that we might die to sins and live for righteousness; by His wounds you have been healed (prayers answered). 1 Peter 2:24 NIV. Amen!!

It is done.......finished.......completed. I encourage you to worship and thank your Heavenly Father for answering your prayers. He loves YOU!

WORSHIP BRINGS CHANGES!

Jehoshaphat bowed down with his face to the ground, and all the people of Judah and Jerusalem fell down in worship before the LORD. Then some Levites from the Kohathites and Korahites stood up and praised the LORD, the God of Israel, with a very loud voice.

Early in the morning they left for the Desert of Tekoa. As they set out, Jehoshaphat stood and said, "Listen to me, Judah and people of Jerusalem! Have faith in the LORD your God and you will be upheld; have faith in his prophets and you will be successful." After consulting the people, Jehoshaphat appointed men to sing to the LORD and to praise him for the splendor of his holiness as they went out at the head of the army, saying:

"Give thanks to the LORD, for his love endures forever."

As they began to sing and praise, the LORD set ambushes against the men of Ammon and Moab and Mount Seir who were invading Judah, and THEY WERE DEFEATED. 2 Chronicles 20:18–22 NIV.

Worship is expressing love to our Heavenly Father. When we pour our love to Him with a heart of thanksgiving, His heart is touched and moved. Worship opens the door for miracles! Worship slays the giants in our lives and removes mountains/obstacles trying to prevent us from being blessed. Worship is telling God how much you love Him, no matter what you are going through at the moment. Worship is trust. Worship is giving (tithing). Worship is surrendering our lives to Him. No, we don't worship to "get" from God, but we know from reading God's Word that we will be blessed when we worship.

I will sing of the LORD's great love forever; with my mouth I will make Your faithfulness known through all generations. I will declare that Your love stands firm forever, that You have established Your faithfulness in heaven itself. Psalm 89:1–2 NIV.

Begin worship by thanking God for Jesus who paid the price that we might be saved and righteous. Thank Him for the many blessings you have received. Thank Him for what He will do for you (faith).

"Give thanks with a grateful hearts.."

GOD IS A GIVER...

He who did not spare his own Son, but gave him up for us all—
how will he not also, along with him, graciously give us all things?
Romans 8:32 NIV.

This scripture reveals that God is a "giver." Yes, He loves us so
much that he GAVE up His son Jesus to be crucified so we might
have eternal life and become righteous. That's love, my friend.

Many feel guilty for asking God to provide for their needs.
Whether it's asking God to save a lost friend/relative, providing
money to pay your car payment, healing in your body, restoring
a relationship, receiving a job promotion, etc. we must believe
His Word that He desires to take care of us. He is our Heavenly
"Father" (Abba Father/Daddy) and we are His children. He loves
to answer our prayers and bless us. God is a giver.

Jesus said, "Ask and you will receive, and your joy will be
complete" John 16:24 NIV.

Yes, there is "JOY" when God answers our prayers, and that
joy of the Lord is our strength.

If our children came to us hurting, wouldn't we take care of
their needs? Why of course we would, because they belong to us
and we love them. How much MORE does God desire to take
care of us?

The Lord will indeed give what is good. Psalm 85:12 NIV.

As we meditate on God's Word, we can believe His promises. If we are praying for a lost relative or friend, we must pray in confidence that our Father hears our prayers and WILL answer. This confidence is our faith in action!

Friends, when we pray for our country, God hears our prayers. When we pray for our church, God hears our prayers. When we pray to receive a physical healing, God hears our prayers. Yes, He hears EVERY prayer and will answer. We must believe that His promises in His Word are true.

Which of you, if your son asks for bread, will give him a stone? Or if he asks for a fish, will give him a snake? If you, then, though you are evil, know how to give good gifts to your children, how much more will your Father in heaven give good gifts to those who ask Him. Matthew 7:9–11 NIV.

God answers prayer.......God is a giver......

Let's believe His Word! Remember, prayer changes everything!

Are Others Blessed By The Words We Speak?

No good tree bears bad fruit, nor does a bad tree bear good fruit. Each tree is recognized by its own fruit. People do not pick figs from thorn bushes, or grapes from briers. A good man brings good things out of the good stored up in his heart, and an evil man brings evil things out of the evil stored up in his heart. For the mouth speaks what the heart is full of. Luke 6:43–45 NIV.

Our daily time with God is so important in developing good fruit in our lives, molding us to be more like Jesus. When we are walking in God's love, we bear good fruit (love, joy, peace, patience, etc). This is a beautiful evangelism tool for the lost. When they view our lives and see the positive, they will be drawn to ask questions and desire what we have (Jesus).

When we bear good fruit, our heart is changed to be like Jesus. Therefore, what comes from our mouth are uplifting, encouraging, and Christ–like words.

Friends, it's difficult to persuade the lost that we are Christians and walking with Jesus when we argue with everyone around us, speaking critical words of others. This paints a negative image of ourselves.

It's important to begin our day with Jesus in worship and thanksgiving. A thankful heart is a humble, loving heart. We should desire to be more like Jesus in what we say and do. This can only come from spending time with Him. Walking in love (God) truly affects those around us.

"Change my heart, O God."

Let's remember we are a lighthouse that needs to shine brightly to offer hope to the lost in this world. That light is Jesus in our lives. Yes, Jesus can change our negative fruit to positive fruit for the world to see and affect what we say and do.

Desire change....Desire good fruit......Desire Jesus.

WE ARE NOT THE JUDGE...

The teachers of the law and the Pharisees brought in a woman caught in adultery. They made her stand before the group ⁴ and said to Jesus, "Teacher, this woman was caught in the act of adultery. In the Law Moses commanded us to stone such women. Now what do you say?" They were using this question as a trap, in order to have a basis for accusing him.

But Jesus bent down and started to write on the ground with his finger. When they kept on questioning him, he straightened up and said to them, "Let any one of you who is without sin be the first to throw a stone at her." Again he stooped down and wrote on the ground.

At this, those who heard began to go away one at a time, the older ones first, until only Jesus was left, with the woman still standing there. Jesus straightened up and asked her, "Woman, where are they? Has no one condemned you?" "No one, sir," she said.

"Then neither do I condemn you," Jesus declared. "Go now and leave your life of sin. John 8:3–11 NIV.

Jesus did NOT condemn the woman in adultery but reached out to her in mercy and grace. Sadly we as Christians seem to feel it's our duty to point fingers at those who sin. But aren't we ALL sinners?

For ALL (that's us) have sinned and fallen short of the glory of God. Romans 3:23 NIV.

Yes, none of us are perfect. When we "judge" someone in sin, we are just as guilty. God's churches should be a loving refuge and a spiritual hospital to everyone regardless of their sin. Restoration, love, and "patience" should be the mission of all God's children.

When Jesus told Zacchaeus that He was going to his house to eat and fellowship, He already knew of Zacchaeus' sins. If He had pointed His fingers at him in disgust or distanced himself from him, there would have been zero change. But Jesus reached out in love and Zacchaeus' life was changed.

Jesus' life is a beautiful example of love and forgiveness for everyone… "Mercy and Grace."

When Jesus said that He was the light of the world, He wasn't referring to His light exposing our sins, but instead offering hope and showing us the way.

Let's choose to walk in love (God) toward everyone around us. Our Heavenly Father loves us ALL the same, regardless of our sins and past. Today, it doesn't matter about personalities or who did what. Let's just love…..and allow God to do His work.

Do You Feel Persecuted?

But I say to you, love your enemies, bless those who curse you, do good to those who hate you, and pray for those who spitefully use you and persecute you.. Matthew 5:44 NIV.

Most of us have wished at various times in our past when we were verbally attacked by someone that this verse would disappear and we could have the freedom to say what we wanted in order to defend ourselves. Well, we might not have argued back, but we're all guilty of thinking it. Our soulish nature, which is our mind and emotions, desires to fight back when we're attacked. But Jesus tells us to LOVE our enemies and bless those that curse and verbally attack us. We should seek God on ways to do good to those that hate us and most importantly, we should pray for them. Most of the time when someone attacks us verbally, there is emotions stirring inside of them and they end up taking it out on those around them. We should ask God to reveal their heart, which is usually deeply wounded. Hurting people and bullies tend to build emotional barricades around themselves to hide what's hurting on the inside of their heart. When we understand this, we can have more patience and empathy.

Rejoice ALWAYS (even though it's difficult), pray continually, give thanks in ALL circumstances; for this is God's will for you in Christ Jesus. 1 Thessalonians 5: 16–18 NIV.

Friends, the ONLY way we can love our enemies and have victory is to give them what we have. If we're praying and seeking God with a thankful heart and walking in love (God), we will be able to rise above any attacks from the devil, who enjoys causing dissension among Christians. We are called to walk in love, no matter the cost. When we ask God to bless our enemies, we are spiritually letting go of the problem and releasing it to God, allowing Him to handle the problem. He will handle it, I promise!

Walking with God in His love is freedom. The next time we are attacked, let's count it all joy and gain victory! We are becoming more like Jesus each day!

GIVING GOD THANKS WILL CHANGE YOUR SITUATION!

You turned my wailing into dancing; you removed my sackcloth and clothed me with joy, that my heart may sing your praises and not be silent. O LORD my God, I will praise you forever. Psalm 30:11–12 NIV.

This scripture reveals that God will turn around our situation that we're going through. No matter how difficult it may be God can and will turn it around. We might feel as if we are at the bottom of a pit, with no way out. But God promises to remove our sadness and fill us with His joy (our strength). This strength from our Heavenly Father will sustain us in the worst of storms facing us.

What do we have to do to get relief? Just believe in the power of His Word and praise Him with a thankful heart. Worship WILL turn around any dark situation trying to cause despair in our lives. God is faithful and full of love, comfort, and joy.

Giving God thanks touches His heart and it should be a priority in our lives. We should praise Him in the good and bad times. When Jesus met with the disciples in the upper room for communion, the first priority was to give His Father "thanks" before He broke the bread.

The Lord Jesus, on the night He was betrayed, took bread, and when He had given thanks (first), He broke it and said, This is my body, which is for you; do this in remembrance of me. 1 Corinthians 11:23–24 NIV.

Yes, even with the horrific storm of death and the cross facing Him, Jesus gave thanks to His Father. This is a beautiful example for us to follow. It's easy much easier to thank God in the good times but when our world is caving in on us, it is a challenge, but necessary for our break through.

When we're facing difficult times we have a choice to make:

1. We can worship and praise our Heavenly Father with a thankful heart, knowing He will turn our storm around. (Give thanks with a grateful heart)

2. We can throw ourselves a pit party and possibly stay in the pit of despair.

But thanks be to God! He gives us the victory through our Lord Jesus Christ. 1Corinthians 15:57 NIV.

Let's choose a heart of thanks. His promises are true....

ARE YOU NEEDING A MIRACLE?

A large crowd followed and pressed around him. And a woman was there who had been subject to bleeding for twelve years. She had suffered a great deal under the care of many doctors and had spent all she had, yet instead of getting better she grew worse. When she heard about Jesus, she came up behind him in the crowd and touched his cloak, because she thought, "If I just touch his clothes, I will be healed." Immediately her bleeding stopped and she felt in her body that she was freed from her suffering. At once Jesus realized that power had gone out from him. He turned around in the crowd and asked, "Who touched my clothes?" "You see the people crowding against you," his disciples answered, "and yet you can ask, 'Who touched me?'" But Jesus kept looking around to see who had done it. Then the woman, knowing what had happened to her, came and fell at his feet and, trembling with fear, told him the whole truth. He said to her, Daughter, your faith has healed you. Go in "peace" (Shalom) and be freed from your suffering. Mark 5:24–34 NIV.

Without a doubt, God placed this event in scriptures to encourage us to believe in His power to bring forth miracles. Our faith can truly make us whole! What do you need today from your Abba Father (Daddy)? Is it physical, financial, relationship, spiritual? Friends, He desires to answer our prayers based on who we are not on what we have done or can do. We are the righteousness of God in Christ Jesus! Jesus paid the price so we could be healed of whatever we have been attacked with and have great peace (Shalom)!

Peace (Shalom) I leave with you; my peace (Shalom) I GIVE you. I do not give to you as the world gives. Do not let your hearts be troubled and do not be afraid. John 14:27 NIV.

"*Shalom* means "completeness", wholeness, health, peace, welfare, safety soundness, tranquility, prosperity, perfectness, fullness, rest, harmony, the absence of agitation or discord. Shalom comes from the root verb *shalom* meaning to be complete, perfect and full. In modern Hebrew the obviously related word *Shelem* means to pay for, and *Shulam* means to be fully paid" Strong's Dictionary.

Today, reach out in faith and touch the hem of His garment for your miracle! His Word confirms His promises to bless us with peace (Shalom) which means completeness (everything).

GOD, YOUR FATHER IS NEAR...

If.....you seek the Lord your God, you will find Him if you look for Him with ALL your heart and with ALL your soul (mind/ emotions). Deuteronomy 4:29 NIV.

You will seek me and find me when you ask me with ALL your heart. I will be found by you, declares the Lord. Jeremiah 29: 13–14 NIV.

God desires a relationship with us. He is NOT unreachable. His ears are attentive to our prayers and He deeply cares about each part of our lives. He still speaks to His children, leading and guiding to truth.

If you desire to know what God is like, read, study, and meditate on God's Word (Bible) about the life of Jesus. Yes, He talked to His disciples, had a relationship with those around Him, had compassion on the hurting, healed the sick, restored those who had fallen away, and most importantly, He loved...

As we seek Him, we must know that there is nothing insignificant about our lives to Him. Yes, we matter to Him! What's important to us, is important to Him. He is full of understanding, compassion, and love.

The Lord is near to ALL who call on Him, to ALL who call on Him in truth (Jesus). Psalm 145:18 NIV.

Sometimes the devil will make us feel as if we're praying/talking to a brick wall, and that God is too busy or not interested in what we have to say. Lies!

Friends, He (God) ALWAYS hears our prayers and ALWAYS has plenty of time for us. He loves having a relationship with us.

Today as you pray, please know in your heart that your Heavenly Father cares about YOU! He WILL answer your prayers. As you pray in faith, never give up!

When Elijah prayed and believed for rain, he sent his servant in faith 7 times to look for the clouds. He never gave up. Guess what? It rained!

God cares about meeting your needs! Pray, seek Him, believe, and don't give up if your answer doesn't come immediately. Your "rain" is coming.....

Has It Been One Of Those Days?

With God we will gain the victory, and he will trample down our enemies. Psalm 60: 12 NIV.

Do you feel your world has caved in? Everything going wrong and you feel like many are against you? It could be so–called friends, a member of your family, co–workers, employers, etc.

God has called us to love our enemies and pray for them. Usually, the strongest bullies that try to attack us are the ones with the deepest wounds in their heart. Their personal hurts cause them to lash out at us. It's not easy to turn the other cheek (which means forgive), but as God's children, we are called to love and forgive. Our Father WILL protect us and will fight our battles for us, if we will allow Him to. Losing our temper and retaliating against those that attack us places us on the same sad level as those attacking. We are called to rise above to be like Jesus. How do we turn the other cheek and forgive? We do so by learning God's ways, reading His Word and seeking His face. No, it's not always easy, but it's His will for us and rewarding.

Beloved, let us love one another for Love is of God…. 1 John 4:7 NIV.

Many people who choose not to forgive allow bitterness to enter their hearts, which can grow like weeds. Eventually, unforgiveness, anger, and bitterness can destroy our faith and trust in God, and even take a physical toll on our bodies.

If you forgive men when they sin against you, your Heavenly Father will also forgive you. Matthew 6:14 NIV.

Friends, life is too short to live a miserable life of bitterness and unforgiveness. The JOY of the Lord is our strength, which gives us peace and a good night's rest. No matter how fierce the attacks are against us or how bad our day seems to be going, we are called to walk in love with our hearts and trust in God. He WILL vindicate us! His Word promises He will take of us and restore our joy!

The next time we are attacked and our day seems to be a mess, let's choose to focus our eyes and hearts on Jesus and allow Him to handle our situation! Remember, the devil loves to use people to say mean, hurtful words to discourage us. Recognizing this inspires us to lean on Jesus in a greater way! Victory is ours through Jesus!

This day belongs to God!

"The Prayer Of A Righteous Man (That's Us) Is Powerful AND Effective" James 5:16.

Our prayers ARE being heard and Will be answered! We don't have to "earn" or "do" to get prayers answered! We are God's (Abba Father) children and we always have His attention and heart. Nothing is too big to present God! Sometimes we look at someone's life and think, "They are too wild or hard for God to change." Friends, God can change anyone or any situation/circumstance! We should NEVER give up believing in the power of prayer! When discouragement tries to attack us, we should fight back by confessing God's promises. His Word is powerful and effective!

You are the God who performs miracles; You display Your power among the peoples. With Your mighty arm You redeemed Your people. Psalm 77: 14–15 NIV.

I will decree a thing, and it WILL be established in my life. Job 22:28 NIV.

Friends, I have personally clung to this verse in Job many times when my life seemed hopeless and I felt there was no way out of a situation. I always knew His Word was powerful, so I would confess this scripture over and over to build my faith in

His promises. God has ALWAYS answered my prayers! He will answer your prayers also! Nothing is too big for Him! Even when you feel you are in the bottom of the pit, He will rescue you!

Remember, John 10:10 says that Jesus has come to give us life MORE abundantly, which includes JOY!

Because the blood of the Lamb (Jesus) was sprinkled on the mercy seat as an offering/sacrifice, we can approach God's throne in boldness knowing that He loves us and truly desires to answer our prayers.

No more nervous hoping and wishing.......Only believing in God's promises (His Word).

DON'T BE AFRAID TO ASK GOD!

Which of you, if your son asks for bread, will give him a stone? Or if he asks for a fish, will give him a snake? If you, then, though you are evil, know how to give good gifts to your children, how much MORE will your Father in heaven give good gifts to those who ask Him! Matthew 7:9–11 NIV.

For some reason, it seems easier to believe in our heart for someone's salvation than to believe God for a material item. Our mindset is God only deals with the spiritual, not the physical. How untrue! Didn't our Heavenly Father feed the children of Israel when they left Egypt? Didn't Jesus feed the five thousand? Nowhere in scripture does it mention that Jesus wore rags for clothing or that He had to beg for food or money to pay His taxes.

What He DID do was put everything in prospective; God first. He obeyed the first commandment, "Love the Lord your God with ALL your heart." Everything else came afterwards. Jesus never lacked for anything because He knew His Heavenly Father would supply everything He needed. He never worried or fretted over needing anything. He never doubted God's ability to provide.

When Jesus turned the water into wine at the wedding He attended, it wasn't really a need. The wedding party would have survived without it, but He did it to bless the wedding couple and family. Yes, He cared about their "desires." Friends, He cares about our desires and truly wants to bless us.

He who did not spare his own Son, but gave Him up for us all—how will He not also, along with Him, graciously give us ALL things? Romans 8:32 NIV.

"All" means EVERYTHING. This isn't just spiritual gifts, but everything! God is Jehovah Jireh, our provider.

Jesus said, "Ask and you WILL receive, and your joy will be made complete" John 16:24 NIV.

Whatever you need today, ask God, who desires to meet your every need and want.

God...richly provides us with EVERYTHING for our enjoyment. 1 Timothy 6:17 NIV.

Thank you Heavenly Father for caring about EVERY part of our lives....Amen.

WE ARE CALLED TO PRAYER

Do you not know that your bodies are temples of the Holy Spirit, who is in you, whom you have received from God? You are not your own.. 1 Corinthians 6:19 NIV.

When we read this verse, we understand that the temple was a place of sacrifice and worship to God; and now our bodies are that temple of worship. We are called to worship God with our whole heart. We should live each day with a thankful heart for all He has done and is doing for us. "Worship moves the hand of God with favor."

My house will be called a house of prayer for all nations. Mark 11:17 NIV.

Yes, He is talking about the church, but also referring to us individually as the "temple of the Holy Spirit." We are called to be prayer warriors, knowing that "prayer changes everything."

The prayer of a righteous man is powerful and effective. James 5:16 NIV.

Friends, let's be encouraged to pray and never give up believing for answers. Our Father loves us and hears EVERY prayer we pray!

The eyes of the Lord are on the righteous (that's us) and His ears are attentive to their prayer. 1 Peter 3:12 NIV.

God will not ignore your prayers! He cares about every thought we have and every word we speak. He truly loves us! Today, let's be encouraged to pray knowing that our prayers will bring results!

YOU ARE NOT ALONE...

...for God Himself has said, "I will never, never let go your hand: I will never, never forsake you." So that we fearlessly say, "The Lord is my helper; I will not be afraid: what can man do to me? Hebrews 13:5–6 NIV.

No matter what we're going through at the moment or season, God reminds us that He is with us whether we "feel" it or not... Obviously, when we're going through a storm or major trial, the devil works hard to make us feel alone, abandoned, and feel God is nowhere near. Friends, this is just the opposite of the Truth (Jesus is truth). He lovingly tells us in His Word that He is with us holding our hand through EVERY trial we face. He protects us as a mother hen protects and shelters her babies.

Yes, even though I walk through the valley of the shadow of death, I will fear no evil, for you O Lord, are ALWAYS with me... Psalm 23 NIV.

Today's Word from God is encouragement and comfort. Even though trials and storms come our way, they can become easier and even turned around to victory "if" we will place it at the foot of the cross and trust Him to be with us AND protect us.

O Lord, my comfort in my suffering is this: Your promise preserves my life. Psalm 119:50 NIV.

When we are facing a fierce storm and our emotions are like being on a roller coaster, and our hearts are broken into, we should reach for our Heavenly Father's hand who is beside us with open arms. He promises He will comfort, shelter, and protect us.

The Lord is close to the brokenhearted and saves those who are crushed in spirit. Psalm 34:18 NIV.

Thank you God for walking with me each step I take…Thank you for wrapping your loving arms around me…Thank you for protecting me in this storm I am facing…

I am not alone..

God's Ways Are Better Than Ours...

Teach me, O Lord, to follow your decrees (Your plans); then I will keep them to the end. Give me understanding, and I will keep your law and obey it with ALL my heart. Direct me in the path of your commands, for there I find delight. Psalm 119:33–35 NIV.

It's a wonderful feeling when we are obeying God. Doing what He desires brings us peace and rest. When we totally surrender to Him, we are filled with His love and peace (completeness).

Choosing to walk in sin and disobedience eventually makes us miserable. We feel like the prodigal son who partied big for a while, but eventually became miserable for choosing to live a life of sin. He became remorseful for disobeying his father's will.

Has there been a time when you strayed away from God and felt miserable and made everyone around you miserable? Sure, we have ALL been there. We have ALL sinned and come short of the glory of God and totally felt lost on decision making. No exceptions. Thankfully, God doesn't categorize sin. Sin is sin. But with Him, there is forgiveness and restoration AND direction.

Come now, let us reason together says the Lord. Though your sins are like scarlet, they will be as white as snow; though they are red like crimson, they will be like wool. Isaiah 1:18 NIV.

God tells us that no matter what we have done or said, we have forgiveness in Him. He will forgive with grace, gently restore us better than before and give us direction. Yes, we will become wiser because we have learned from our mistakes.

As the prodigal son repented to his father and was restored to his rightful place, we also will be restored to our rightful place. Friends, God forgives and NEVER holds grudges against His children for what we have done. We should follow the life of Jesus and do the same for others.

Loving God with all our heart is the key to obeying. Listening to God is the key to following Him down our path of life.

You are my friends if you do what I command. I no longer call you servants, because a servant does not know his master's business. Instead, I have called you friends, for everything that I learned from my Father I have made known to you. John 15:14–15 NIV.

Since we have all made mistakes and made wrong decisions by not following God's plan at some time in our lives, let's choose to follow His will and plan. His ways are truly better than ours.

It's A New Day!!

Forget the former things; do not dwell on the past. See, I am doing a new thing! Now it springs up; do you not perceive it? I am making a way in the desert and streams in the wasteland, declares the Lord. Isaiah 43: 18–19 NIV.

God is speaking to us, His children, to focus on the now and what's ahead and NOT to look back at our past failures and mistakes (sins). God is NOT into "branding" an individual for life because of bad choices in the past. God is a "restoration" Father who loves us so much. Because Jesus paid the price on the cross, we are already forgiven. Our past sins are remembered no more. My dear friends, we should never live our lives dwelling on our past, but be excited about our future with God. He has special, unique plans just for us! Don't let the devil talk you out of your blessings and favor with God by making you feel unworthy. Remember, the devil is the accuser, NOT God!

Here's an FYI: There are NO perfect Christians. We have ALL sinned and come short of the glory of God. Romans 3:23 NIV. So we do NOT have the right to judge others over their past. If God says He remembers no more (Hebrews 8:12), do we have the right to remind people of their past or hold former sins over their head? I believe, as Christians, we know the answer. We are called to be loving, forgiving, and compassionate with a heart to see others restored by God. When God restores us, it's usually greater than before. Most successful individuals have learned more valued life's lessons from their failures than successes.

Let's look with excitement to the plans God has for us! By reading His Word and praying, we will understand our purpose and reason for living. God is a God of Restoration. He is a God of HOPE. He is a God of COMPASSION and FORGIVENESS. He is a God of LOVE............p.s. Don't look back.....It's a new day in our lives!

Are You Ready For Some Joy?

Jesus said, Ask and you will receive, and your joy will be complete. John 16:24 NIV.

The joy of the Lord is your strength. Nehemiah 8:10 NIV.

When we praise and worship God with a thankful heart, joy flows from our heart to others. Joy also strengthens us to fight the devil's attacks. With joy, we are overcomers. Living in joy isn't just about putting a smile on our face, but truly living a life of love (God). As we spend more time with our Heavenly Father, the joy will increase and strengthen us. Joy comes from love.

In the midst of our darkest trials and storms, we can be reassured that storms are only temporary and trusting God gives us peace. We may not know what the future holds for us but trusting our lives in His hands calms our fears and worries and gives us peace.

You turned my wailing into dancing, O Lord; you removed my sackcloth and clothed me with joy, that my heart may sing to you and not be silent. O Lord my God, I will give you thanks forever. Psalm 30: 11–12 NIV.

Friends, let's give thanks to God for His goodness. No matter what you are going through, reach out to Jesus who will calm your storm with peace. Thank Him for His joy that strengthens you to succeed through the darkest nights/storms. We have victory! We have Joy!

Do We REALLY Have To Love Everyone?

Love the Lord your God with all your heart and with all your soul and with all your mind and with all your strength.' The second is this: 'Love your neighbor as yourself.' There is no commandment greater than these. Matthew 12:30–31 NIV.

When we meditate on God's Word, we find that basically everything falls under these two commands from God. Did you know that the Ten Commandments are given in two parts? The first part deals with our love for God and the second deals with our love for our neighbor. So when Jesus gave the two commands in Matthew, He wasn't negating the other commandments. They are part of loving God and loving our neighbors.

Do we REALLY have to love those that are mean to us? Yes, we do. I'm sure each of us have given God more than one excuse why we shouldn't have to love a particular person since we were so badly treated by them. But our loving Heavenly Father commands us to look beyond what they have done and love them because they are His children. Siblings SHOULD get along in a family and since we're part of God's family, we should get along also. Is it easy? NOPE, it's not. We must spend time in prayer and worship with our Father in order to have love to give them.

Remember, when we give love to someone, we are giving them God because "God is love."

But I tell you, love your enemies and pray for those who persecute you.. Matthew 5:44 NIV.

I know there have been times in my own life when I was mistreated, falsely accused, hurt, angry, etc., that I wanted to rip these verses from the Bible but God would gently speak to my heart. Over the years, I've discovered His ways are much better than mine.

Bless **them** that curse **you**, and pray for **them** which **despitefully use you** ... Love your enemies, **do good** to **those** who hate **you**.. Luke 6:28 NIV.

By choosing to love and forgive those that hurt us, we are giving our pain and emotions to God who WILL handle the situation! By doing this, we are winning the battle and celebrating the victory.

Again, is it easy? No, but the more we choose to forgive and love those around us, the easier it becomes. Most of the time when we look back over a situation years later that had caused us to get upset, we see it was a smaller problem than we had thought and not worth losing our joy over.

Friends, God is love. Let's give God (Love) to those who hate us.....When we do, we will feel the weight of the burden lift from our shoulders.

Do We Really Care?

For I was hungry and you gave me something to eat, I was thirsty and you gave me something to drink, I was a stranger and you invited me in, I needed clothes and you clothed me, I was sick and you looked after me, I was in prison and you came to visit me. Then the righteous will answer him, 'Lord, when did we see you hungry and feed you, or thirsty and give you something to drink? When did we see you a stranger and invite you in, or needing clothes and clothe you? When did we see you sick or in prison and go to visit you? The King will reply, 'Truly I tell you, whatever you did for one of the least of these brothers and sisters of mine, you did for me. Matthew 25:35–40 NIV.

As Christians, we are called to be givers, bottom line.....We should live our lives with a heart to give to others as God leads us. We shouldn't judge a person by the way they look or by how much money they have or don't have, but instead allow God to show us the heart of the individual in need. This verse in Matthew 25, tells us that when we bless others, we are blessing Him.

God's Word tells us that whatever we sow, we shall reap. When we give to others, we are sowing into God's kingdom and we WILL reap a harvest. Friends, we can't out give God. The more we give, the more God will bless us in return. It's a win/win! As the verse in Matthew states, it's not just about giving money, but also giving of our time and heart to help others.

Jesus replied, "Love the Lord your God with ALL your heart and with ALL your soul and with ALL your mind. This is the greatest commandment. This is the first and greatest commandment. And the second is like it: Love your neighbor as yourself. Matthew 22: 37–39 NIV. Do we really love the unlovable? This is tough, but we can "do all things through Christ who strengthens us." Philippians 4:13 NIV.

Serving God in love means we choose to serve unselfishly with a heart to help, leaving the results to our Father.

Today, let's reach out to those around us in love with a heart to help.

Don't Doubt What God Can Do

You are the God who performs miracles; you display your power among the peoples. With your mighty arm you redeemed your people. Psalm 77: 14–15 NIV.

Need a miracle in your life today? Desiring a turnaround in your situation? Friends, grasp this scripture and keep it in your heart daily. His Word does NOT lie. He is the God of miracles! Our Father can turn ANY situation that you feel is hopeless around. Nothing is impossible, nothing too difficult!

With God all things are possible. Matthew 19:26 NIV.

He only asks that we believe His Word and trust Him.

If you believe, you will receive whatever you ask for in prayer. Matthew 21:22 NIV.

That's strong truth! God doesn't need our doubts and fears. He desires our love and trust that He can and will provide a miracle. It might not be at the exact timing that we want, but since He knows what's best for us, we must trust Him and not worry. Our Heavenly Father will not abandon or forsake us.

God is not a man that He should lie, nor a son of man, that He should change His mind. Numbers 23:19 NIV.

Begin believing that you have already received your miracle! Begin thanking God that it's done! No, you might not can see it, but your faith will make your situation whole (complete). Don't give up thanking Him until you see your miracle! It's coming!

He is With Us

May the Lord answer you when you are in distress; may the name of the God of Jacob protect you. May He send you help from the sanctuary and grant you support from Zion..........May He give you the desire of your heart and make ALL your plans succeed... May the Lord grant ALL your requests. Psalm 20: 1–5 NIV.

Our Abba Father (Daddy) cares so much for His children (us). His desire is to give us the desires of our heart (that's love). We don't have to "earn" his love and blessings because they are free! We have received the "gift" (free) of righteousness because Jesus paid the price on the cross. It's paid in full. No debt owed. His blood covers our sins and failures. We can rise each morning redeemed and free! Praise the Lord! His love for us NEVER fails. He is ALWAYS with us, never leaving our side!

Yes, even when I walk through the valley of the shadow of death, I will not fear, for You, O Lord, are with me. Psalm 23 NIV.

This is our promise from our Father. We are NEVER alone. This promise is our hope as we face trials and storms.

My hope is built on nothing less than Jesus' blood and His righteousness...

Today, live in victory, expect God's blessings, and choose to love others with the love God has given to you.....And know He is with you, guiding and protecting each step you take. Remember, you're never alone.

BECOMING THANKFUL WILL CHANGE MY CIRCUMSTANCES

Enter His gates with thanksgiving and his courts with praise; give thanks to Him and praise His name. For the Lord is GOOD and His love endures forever (unconditional); His faithfulness continues through ALL generations. Psalm 100: 4–5 NIV.

The Lord recently spoke to me to be thankful in ALL matters, not just in the good times. Rejoicing in the victories is easy, but it's a challenge to be thankful during the storms of life when we feel our heart is broken in half. A thankful heart (even when our heart is hurting) will make us stronger. Our thankfulness is in knowing that He is with us each step we take. He will NOT abandon us! No, He will NEVER leave our side!

If you're hurting today, feeling your heart is crushed, I encourage you to meditate on this scripture, "He WILL respond to the prayer of the destitute...." Psalm 102: 17 NIV.

Friends, I can personally testify that God will hold you tight during your storms. During the loss of our son three years ago, He never left our side. Even in my deepest/darkest moments of despair, when I didn't think I could even breathe, I just knew He was there sitting beside me. It was difficult, but I recall mustering the words through my horrific pain, "I thank you Father that you know what's happening to Teri, Lydia and me..... and, I love you God...." It was the beginning of my healing journey.

Dear friends, nothing surprises God, nothing. I encourage you to trust Him with every part of your being. Give Him thanks that He is gently leading and guiding you and that He holds your broken heart in the palm of His hands.......Look to Jesus, your redemption (healing) draws nigh.....

Be joyful always; pray continually; give thanks in ALL circumstances for this is God's will for you in Christ Jesus. 1 Thessalonians 5:16–18 NIV.

Also remember, if you will allow, God will use your storm experience to help others going through the same. When you reach out and help others, you become stronger. If I bought a boat and desired to sail, I would first seek advice from experienced sailors who had weathered storms. Yes, our Father will use you to help others.

Give Him thanks in ALL situations and circumstances.......

HE WILL NOT FORSAKE US!

O great and powerful God, whose name is the Lord Almighty, great are your purposes and mighty are your deeds..........You performed miraculous signs and wonders in Egypt and have continued them to this day, both in Israel and among ALL mankind, and have gained the renown that is still yours...........I am the Lord, the God of all mankind. Is anything too hard for me? Jeremiah 32: 18–27 NIV.

God is STILL in the miracle business, blessing His children. We mustn't limit God by our lack of faith. Let's believe He will do what His Word says He will do.

Those who know your name will trust in you, for you, Lord, have NEVER forsaken those who seek you. Psalm 9:10 NIV.

He will NOT forsake us! He will NEVER leave us! Friends, most of us are praying and believing for a miracle in our lives. Whether its job related, relationship, etc., God can and will turn our situation around, if we will trust Him.

Sometimes when miracles don't happen instantly, we think He's not answering. Most of the miracles in our lives are gradual. Yes there are some that are instant, but the majority comes with time. God always knows what He is doing and His timing is always perfect. We might not see it at the time, but later we will realize that He's not late, but right on time according to His will.

The process of waiting requires trust and faith. But trusting AND waiting creates a renewed strength in us so we can soar like an eagle above the problems. Our doubts fade away because our focus is on Our Father God......

Today, trust and believe for your miracle. Begin to give thanks for what he will do....Friends, He WILL answer!

BILL'S DAILY STORM DEVOTIONS 365 MINIDEVOTIONS TO HELP DRAW YOU CLOSER TO THE FATHER.

I pray these 365 daily thought provoking minidevotions will jump start your mind to live closer to God. Meditate on 1 devotion each day and allow God to work in your life. God has called us to be more like Jesus each day. Not only does he desire to help you grow spiritually, He desires to use you to help others. Be blessed as you meditate on His Word and listen to His voice.

January 1

Happy New Year! Some believe that it's the opportunity to begin a fresh start with their lives. "The steadfast love of the Lord never fails. It's new EVERY morning. Great is your faithfulness, oh Lord" Lamentations 3:22.

With God, beginning a new start is instantaneous. God forgives the moment we ask. We are covered in mercy and grace. Our sins are under the blood of Jesus. Forgiveness is for the asking...What a beautiful gift from our Father....Today, hold your head high and smile, knowing you are loved by God. Truly, it's a new day!

January 2

We are loved and important to God! We are created to be unique. God's not concerned with carbon copies, we are each different. We should spend more time with Him, our loving Father discovering who we are and our purpose. We aren't created to merely exist as so many do. We are created to LIVE our life pleasing to Him, making a positive difference in others' lives. We ARE important to God! A CEO needs his workers, a pastor needs his congregation, a general needs his army, a teacher needs their students, and children need their parents. We are "needed".... Let's live this day with purpose, offering HOPE (Jesus) to those only existing, not living.

"Let us hold unswervingly to the hope we profess, for God who promised is faithful" Hebrews 10:23.

January 3

Forgiveness must operate within us 24/7. We are bombarded daily with actions and words that can irritate and aggravate us to the point we become bitter and unforgiving. So why do we allow these emotions to build in us? Let's realize: 1. We can't change one another. 2. Most people don't hear the tone of their voice when they speak. But God's Word is clear...We must forgive others so we may be forgiven by our Father, looking for the good in others. When someone's words or actions offend us, let's begin by asking God to bless them. Learning to rise above daily chaos and drama, and forgiving others brings peace and calmness to our lives. "Forgiveness"

"If you forgive men when they sin against you, your heavenly Father will also forgive you" Matthew 6:14.

January 4

To be like Jesus doesn't mean we're called to be a "doormat" for some to trample on over and over. Yes, we are commanded by God to love and forgive those who hurt us, but forgiving doesn't mean we have to continue to receive hurt. That's not the heart of God. In the movie "Ever After" Danielle (Cinderella) tells her step mom, "I forgive you for all the hurts, but from this day forward, I will never think of you again..." She forgave, but chose to never allow it to happen again. Jesus instructed His disciples in Matthew 10:14 to shake the dust from their feet when not received and move forward. We should pray and God to bless those who have a bused and persecuted us, but be wise and never let it happen again. Forgive and begin a new day!

"If anyone will not welcome you or listen to your words, shake the dust off your feet when you leave that home or town" Matthew 10:14.

January 5

"Ask (ask means we take the 1st step) and it will be given to you; seek (seek means take the 1st step) and you will find; Knock (we knock 1st) and the door will be opened to you. For everyone who asks receives; he who seeks finds; and to him who knocks, the door will be opened" Matthew 7:7.

Too many of us are standing on the sidelines quietly waiting to play the game, waiting for God to do something. When in actuality, God is waiting on us! He wants to bless and use us! Let's be spiritually bold to ask, seek, and knock on His heart's door. He loves us and is ready for us to jump in the game....

January 6

Truth=integrity=honesty=holiness. When we walk in truth (doing what's right in the sight of God) we feel good. Lying and dishonesty makes one miserable. Desiring to be more like Jesus should encourage us to walk in truth. This includes what we say, do, and how we treat others. Also, truth challenges us to be like Jesus when we're driving, doing our taxes, shopping, etc. Truth brings freedom. It's time for Christians to walk the walk and talk the talk. Today, let's ask the Holy Spirit to keep us walking in truth. Remember, truth sets us free!

"Kings take pleasure in honest lips; they value a man who speaks the truth" Proverbs 16:13.

January 7

When we hear negatives regarding the awesome power of God, we must remain focused on His Word and not lose our faith. There are many around us who don't believe in miracles and faith. Faith comes from hearing, believing, and acting on the Word of God. We begin with small steps of trust, which increases to bigger steps of faith. Trusting God is our faith in operation. Anyone need a miracle in their life? Begin believing, trusting and obeying His Word. The result will be miracles in our lives!

"Commit your way to the Lord; trust in Him and He will do this: He will make your righteousness shine like the dawn, the justice of your cause like the noonday sun" Psalm 37:5–6.

January 8

By daily submitting our lives to God, we release every part of ourselves to Him. We don't need to fret over issues as, "Will God provide a marriage partner or boyfriend/girlfriend for me?" He has plans for us, if we'll trust Him. We don't need to wring our hands about our jobs and careers. God tells us He has plans to prosper us. We should prepare, work hard and leave the rest to Him. Our Father will lead us to the right career position, if we'll trust Him.. He can open doors in our lives that we can't open. We should walk in peace, knowing it's all in His hands. Our job is to trust Him and believe His Word....Begin today...

"Those who know your name will trust in you, for you, Lord, have never forsaken those who seek you" Psalm 9:10.

January 9

Dear God, we pray you will fill us with your "compassion." Give us compassion for those who are hurting so we may love and pray for them through their darkest storm. Gracious God, give us compassion for those who have made mistakes, that we may love them with your love instead of lecturing. May we be there for one another through trials. May your churches be flooded with compassion for the lost and hurting instead of constantly arguing and fighting over religious laws. Help us, oh God, to understand that the church represents Jesus, full of love and compassion. Father, fill us with compassion for the people we come in contact with today. In Jesus' name....

"The Lord is close to the brokenhearted and saves those who are crushed in spirit" Psalm 34:18.

January 10

Judging others is NOT God's plan nor His heart for us. When someone does something that's not in our descriptive of a Christian, we tend to judge them and declare they're not saved. Friends, God looks at the heart. We mustn't judge others by their actions. We can look at the disciples' lives and see they were not perfect. No, they didn't fit into the Christian mold, but God in His mercy and grace used them to minister and bless others. Let's begin today by loving and accepting others, allowing God to judge, not us. Father, help us to love unconditionally as we're around others. In Jesus' name, Amen.

"Do not judge, or you too will be judged. For in the same way you judge others, you will be judged, and with the measure you use, it will be measured to you" Matthew 7:1.

January 11

"My hope is built on nothing less than Jesus' blood and His righteousness. I dare not trust the sweetest frame, but Holy lean on Jesus' name. On Christ the solid rock I stand, all other ground is sinking sand." The writer of this powerful hymn probably faced a major storm in his life, but took a stand and clung to Jesus, his solid rock. Let this old hymn encourage us as we face uncertainties today. All other ground (other than Jesus) is sinking sand. No matter the economy, bank accounts, family situations, careers, etc., let's trust God today. He WILL NOT fail us!

"Those who hope in the Lord will inherit the land" Psalm 37:9.

January 12

Today's Word is "Passion." We must spend time with our Father, understanding His will for us, not listening to the doubters, and begin to pursue our passions with our whole heart. God is in the prayer answering business but we must pursue Him like the woman with the issue of blood (Mark 5:25–28). She didn't give up and received her healing! We need this strong determination (passion) also!

"Be strong and do not give up, for your work will be rewarded" 2 Chronicles 15:7.

January 13

Straying from God's Word (the bible) can create confusion about God's will for us (note: the devil loves to confuse us). The Word of God is the will of God. When we read and meditate on scriptures, we receive life and power to our prayers. Prayer and God's Word work "together." Many times God speaks to us through scriptures. We may read the same verse each day but receive new revelation from the Holy Spirit each time we read it. Friends, it's time to "blow the dust" from our Bible, open it, and begin to hear God's voice through His Word. He is always speaking. Are we listening?

"Thy word is a lamp unto my feet and a light unto my path" Psalm 119:105.

January 14

Some of the most satisfying moments are when we reach out and help someone. Yes, it's a wonderful feeling to help and give of ourselves. This is truly the heart of Jesus, taking the focus off ourselves and blessing others. Friends, a giving heart is a happy heart, but the devil likes for our focus to be centered on ourselves. This can cause us to be self-centered. Today, let's fight this mode of thinking and be givers whether it entails a call, visit, an errand, a smile and hug, financial, or even a listening ear. Giving people have peace knowing they are walking in the steps of Jesus.

"Serve one another in love" Galatians 5:13

January 15

Today, let's choose to spend time with our Father worshiping, praying, and "listening." The result will be a sensitive spiritual ear to hear the voice of the Holy Spirit as He speaks. When we sin, He will gently speak to our heart so we may repent and continue growing. When someone needs an encouraging word today, He will speak to us to say the right words. His voice can also save our life as He will warn us of danger ahead so we may choose a different path. He promises to lead and guide us each step we take, if we'll listen to His voice........Holy Spirit, you are welcome in this place (my heart)....

"I will instruct you and teach you in the way you should go, says the Lord" Psalm 32:8.

January 16

"Let us love one another for love is of God....and everyone that loves is born of God and knows Him. God is love...."true" love comes from Him because He is love" 1 John 4: 7–8.

Bottom line.....if we don't love others, we don't really know Him. And we can't love others if we don't love God because loves comes from Him......He is love. Relationships built on Love (God) are built to last...Let's be obedient to His Word, choosing to be like Jesus. Today, we will love everyone, even the unlovable.

January 17

Choosing to trust God and believe His Word, means we trust
Him in the sunshine AND the storms. No matter what happens,
we must keep our eyes fixed on Jesus. God proves Himself over
and over because He loves us. We must not get weary, discouraged,
or angry because He doesn't answer on OUR timing or the way
WE want it answered. I promise, He knows best and His timing is
never wrong. Today, please trust Him!

"Trust in the Lord at all times, O people; pour out your hearts
to him, for god is our refuge" Psalm 62:8.

January 18

Each day God touches our hearts with more healing from our
pain and grief. If we'll spend time with Him, we can feel His love
and peace surrounding us. Let's make a commitment to not run
from God, but instead to run to Him. Too many times in a crisis,
we panic and run from God. He's a God that answers prayers...If
we're hurting today, let's run to Him and not let go of the hem of
His garment till we feel His touch. He loves us and doesn't desire
for us to live our lives in pain..

"You O Lord, have helped me and comforted me" Psalm
86:17.

January 19

Jesse Duplantis–"You will find success in anything you do if you
listen to God's Words and follow the revelations He gives you. If
you are willing to simply listen, I can tell you that faith will rise
up in your heart. Listening changes everything!" Today, listen to
God. He's a God of success. His desire for us is prosperity. Let's
listen to His voice of success, He's speaking. How do we hear His
voice? Reading His Word, the Bible....

"Listen to his voice, and hold fast to him" Deuteronomy
30:20.

January 20

Isn't it wonderful that when we "blow" it (sin), and we all do, that we have the opportunity to come before God's throne and repent. Nothing we do or allow out of our mouth surprises God. He knows everything...and still loves us.."Amazing Grace, how sweet the sound..." God is a God of hope and restoration. It's never too much for Him. Today, knowing that our loving Abba father (Daddy) loves you, bring your burdens, brokenness, and pain to Him. He will heal and restore you...."Restoration"

"Through Christ we have now received reconciliation" Romans 5:11.Remove Post

January 21

Why are we selfish & demanding, wanting our way? We say we love God and attend church regularly, but we want things our way and for people to agree with us. Hmmmm.....isn't the Christian life about giving of ourselves and putting others' needs before ours? The Word never describes Jesus as selfish, but always giving.....I believe it's time we act like Jesus and truly serve God by loving and caring about other's needs. What a wonderful feeling when we give of ourselves.

"Humble yourself before the Lord, and he will lift you up" James 4:10.

January 22

Do we sometimes feel as if we're all alone in a desert? Yes, we do go through 'dry' periods where we feel we can't hear from God etc. Let's rest assured in His promise that He hasn't left our side. We can't base our spirituality on feelings or emotions as they can deceive us, but we can look to the Word of God and the assurance that we belong to Him. No matter how we feel at the moment, we just have to know in our heart, "Blessed Assurance, Jesus is Mine."

"If God is for us, who can be against us?" Romans 8:31.

January 23

When those around us begin to speak negative and critical remarks about others, we should first try to turn the conversation around. If that doesn't succeed, we should remove ourselves from the conversation. To listen is to agree....Let's not allow ourselves to be caught up in ungodly talk. It's poison..Today, let's keep our hearts and minds pure with Godly, encouraging conversations.

"But just as he who called you is holy, so be holy in all you do; for it is written: Be holy, because I am holy" 1 Peter 1:15–16.

January 24

"When we walk with the lord in the light of His Word, what a glory He sheds on our way. While we do His good will, He abides with us still and to all who will trust and obey. Trust and obey for there's no other way to be happy in Jesus, but to trust and obey." It took many years of singing this hymn before it finally came alive in my heart. What a beautiful message to us. If you desire to be happy, trust & obey...

"Those who know your name will trust in you, for you, Lord, have never forsaken those who seek you" Psalm 9:10.

January 25

"When peace like a river attendeth my way. When sorrows like sea billows roll. Whatever my lot, thou hast taught me to say, It is well, it is well with my soul." There are days (seasons) we go through storms and we want to question God and ask Him why... Learning to trust God in the storms, as well as the sunshine days, is victory. Knowing that He knows what's best for us gives us peace. Today, trust Him and say, "It is well with my soul".

"May the lord of peace himself give you peace at all times and in every way" 2 Thessalonians 3:16.

January 26

Giving thanks with a grateful heart is the first step to entering the presence of God. It's so easy to find an audience when we want to complain or "get it off our chest." But we must know that

God isn't pleased with that attitude. Sometimes we need to "shut" our mouths and not say anything, which can be uncomfortable. But I'd rather be blessed by God. Today, give Him sincere thanks from our heart and watch what comes forth from our lips .

"Enter his gates with thanksgiving and his courts with praise; give thanks to him and praise his name" Psalm 100:4.

January 27

When God calls us to go in a direction, we just need to go and not look to the right or to the left. We must keep our heart and mind focused on the One who called us. People, who mean well, might try to discourage us with, "It'll never happen, etc" but we mustn't be moved by what we hear or see. Be moved only by the Word of God. He takes the impossible and makes it possible! He's a miracle–working God! Begin now believing His promises….

"Your word, O Lord, is a lamp to my feet and a light for my path" Psalm 119:105.

January 28

Whatever you're facing today that seems to be an overwhelming challenge, remember you have the "mind of Christ." You "can do ALL things through Christ who strengthens you" and "He will supply ALL your needs." These are strong, powerful verses from His Word. God desires for you to have victory so don't allow fear and doubt to creep in. Trust Him to "make a way where there seems to be no way." He WILL provide a way out of the darkest tunnel. That's His promise!

"God's divine power has given us everything we need for life and godliness through our knowledge of him who called us by his own glory and goodness" 2 Peter 1:3.

January 29

It's amazing to think about God's love and grace. It's overwhelming at times. "He looked beyond my faults and saw my every need." If we just try to be good, we'll fail. We can't do it on our own merits, but we can "do all things through Christ who strengthens us." God knows we're not perfect. He knows when we'll fail. And yet, He STILL loves and forgives us when we ask....Amazing love... Amazing Grace..If we're facing guilt and shame after repenting, we must remind ourselves of mercy and grace and move forward. Remember, God's voice isn't one of shame and condemnation. He offers us life and life more abundantly.

"Grace and peace be yours in abundance through the knowledge of God and of Jesus our Lord" 2 Peter 1:2.

January 30

When we've done all we can do and prepared in every way possible, we should just rest in God knowing His will is most important and He truly knows what's best for us. Our choices and decisions, whether good or bad can teach us the importance of accepting His will, even though we sometimes don't understand. We can rest assured that He loves us and wants the best for us. This we know.. His decisions are for our best. Let's trust in the Lord with our whole heart....

"The Lord is my strength and my shield; my heart trusts in him, and I am helped" Psalm 28:7.

January 31

We can't judge people, BUT we can judge their spiritual fruit. We are like trees bearing fruit. Good fruit is love, joy, peace, patience, kindness, goodness, faithfulness, gentleness, and self–control. We are known by our fruit. If we're NOT spending daily time with God, our fruit could be the opposite i.e. hatred, meanness, selfishness, etc. What kind of fruit do we bear to those around us? Spend time with God and allow His love to change you! "Good fruit"

"But the fruit of the Spirit is love, joy, peace, patience, kindness, goodness, faithfulness, gentleness, and self–control" Galatians 5:22–23.

February 1

When we have been praying for someone and not seeing immediate change, we need to confess this verse in our heart. Philippians 1:2 *I'm confident of this very thing that He (God) who began a good work in _____, will continue it till the day of Jesus Christ (Philippians 1:2).* We're saying that we trust God with our whole heart to change this person. His Word is true. He began the work and WILL continue it. Let's be confident & believe that he's working in their lives!!

February 2

God has called us to love one another. This call of love has no limits or boundaries, and is unconditional. As Christians, we should believe the best in others, choosing not to judge or even gossip. Loving others like Jesus is not choosing to like only our friends, but being obedient to love everyone, even the unlovable. As we begin our day, let's choose to truly love. Someone may be hurting, feeling all alone and need the love of Jesus. Let's share love (God) with them and make a difference......

"Friends, let us love one another, for love comes from God" 1 John 4:7.

February 3

Two main enemies we encounter as Christians are "fear & doubt." Satan loves to steal from us. When we know we've heard from God about a particular matter, we can be assured that fear & doubt will try to creep inside our door and steal our faith in God's promises! Don't let it happen! Remember we are God's precious child and He desires to bless us so let's keep our eyes on Jesus and trust!!

"I trust in God's unfailing love for ever and ever" Psalm 52:8.

February 4

Why do we doubt God's goodness or believe we don't deserve God's very best? When we present our petitions to our Jehovah Jireh (Provider), we shouldn't ask for 2nd best, but rather come before His throne with loving boldness and ask for the best. We ARE His children and He desires to give us the best. Nothing is impossible to him who believes and trust! "With God, ALL things are possible!" Today, believe His promises! They are true!

"Remember the Lord your God, for it is he who gives you the ability to produce wealth" Deuteronomy 8:18.

February 5

We shouldn't scoff at those who make end time predictions. We know the Word and it doesn't lie. No man will know the hour or day. I do believe that God will reveal when the rapture is close. That's because He is a loving God and desires that none should perish. Let's stay in the Word, ignore "in love" those who miss the mark with their predictions, and continue living a life like Jesus. That's evangelism!

"Set your minds on things above, not on earthly things. For you died, and your life is now hidden with Christ in God. When Christ, who is your life, appears, then you will also appear with him in glory" Colossians 3:2–4.

February 6

If you're not feeling attacked by Satan, then you need to check your spiritual life. He doesn't go after the lazy, complacent souls, but the Christians who are serving God to discourage and distract them. If you're being attacked, please know you're a worry to the enemy. I encourage you to draw your sword (Bible) and fight back. "Greater is He (Jesus) that's in YOU than he (Satan) that's in the world." WIN!

"Thanks be to God! He gives us the victory through our Lord Jesus Christ" 1Corinthians 15:57.

February 7

Spending time with God should never be drudgery. Yes, we need to discipline ourselves to have quality time with Him, but understanding that it's a major help to our lives. His Word will keep us on the right victorious path of living. We should look forward to that Rhema (fresh) Word and not a dreaded habit. Today, get excited about your time with God knowing that His Word can change your life.

"Do not merely listen to the word, and so deceive yourselves. Do what it says" James 1:22.

February 8

We shouldn't believe in luck, but believe in God's blessings. Carrying a 4–leaf clover in our shoes or even wear a cross around our neck for good luck isn't going to bring results. The cross is only a reminder to give thanks for the price Jesus paid for us. Let's focus on living as victorious Christians, believing in faith for God's blessings and not waste time crossing our fingers for luck. Have faith in God and believe His promises and blessings!

Jesus said, "If you have faith as small as a mustard seed, you can say to this mountain, 'Move from here to there' and it will move. Nothing will be impossible for you" Matthew 17:20.

February 9

A powerful scripture that can help through storms is, *I am established in righteousness, and oppression (depression & grief) is FAR from me. (Isaiah 54:14).* Continually quote this Word over and over when you feel yourself sinking into deep grief. God will comfort and given you JOY! His Word (our manual) will deliver from oppression, comfort and protect you! It's His promise.

February 10

When God speaks to our heart and gives us direction, we must remain close to Him and not allow circumstances or people (even friends & family) talk us out of our vision or dreams. People mean well with the things they say, but their negative words can cause us to waver in our faith, creating fear and doubt, if we listen. Staying in God's Word with prayer, will keep us focused and our vision fresh, allowing us to have victory.

February 11

Because the Lord is my Shepherd (my Daddy), I have everything I need (You supply ALL my needs). Even when I walk through the valley of the shadow of death (storms in our lives) I won't be afraid because You are with me every step of the way. Your rod and staff comfort me (Sometimes you discipline me, because you love me). You make me lie down in green pastures (rest) & you restore me (Psalm 23). What a promise from God! He truly cares!

February 12

Love the Lord your God with all your heart and with all your soul and with all your mind. This is the first and greatest commandment. And the second is like it: Love your neighbor as yourself. (Matthew 22:37). Our goal each day should be to make a difference in someone's life. Many around us are starving for love and a reassurance that someone cares. Let's touch lives today with God's love. Helping others also prevents us from being self–focused, which can lead to pride. Let's follow Jesus' ministry by touching lives for Him. It's His will for us...Choose to love & encourage...You'll be glad you did...

February 13

Valentine's Day should be celebrated by all. It's not just about romantic love....It should also be celebrated by close friends and family members. It's about giving LOVE to others...It's for everyone to enjoy. We had students at school who literally got depressed because they didn't "have someone" for Valentine's Day. It's okay!! Enjoy the life God gave you. Enjoy being you.... Celebrate Jesus!

February 14 –Valentine's Day

On this day let's be reminded that we are not alone, whether married or single. Jesus died for everyone and stands with open arms ready to accept us. God's Word tells us that He supplies all our needs. That surely means love. As many celebrate Valentine's Day with that special someone, know that we are God's children and He loves us. Yes, we are loved! Yes, we have a relationship! No need to feel alone again. Let's enjoy this day and celebrate Jesus!

February 15

What a beautiful Biblical story of the woman with the blood disease who was determined to see Jesus, even though the crowd was massive. She "knew" in her heart that if she could even touch his garment, she would be healed. That's FAITH! She had no doubt! Her FAITH made her whole (healed) when she touched him. That's 'mountain moving faith.' If we're ready for miracles, let's reach for Jesus and don't give up! FAITH!

February 16

Life is a daily lesson as we walk with Jesus, learning more each day to be open to the Holy Spirit. Because everyone thinks differently, we should exercise patience as we deal with them. Just because someone doesn't think like us, doesn't mean they're wrong, just different. Let's spend time with the Father and allow His love to flow through us to others with patience and acceptance of their personalities.

February 17

Sometimes we allow ourselves to get so worked up over matters that really aren't that important. Is it because situations aren't going OUR way that we get so bent out of shape? Let's get back to trusting God for everything. He knows what's best for us. He knows us personally since He created us! God is PEACE. As we spend time with Him daily, His peace will flood our heart. God is stress–free! Let's be like Him!

February 18

Sometimes when we read the same scripture over and over we get bored or very used to it. The same applies to familiar sermons. The key to a Rhema (fresh) Word is "relationship" with our Father God. As we commune with Him, He may speak to us through verses we already know well. We must keep ourselves open and teachable. Each time we read a verse, He may speak something new. Today, let's listen as we read. He's speaking..

February 19

We should be thankful that God forgives and pours mercy & grace on us when we sin. Thankfully, when we repent, Jesus' blood washes away those sins, and God remembers them no more. Like Jesus, we must forgive and remember no more. No matter how much someone hurts us, we must learn to forgive and move on with our life. Unforgiveness will chain and entrap us. Today forgive and live in freedom!

February 20

Our time with God shouldn't be optional. We should pray and worship our Father whether we "feel" like it or not. It needs to become a discipline in our lives, knowing that prayer changes EVERYTHING. Our prayer time is vital to seeing miracles and answers. Today pray, seek His face, & worship, no matter what mood you're in. Someone's life could be changed because of our prayer. Prayer WILL make a difference! Be blessed and pray!

February 21

If birthdays and other special holidays cause us emotional pain, then we should choose to look at the beautiful memories we have instead of our pain or loss. Memories are a beautiful gift from God. (Thank God for technology so we can enjoy our memories through videos, pictures, etc.) Today, let's give Him thanks for the gift of memories, whether immediate family, friends, or church family. Give thanks for those around us today and choose to be a blessing!

February 22

With God ALL things are possible. "We thank you Father for always blessing and caring for us in storms and sunshine. We believe Your Word. It's truth! We confess fear and doubt as sin. Help us daily to draw our sword of the spirit (God's Word, the bible) and use it to gain victory against the enemy. We declare that we are over comers and will not give up! We know Jesus is with us during the worst of storms. We choose to trust. In Jesus' name. Amen."

February 23

There's room at the cross for you" It's refreshing and comforting to remember old hymns that are powerful and meaningful. If you're hurting today, there's room at the cross for you to come and give it to God. If you're fighting resentment, anger, frustration, discouragement, there's room at the cross for you. Friends, whatever needs you have, Jesus is waiting for you to come and surrender it all. He paid the price just for YOU! Come home...

February 24

Sometimes after our prayer time with God, we vow to trust Him in a particular situation only to begin trying to "figure it out", as if God needed help. It's a difficult lesson for each of us to learn. Trust God in ALL things. ALL means everything. That means we must remove our hands from "helping" and allow Him to work. God really can do a much better job than we can do. Let's REALLY trust & believe Him. He won't let us down, that's a promise!

February 25

It's a beautiful feeling of peace that comes from God after a raging storm hits. After the storm and raging sea of problems, we can get exhausted from fighting to keep our ship from sinking. God gently puts His loving arms around us and comforts us with love and peace. Remember, not only do we grow with each storm, but we become wiser and a more skilled navigator of our life's ship.

February 26

Let us rejoice in God's goodness and power. Let us continue praying for freedom and peace in this world. One death of a world leader will not stop terrorism. Let us intercede for our country, praying for our leaders and troops and continue praying for safety in our country and the world. God bless our nation! We will not give up praying no matter how bleak the situation gets. Prayer changes everything!

February 27

The old hymn "Wherever He leads I'll Go" speaks volume– "Take up thy cross and follow me" I heard my Master say. "I gave my life to ransom thee, surrender your all today." Wherever He leads I'll go. Wherever He leads I'll go. I'll follow my Christ who loves me so, wherever He leads, I'll go......" Friends, let's allow the Spirit of God to lead us in all we do. His Word says He will lead us into ALL truth.....Jesus is truth........Believe and trust His voice..Let's be willing to do, say, and go where He leads.

February 28

"Bless those that persecute you." Hmmmm, why did God put that in His Word? Ha! It would be easier to hate and be mean in return, BUT, God has commanded us to love because He is love. It brings us peace when we pray for our enemies. God is teaching us to keep our eyes & hearts focused on Him and allow Him to deal with those who are against us. So relax, it's in His hands! He'll deal with it, that's His promise. Relax, have peace and be blessed!

March 1

How awesome is the power of God's Word (Bible). If we could grasp the true power that His Word holds. It can move mountains! Today, let's believe with our whole heart in His promises and not allow fear and doubt to creep in and steal our joy. The devil loves to tell us it won't work. Lies, lies, lies. Friends, we are a beautiful creation of God with plans and gifts inside us. Let's walk in confidence today that He loves us! We are His children! We are blessed!

March 2

Trusting God is a journey. We trust with our whole heart, conquering mountains, etc. then all of a sudden, Satan attacks. At this point, we pick ourselves up, keeping our eyes on Jesus and continue trusting that He knows best and will make a way for us where there seems to be no way. Let's finish this race with victory! If we stumble or get hit by a storm, let's choose to keep our eyes on Jesus and trust! Storms are only temporary. Choose to trust! We WILL win!!

March 3

Sometimes we come across a big mountain in our journey. It might look like we can't keep going. We have to trust God and by faith in His Word, believe that this mountain will be removed! It might also appear as a giant as David faced, but by faith in God, we will slay the giant that comes against us. God has purpose for each of us. Today, believe for that purpose and have victory! The devil will NOT win!

March 4

If you abide in me, and my words abide in you, you will ask what you will, and it will be done unto you (John 15:7). This is where faith kicks in. We must believe that God truly wants to bless us. Abide means to spend time with God, thanking, worshiping, and praising Him. He desires our love, so let's begin each day in His presence. Let's love Him and believe His word! Today is OUR day for a blessing!

March 5

Today, give God thanks for life, salvation, mercy & grace, our family, jobs, etc...He's a loving Father who cares so much for us. Thank you Jesus for the price you paid just for me. Today let's choose to celebrate! Celebrate & enjoy your praise and worship to God! Celebrate & enjoy your family & friends! Celebrate & enjoy the plans He has for you! Celebrate & enjoy Jesus!!! Tell Him you love Him!

March 6

We must be careful and not allow ungodly talk to come from our mouth, whether it's about something or someone. We can't go to church with a heart to praise God, then head to lunch and talk about everyone we saw in a negative, gossip way. God will not bless that lifestyle! But "if" we want to be blessed, we must guard our tongue, saying only what will edify someone, not tearing them down. Let's be like Jesus and guard our mouth!

March 7

"Jesus paid it all...All to Him I owe..Sin had left a crimson stain, but He (Jesus) washed it white as snow.." Today, let's be reminded of what Jesus did for US. He thought of US while on the cross....He paid the ultimate price...Now we have mercy and grace...Thank you Jesus for loving us enough to die. Because of His death and resurrection, " I can go into the Holy of Holies...I can boldly approach God's throne." No more carrying sin on our shoulders. We have freedom!

March 8

Psalm 37:22 "Let me inherit the land." We should confess this verse 24/7 from our heart and BELIEVE in faith that we are God's children and that He desires to bless us. The word "land" represents a relationship, job promotion, financial blessings, & etc. Whatever our need is, let's begin to believe God and His Word. His promises are true! If we love blessing our family, how much more does God desire to bless us!

March 9

When we're facing a storm in our life, we mustn't allow the devil to isolate us away from other believers who desire to help us. When storms hit, whether it's a death of a loved one, job loss, divorce, etc., it's difficult to navigate your ship alone. This isn't referring to prayer, which is good to get alone with God, but more about allowing others into your life to pray, support and guide you to safety. Bottom line..We need one another...God wants to use you today! Open your heart's door to others who care and want t be there for you. They might not say the right words, but in our hearts we know they care.

March 10

Spending time with God not only strengthens you, but tunes your ears to the voice of the Holy Spirit. God desires to talk to us but we must learn to listen. Unfortunately, it might not be the same big voice we heard on the Ten Commandments movie. Ha! God speaks in that soft, still voice. Taking time to be alone with Him is the 1st step in hearing His voice. Today, listen.... He speaks.

March 11

When Jesus talks about us abiding in the vine, He doesn't mean just on Sunday mornings in church. He's referring to 24/7. We need Him! He is the vine and we are the branches. A branch dies without nourishment from the vine. That describes us. There is no life without Jesus, so stay close praying and praising Him throughout the day. He truly cares and is ready to answer your prayers! Abide!

March 12

There are times we encounter those who are mean and vindictive, seemingly out to get everyone. You probably know a few! Many times we wish God would just squelch them with a giant fly swat! But, as we grow in Jesus, we realize they truly need God. The Bible tells us to pray for them. And yes, to love them also. Instead of wanting God to "get" them, we should pray that He will change them. God's ways are much better than ours.....

March 13

Today, allow Jesus to shine through you to make a difference in someone's life. We live in a hurting world. Be a minister for God and allow Him to work through you to touch someone. It's a wonderful feeling to be used of God. Today, be the lighthouse on the hill in the dense fog of life. Shine your light for Jesus (the way we live) so that others can see and have hope.......Shine!

March 14

Do you ever think about how time is flying by? Maybe that's a sign that we're getting older or busier. Many times we look back and realize that we wasted alot of time that we should have spent serving God more faithfully. Thank God that all our yesterdays are under the blood of Jesus. Gone..Starting today, make each day count for Jesus. God has a plan for us. Let's don't look back at our wasted days, but get excited about serving Him today! Choose to live for HIM!

March 15

It's important as God's children to spend time in the Word and prayer. We face many obstacles in our day that can irritate and anger us. This can cause unforgiveness to grow in our heart. We must treat these feelings as weeds and kill them at the root, with our spiritual weed eater (love). Let's love and bless those that persecute us, cleanse our hearts of any sin, & spend time worshiping God. He will take care of the problem, and that's a promise.

March 16

Today, with a heart to worship our loving Father, let's give Him thanks for all He has and is doing in our lives. Let us love those around us, even the unlovable, as Jesus loves. As Christians, we are all called to serve & love others. This is our ministry, our calling. Let's not be bullies demanding our own way or complaining about situations or people. Let's make a decision to live today with clean hands & a pure heart ready to love. Love (God) changes everything. Let's make a difference!

March 17

Can you imagine what this world would be like if everybody had a giving heart? It would be a taste of heaven...God has called each of us to lay our lives down & be willing to give of ourselves to help and serve others. It's rewarding to help someone in need, plus it's God's heart. This was the impact of Jesus' ministry on earth. He gave himself to touch others' lives. Let's follow His ministry and reach out in love to someone today. Someone needs a touch from Jesus and God desires to use us.

March 18

It's difficult to always feel we always have to make the first move in reconciliation with someone, especially when we feel we've done nothing wrong. God blesses our obedience when we listen to His voice and reach out to that person who is offended. Friends, it's not important whose fault it is.....It's Christ–like to reconcile and move forward. Love conquers all. Today, let's choose to forgive, make the first move, love & leave the results to God. We'll be blessed in return.

March 19

"Grace that is greater than all our sin." Wouldn't it be nice if we were perfect and never sinned? Unfortunately, the Word says we have all sinned and come short of the glory of God. The good news is God's grace covers our sins when we ask for forgiveness. We do NOT have to live in condemnation (guilt and shame). To many Christians spend years beating themselves up when they falter. This isn't God's plan for us. He desires to set us free from the guilt and restore us better than before. That's freedom, that's "Grace"..Receive it now!

March 20

Pain is a terrible thing that affects so much of who we are. It affects our health, minds, and our hearts. Pain, whether it's a loss of a family member, job loss, physical, broken relationship, etc is real and it DOES hurt. Pain has no age requirement. It affects everyone at sometime in their life. Please know that God is a "healer" and promises to heal our pain, if we will give it to Him. That's love........

March 21

When we accept Jesus as our Lord and Savior, we become God's children. We are His! Just like our children are ours and no matter what they do, they still belong to us, this is the way our loving Father is. We might rebel into sin & etc, but we are still His children. That, my friends, is "Grace." God does not intend for us to walk on egg shells our entire life worrying if we'll make into Heaven. God doesn't divorce His children! There are some religions that disagree with this belief. Just know Grace....God's grace is greater than our sins. "Jesus paid it all and all to Him I owe. Sin hath left a crimson stain, He washed it white as snow...." Be blessed and be free....

March 22

The most spiritual growth we experience is when storms are raging against us. We have choices to make. We can hold tight and ride the storm until it's over, or we can give up and sink. The only way we can become an expert sailor (Christian) is to learn to allow the Holy Spirit to guide our boat during a storm. Some believe that becoming a Christian makes us immune to problems. Not so. Storms will come. We must learn to trust God in our storms. Learning to be an over comer is growth! He is ALWAYS with us! Remember, God can steer our ship much better than we can. Let's turn it over to Him

March 23

God is calling us to surrender every aspect of our lives. Many believe this means they will end up with no life, which is just the opposite. When we surrender to our Father, our life just begins! He replaces the 'yuck' with newness and joy! God is a God of 'new beginnings!' Yes, no matter our past, God can and WILL turn it around. The joy of the Lord is new every morning! Let's start today & give Him our all. It's a new day!

March 24

Can't you hear your Father calling to you to come to Him? Yes, He already knows everything in our hearts and mind, but by sharing our heart to Him, it opens the door for Him to minister to us. He desires a relationship with us that's built on love and communication. Let's spend quality time with God and allow Him to minister to us. He's ready to answer our heart's request, if we'll just believe. Today, believe!

March 25

When people get into sin and "run away from God", where do they think they will run to if God is omnipresent (everywhere)? I think of a small toddler running the other direction when you call them. We are right behind them making sure they don't get too far. Isn't that what God does? He's always there with such love and compassion. Today, let's quit trying to run and just enjoy God's presence. He loves us!

March 26

God's Word cannot and will not fail! "If" you seek Him, you WILL find Him! God promises to be a rewarder of those who diligently seek Him. Emmanuel! God with us–God in us–God in ME! If you have strayed away from God, run back into His arms today as He is waiting! My friend, there is no life without God! He is loving, forgiving, and faithful....Come home to Jesus....He's standing with open arms. What a loving Father..

March 27

Jesus loves us so much. He cares about every hurt, pain, worry, etc. He chose to suffer and die on the cross for these issues that weigh us down. God desires for us to walk in freedom and not be burdened down with life's issues. Today, let's tell Him we love Him and surrender every part of ourselves to Him. Yes, every issue that is worrying us. He is waiting with open arms to set us free. *The way of the Lord is a refuge for the righteous (Proverbs 10: 29).*

March 28

The Lord asks, "Why do you not trust me to handle your situations?" Many times we are guilty for trying to "help" God solve our prayers. Friends, when we pray and give it to God, we don't need to pick it back up and help God fix it. He really doesn't need our advice! Today, be encouraged to totally trust God by giving Him your problems and allowing Him to answer. He'll answer! He's never broken a promise. *Whatever we ask in prayer, believing, we will receive (Matthew 21: 22).*

March 29

One of the greatest challenges for Christians is keeping our minds & hearts focused on God's promises and not allow fear & doubt to creep in. Many believers lose their blessings because of doubting that God will answer their prayers. We must stay focused on His Word, knowing God doesn't lie and that He desires to bless us. We are His children so stay focused on His love & promises! Believe, no matter how long it takes! *God watches over his Word to perform it (Jeremiah 1: 12).*

March 30

Do you know of someone in your school class, work place, or home that is loud, blunt, outspoken, and grinding on everyone's nerves? We all know this person! Well, under that tough & brazened skin is a very tender heart crying to be loved. Today, instead of avoiding or confronting this person, let's pray and love them, asking God to soften their heart. Let's remind ourselves that they are God's children also & dearly loved by Him. *We* should *love one another (1 John 3: 11).*

March 31

When people become critical & judge us, we mustn't retaliate. Our job is to "love", knowing that God is Love. Satan is always looking for an open door to slide his nasty foot in. We mustn't allow him access in our lives. Keeping the "Joy of the Lord" in our heart defeats the devil. Today, let's don't be moved by what others say or do against us. Forgive, love and let God handle it. Let's choose to keep our joy & have Victory!

April 1

"Mercy said no! I'm not gonna let you go. I'm not gonna let you slip away, you don't have to be afraid. Mercy said no! Sin will never take control. Life and death stood face to face, darkness tried to steal my heart away.....Thank you Jesus, mercy said no!" What a beautiful song...What a beautiful message........Thank you Lord for your mercy. He will not let us go...Today, rest in this promise that no matter what we have done, God forgives..

April 2

It's sad to hear of some Christians moving from church to church on a continuous basis due to the church not meeting their needs. Maybe your church doesn't have great Praise and Worship, but aren't we to worship our Father on a daily basis...If things don't happen the way we think they should, we should seek God with all our heart and be sure that we hear from the Holy Spirit in regards to moving to a new church. He promises to lead us into all truth. Let's listen to His voice and obey.

April 3

The Lord is our helper. *God WILL NOT turn away our prayers (Ps. 66:20). God will not despise our prayers (Ps. 102: 17). The prayer of the upright is God's delight (Prov. 15:8). He is near to all who call upon Him (Ps.145:19).* May these scriptures encourage us as we pray. We have power when we pray! But more importantly, we have God's ear and heart. Let's talk to Him..now..

April 4

Not too long ago, I was "Shackled by a heavy burden. (I was) beneath a load of guilt and shame, but then the hand of Jesus touched me and now I am no longer the same. (My friends,) He touched me, oh He (Jesus) touched me, and oh the joy that the floods my soul. (You see) something happened and now I know,

He touched me and made me whole." Ask God to touch you today. One touch from God is life changing..

April 5

This is a great day to rejoice in Jesus and be thankful. It's so easy to moan about our lives and how things are going wrong, but being thankful that God is in control, gives us peace and can turn it around to a blessing. Let's trust, trust, trust, and thank our Father for what He has done, is doing, and is going to do. His plans are the best and He won't let us down. *I delight greatly in the Lord; my soul rejoices in my God. For he has clothed me with garments of salvation and arrayed me in a robe of righteousness (Psalm 61: 10).*

April 6

We need to give thanks for those around us. No one's perfect. Yes, we ALL have faults, but thank God for changing us each day to be more like Jesus. We should be thankful that God has placed certain individuals in our lives to help us grow. Some people are considered good experiences and others, not so good. God has ways to mold us & help us be like Him. He knows more than we do so let's desire His ways to be our ways and be thankful for those around us…*Being confident of this, that he who began a good work in you will carry it on to completion until the day of Christ Jesus (Philippians 1: 6).*

April 7

When you don't believe it can happen, when you can't figure it out, when you can't "see the forest for the trees", then it's time to TRUST God in faith. "ALL" things are possible to him who believes! It's time to trust God for your miracle. He loves for us to believe the impossible. Your obstacle, which appears as a big mountain, is only a hill in the way. God can and will remove it, if you'll trust! *It is through faith and promises we inherit the promises (Hebrews 6:12).*

April 8

We should live our lives with purpose, continuously setting goals. A man with no direction is like a ship without a rudder, floating aimlessly on the water. The churches today are full of Christians who are status quo, no desires to grow in the Lord. Friends, we're either moving forward or backward. There's no middle ground. Let's begin to seek God for purpose in our life. Our Father has plans for each of us but living a non-existent status quo life helps no one. We are called to be conquerors for Christ, over comers, achievers, winners, soldiers, evangelicals. Today, allow Him to give you purpose so you may bless others.

April 9

When we've done all we know to do with a situation and pray "Father, Your will be done", we have to accept what He sees as best. We might not always agree at the moment, but God sees the big picture. We only see the moment. When we turn it over and trust Him, we can step back and relax knowing He's doing what's best for us. "TRUST and obey, for there's no other way to be happy in Jesus!"

April 10

The Bible states that we are daily sowing seeds. This can be good or bad, but we are going to sow with our lives. If we sow love & kindness, we will be rewarded openly. Sow love & forgiveness, and reap the same. Sow generosity & gratitude, and never feel poor. Sow hope, and reap fulfillment. Sow praise, and reap joy, well-being & a strong faith. Sow bountifully, and reap bountifully. Today, sow good seed.

April 11

When the storms of life hit like death, divorce, broken relationships, job loss, etc., we must trust God with our whole heart to lead us through the grieving period to stand strong again.

Psalm 147:3 "He heals the broken in heart, and binds up their wounds." There is no true healing without God's help. We should visualize in our mind handing God our heart and allowing Him to heal and restore our joy! Remember, he is the "Potter." Storms are only temporary.

April 12

"Count your blessings, name them one by one." What a wonderful hymn to remind us to be thankful in ALL things. When we surrender completely to God, we can rest in His promises, knowing He knows what's best for us. Isn't it a relief that we don't have to rack our brain trying to figure out our lives and what God desires for us to do? We can trust Him to lead & guide us. He will NEVER steer us in the wrong direction..Be thankful and trust His leading. He leads much better than we do. Choose to trust!

April 13

Sometimes when we listen too much to the media reports of negative happenings around us, it can create fear in our heart. When we dwell on the negative, we begin to feel that our world is at it's worst. Friends, we must look to God's Word which offers hope. Prayer and the Word can and will fight fear. "I do not have a spirit of fear but power, love, and a sound mind" (2 Tim 1:7). God is moving during these last days before Jesus returns. Many are being saved, healed, and restored! God has equipped us to fight the enemy and WIN!!! Let's rejoice today with praise and worship, dwelling on Jesus, rather than reports of doom and gloom! (Read the last chapters of Revelation.......we win!)

April 14

Remember the story in the Bible of Mary & Martha (Luke 10: 38–42)? Martha spent her time working and preparing a meal while Mary spent her time with Jesus. As Christians, we must be careful not to confuse church activities with our relationship with God. It's good to volunteer and work in the church, but it mustn't take precedent over our time with God. God desires for us to "walk with Him and talk with Him....He loves us!

April 15

Sometimes it doesn't take much to stir our pots of irritation and unforgiveness and get us worked up over something that's not of major importance. The reason we get irritated at others is they don't do things the way we think they should. Deep inside we feel our way is best. We must understand that everyone thinks differently and acceptance is the best. It's not always about us! Forgive and accept others' way!

April 16

Praising God can be the best medicine to take when we're feeling down & depressed. The Word says "The JOY of the Lord is our strength." This verse is LIFE. Praise and Joy keeps us focused on the present and the future, not the past. Praise is like tulips blooming. When they begin to open we see their beauty and think ahead to the spring, never looking back to winter. Let's begin our day with Praise to God! It's a NEW day!

April 17

Praising God is not always fun in the beginning, but once we get started, we get filled with joy. We have to make a choice, a decision to praise God, knowing that by doing so, there are benefits. He loves and desires for us to praise Him. Looking back on certain situations in our life can be painful, so let's focus on the now and what's ahead. We might be experiencing a "winter" in our life right now, but let's choose to praise Him, it's only for a season!

April 18

It's a new day, a new year for us in so many ways. We should be excited about what God has in store for us, His children. His plans are usually not our plans, thank goodness. His plans are always better than ours. Let's learn to depend on Him for decisions to avoid making mistakes and not get into a state of worry or stress, but listen to His voice as He speaks to us through prayer and His Word. Praise Him today for His goodness! Remember, He truly has a special plan...trust.

April 19

Today, don't give up on pursuing what God has put in your heart. Satan doesn't like us and will pull out many stops to prevent us from achieving our dreams. BUT, The Word states *Greater is He (Jesus) that is in us, than he (Satan) that is in the world (1 John: 4:4)!* Don't throw your hands up and cry when he attacks! Draw your sword (God's Word) and fight back to win! The word WILL stop Satan! Today is VICTORY!

April 20

Today, let's ask the Holy Spirit to reveal to us if there is any unforgiveness in our hearts. It could be toward a person, a business or restaurant. If we have ill feelings toward someone or something, it's time to check our heart. There's probably some hidden unforgiveness there that needs to come out. We need "clean hands and a pure heart" to forgive, so we can receive God's forgiveness. Be blessed today!

April 21

To all those who have suffered a loss of a family member, divorce, job loss or tragedy of any kind, the Word is don't allow Satan to ruin our day whether it's a holiday or a regular working day! We must take the first step which will lead us to victory. Let's plan to be with friends or family if we're alone taking time to worship our Father which brings JOY! God desires for us to be happy!

Dr. Bill Myers

April 22

"His eyes are on the sparrow, and I KNOW He watches over me."
What a great song. What a great testimony that God cares about
every detail of our lives. He's our loving Father who truly cares
about His children. If you're hurting or going through a storm in
your life, please lean on Jesus. Trust Him to rescue you and He
will. No storm or crisis is too big for Him. "Oh how he loves you
and me." Peace comes with trust....

April 23

If an intruder came into your house, wouldn't you do everything
possible to get them out for the safety of your family and
possessions? We must recognize that Satan, the deceiver, comes
to "steal, kill, and destroy." We must put our spiritual foot down
and say "No more!" Rise up and fight for what is yours in the
name of Jesus. Don't let the devil rob you anymore! You are a
child of God! AMEN! *I take the shield of faith, and I quench every
fiery dart of the enemy (Ephesians 6:16).*

April 24

Today's questions: What can I do for someone else today to help
or make them feel special and loved? Who can I encourage today?
Who can I give a loving hug to? Who can I give a listening ear
to? Can others see Jesus in me? Do I treat those around me with
the love of Jesus? ....Many questions, one answer. "Change my
life O God, make it ever new. Change my life o God, may I be
like you." There's no greater feeling than helping someone. Today,
God desires to use US!

April 25

Today's devotion isn't fuzzy warm words, but a charge to us that
there's power in the name of Jesus! Mountains can be removed,
the sick can be healed, lost souls can be saved, all in the name

402

of JESUS! His blood He shed at Calvary has power! In today's world many refrain from speaking about the blood of Jesus, but I'm telling you, there is POweR in His blood! JESUS! Speak it today! *I tell you the truth, if anyone says to this mountain, 'Go, throw yourself into the sea,' and does not doubt in his heart but believes that what he says will happen, it will be done for him (Mark 11:23).*

April 26

Why do we expect our children to be superstars in everything they do? Yes, they should strive for excellence BUT they must "enjoy the ride" while working toward goals. Children aren't perfect. God made each one different and special. Let's ENJOY our children and be thankful for the gift they really are. Sadly, our disappointments sometimes come from what we, as parents, didn't do ourselves. We mustn't live our lives through them or "use" them to make us look good. Remember, awards do not make children happy. It's the quality time we give them that puts a smile on their face.

April 27

Many people perceive God according to their upbringing. Some raised in hard lined religion, view God as stern ready to beat us when we get out of line. Others, who were raised in a very liberal environment, believe God allows everyone to go to Heaven. Bottom line: We must read God's Word (Bible) and find for ourselves His nature and personality. He is a "good" God, a loving "Abba Father" who loves and so desires to bless His children with blessings and favor. Not because we deserve it, but because we are His children and His Word says so. God (Love) gives everyone an opportunity (choice) to be with Him in Heaven for eternity......
That opportunity is Jesus Christ, the ONLY way....Let's read the Word, discover "truth" about God, and chooses Jesus.

April 28

Ever know someone who always wants to be like others or have what they have thinking it will make them happy? They look at others and envy their families, jobs, possessions, etc. News flash! The grass isn't greener on the other side! We must quit looking at others and their situations and began thanking God for who we are and what we have. Give thanks to Him for designing a special plan for us and choose to believe His promises!

April 29

If we're hurting for whatever reason and dreading special holidays, let's follow this advice: 1. Stay busy, too much "down time" will cause our mind to ponder over our hurts. 2. Keep ourselves surrounded by supportive and positive people, not negative complainers. 3. Worship, worship, worship. Praising God will lift the pain and struggles off our shoulders, but we must "abide in the vine" for relief. God will bless us! I believe!

April 30

"Oh give thanks unto the Lord, for He is good..." Yes, He is a good God (Father) who loves His children. We mustn't blame everything bad on God. John 10:10 tells us Satan comes to steal, kill, and destroy, BUT Jesus comes to give us life and life more abundantly (Blessings). Let's keep our eyes on Jesus daily, trusting Him each step of the way, and give Him thanks because he is good. God's GPS (Holy Spirit) will lead us in the right direction, and that's a promise. Trust, He knows best!

May 1

Even when we're going through a storm in our lives, it's important that we don't become extremely self-focused on our own problems, but take notice that there are others hurting also. If we'll take time to pray for and love those hurting, we'll began to sense healing in our own life as well as blessing others. Today, let's look outside of our "shell" and see a hurting world that needs us.

May 2

Reading and meditating over God's Word (Bible) can reveal His will for our lives, which is ALWAYS confirmed through His Word. The Bible IS His spoken Word. God has His divine plan for us "if" we'll just listen and trust. We are such a NOW generation. God's will is to teach us to trust Him, which may cause us to wait. That's ok. It's worth it! Let's pray and read His Word for His perfect will in our lives. *It is through faith and promises we inherit the promises (Hebrews 6:12).*

May 3

King David didn't receive his promises from God instantly as there was a waiting and growing process while God was taught him to trust. He even had two opportunities to take Saul's life, but refused and left him in God's hands. All during his times of storm and strife, God was molding him to be a great leader for Israel. This process taught him to become a "man after God's own heart." Let's begin to look at our storms as times of molding us into the character of Jesus. Dear God, mold me into a man/woman after your heart. Amen.

May 4

Self–pity isn't an attribute of God. It doesn't glorify Him and nor get the problems solved. We must recognize it creeping on us when we're faced with a storm. The devil enjoys making us feel sorry for ourselves, the only ones having to suffer. We must focus our attention on Jesus, not ourselves. Even on the cross, Jesus did NOT display self–pity. The antidote for self–pity is "JOY" derived from praise and worship to our loving Father. The joy of the Lord puts the focus on God and brings victory to our lives.

Today, let's look in the mirror and remind ourselves that storms are temporary and self–pity isn't an attribute of God. Joy=victory!!

May 5

Rising above a situation when you've been personally attacked is a step in spiritual growth. Yes, our flesh wants to lash out when others attack us, which often comes through words, gossip, actions, etc. When we read in the bible about King David taking the spiritual "high road" in the many attacks from Saul and even his own son, Absalom, we see a man after God's own heart. Allowing God to fight our battles brings us peace and assurance that He WILL handle the situation. Do we trust Him today that He can and will take care of it? Our faith in His promises will make us 'whole.'

May 6

Let's be thankful we are a Christian. Our lives are short on earth compared to eternity in Heaven with Jesus. It's comforting to know our decision to follow Jesus gives us the right to be called a son of God, an heir and joint–heir with Jesus. Being a Christian gives us access to the throne of God with our prayers. God loves and desires to bless us. WE ARE HIS CHILDREN!!!!! Today will be exciting just knowing in our hearts who we are in Christ!!

May 7

Let's choose today to be a blessing to someone. Let's ask Holy Spirit to show us and open the door of opportunity. It could be a smile, a hug, an encouraging word, etc. May our desire be to finish the day knowing that we submitted to our Father and He used us to touch someone's life. It's not about us today, but us helping someone else. What a great feeling! What Joy and Peace! What "obedience." Blessings!

May 8

When facing conflict or a big mountain in our life, we have 2 choices: 1. We can take the world's view, using harsh words & actions but not accomplishing anything and feeling worse than when we started. 2. We can humble ourselves, getting rid of pride, walk in love because God is love, and allow His Love to stir our faith. Our faith in God can move mountains! I choose method #2 in handling my conflicts. It's God's way.

May 9

When we trust God with our lives, He not only brings direction and answers, but gives us a beautiful river of peace that calms. I'm still learning that God knows more than me, so I continually trust Him. I have peace like a river......Trust equals peace. Peace is a choice. If turmoil arises, and it will, we will conquer with peace. Peace=Letting it roll off our shoulders. Peace allows us to smile more during the day and sleep better at night. Peace....

May 10

Two great songs with a powerful message. "Jesus, Jesus how I trust you, how I've proved you over and over. Jesus, Jesus, precious Jesus, oh for grace to trust Him more." And, "Learning to lean on Jesus. Finding more power than I've ever dreamed, learning to lean on Jesus." We must allow God to take charge of our life including this day. He loves & wants us to walk in victory, His victory. Trust Him with your problems & believe His promises..........He will NOT fail. Never has, and never will. Today begins with us making the decision to let him lead our life.

May 11

Learning more about being an heir of God and a joint–heir with Jesus is helping me be victorious in my life. God's promises are ours so we must began to walk in who we are and what we're destined to be. Just as our children are heirs, we are God's heirs.

His kingdom is ours because we are His children and He loves us. Don't allow Satan to convince you that you are worthless. God doesn't intend for you to just exist, but to have life more abundantly! Rejoice! *Romans 8: 17 Now if we are (God's) children, then we are heirs and co–heirs with Christ.*

May 12

One of the hardest aspects of being a Christian is turning the other cheek when someone attacks you, but this is the very nature of God. Of course, Satan knows the attacks that can hurt the most. We must be doing something right for him to attack us so much. Instead of cowering, running, or even fighting back, we must put on the armor of God with praise and worship on our lips, and see God bring victory in our life. Obeying God brings peace to our lives. *Matthew 5:39 If someone strikes you on the right cheek, turn to him the other also.*

May 13

Our daily tendency in dealing with negative, complaining people is to back away and remove our self from the conversation. Yes, we shouldn't get involved in a negative conversation or allow it to influence us, but God DOES desire to use us to plant a LOVE (God) seed inside them. Allow God to use you the next time someone talks negative. Love (God) changes everything...Yes, we have the ability to refocus a negative conversation to a positive one by allowing God to be in charge. Remember, Jesus even loves the complainers! We must love also....

May 14

Let's don't start our day or even go to bed tonight without thanking our Father God for all He has done in our life. God loves a thankful heart. Choose joy! Choose to love! Choose Jesus! These biblical choices will bring us victory and joy. Give Him thanks with a grateful heart. Complaining doesn't bring results to our prayers. When we are grateful, we are happier..

May 15

Jer. 29:11 tells us that the thoughts of God are peace and prosperity. Why is it that some folks don't mind hearing sermons on peace, but get irritated about sermons on prosperity? Aren't they both in the Word? Do we separate and choose? I think not. God truly wants to bless us. Prosperity deals with EVERY area of our lives, so let's believe for prosperity and walk in peace. Amen!

May 16

A challenge for us as Christians is to ALWAYS look for the best in others. Like the scenario of lemons making lemonade. Instead of judging others with pointed fingers and whispering ear to ear, we should focus on the goodness of God and His loving ability to make us like Jesus. We never know what God is doing in others' hearts. Sadly, we tend to judge when it's not 'our' norm. Let's choose to love and leave judging others and situations to God. Remember, being Christ–like is a beautiful, evangelical tool. I don't believe too many lost souls have been won to Jesus through judging and pointing fingers. Love is the key........

May 17

"This is the day that the Lord has made, I will rejoice and be glad in it." Yes, it's a conscience decision we make to walk in peace and the "Joy of the Lord", even when you feel your life is falling apart. There's an old song that speaks to us, "Only JESUS Can Satisfy Your Soul." Let's don't waste our time searching for some sort of happiness in this world, but instead look to Jesus who supplies all our needs. He's true joy and PEACE.

May 18

When dealing with people in general, you'll face "drama" or gossip/backbiting. This is life in a world of sin. If we allow ourselves, we can get bent out of shape over nothing! We must lay our emotions at the foot of the cross. Let's strive to be like Jesus and let things roll off our shoulders and not be offended over remarks or gossip. We can't change people, but we CAN pray for and love them. Rise above today!

May 19

Thank you Lord for your "joy" that fills us each day. When we worship God with a sincere heart, His love fills us to where the worries of this world seem unimportant. Let's focus on the love of Jesus and plan to have a wonderful day, asking God to use us to bless others. What a wonderful feeling to be used of God! "Joy to the world."

May 20

When we get attacked by people, we have to choose to fight back or give it to God. Rising above an attack (we ALL get attacked) and giving it to God will bring victory and peace in our lives. Arguing, fighting, and being negative, which the devil loves, will keep us frustrated and exhausted. When people attack us at school, work, or even church, choose to follow Jesus and win! Remember, our battle isn't with people, but with the devil. Today, smile and rise above for the "Joy of the Lord is your strength!"

May 21

Truthfulness and integrity: When someone asks us to pray about a matter and we agree, we should pray. Too many Christians use the phrase "I'll be praying for you" as conversation words instead of actually praying. If we would commit to pray for one another (not just saying it) when someone asks, we would see many more miracles. Today, let's be truthful with the words that we speak..

May 22

God is in the restoration business! No matter what we've done or been through, God can and will use us, if we'll surrender our will. He can take the hurts, mistakes, shortcomings and use them to strengthen us to help others. Our past is in the past. God desires to use us in the now! If He had wanted perfect, there wouldn't have been disciples. Today put your eyes on Jesus! He wants to use YOU!

May 23

When we repent from our sin, God, in His amazing love for us, forgives and restores us. I think about the prodigal son who sinned, repented and came home to his father. His father went to meet him (left his house), embraced him (stink and filth), forgave him, and restored him by presenting him with a ring and robe. This story reflects the character of OUR loving, forgiving and restoring God. Amazing!

May 24

Today, let's sow love and kindness into as many people as possible, expecting nothing in return. Many times we get offended when we're speaking kindness and love to someone and they grumble or snap back. Their response should not affect us. We are called to love. The seeds of kindness and love WILL affect others, even though we don't see it at the time. So don't get offended at someone's reaction. Just love.

May 25

What's our purpose and mission today? We should begin each day with a desire to serve God, which includes others around us. To do His will, is to love and help others. If we desire for God to take us to the next level in our life, we must determine how that promotion will involve ministering to others. God's will for us isn't isolation, but serving others through His love. Let's touch someone's life today!

May 26

In our Journey with God, there are times when we "blow it" and times when we think or do "stupid." But God, in his mercy and grace, forgives and helps us get back on track. Remember the hymn, "Mercy there was great and grace was 'free'…at Calvary" We don't have to 'earn' His grace, so let's quit beating ourselves up when we stumble. Let's stand up, dust ourselves off, and keep walking toward the cross. We WILL win!

May 27

Today's message is a reminder. Prayer changes EVERYTHING!! When you feel you're stuck, bogged down, up against a wall, etc., pray with strong faith believing for a miracle! He will make a way where there seems to absolutely be no way! He's the God of the possible when it seems impossible! Don't lose your faith in Him. Pray! He can and WILL provide, "if" you'll put faith and trust in your prayers!

May 28

"Take up thy cross and follow me, I heard my Master say.... Wherever He leads, I'll go…" I love this hymn as it's a reminder that God is calling us to a closer walk with Him, a Walk of love. We don't have to "do anything" first, just come to Him as we are. He's waiting with open arms to receive us. Today, come to Him with your hurts, burdens, anger, frustrations, sins, etc and allow His love to change you. He will...

May 29

When we "sell out" to God, it means no longer are we in charge of our lives. (That's a relief) We must learn to listen and follow His voice, learning to follow His will, not ours. Many people are like bumper cars bouncing and bumping into every wall. God has a chosen a clear path for us to follow. Let's surrender our will to Him and listen. His plans are much better than ours. Amen!

May 30

How can I touch someone's life today?" "What can I say or do to make a difference?" These are the thoughts we should pray about each day. God never wants us to waste a single day. He has called us to be a beacon light in a world of darkness. SOMEONE needs hope...SOMEONE needs love..SOMEONE needs JESUS... Let God use you today to make a difference....That, my friend, is ministry.

May 31

When we surrender to God, He'll take us where we are and use us to touch others. Even when we feel like a complete failure and feel we have "blown" it, God will turn it around and use us. In the Bible, He used imperfect people to make a difference. He just needs a willing soul that will say "yes, Lord"...Today, be that person who says, "Take me Lord, I'm yours." You won't be disappointed.

June 1

There are times in our walk with God that we might desire to revert back to old thinking and feel that we must perform for God, or we're not "good" enough to be blessed. That mentality doesn't come from God. We don't "earn" his blessings by being good, we are His children, saved by grace! We do things for our children because we 'love' them.....Abba Father (Daddy) loves us! Matthew 7: 11 If you, then, though you are evil, know how to give good gifts to your children, how much more will our Father in heaven give good gifts to those who ask him!

June 2

What a great day to be thankful! On our way to God's "promise land" we must learn to enjoy the journey. There are lessons of faith and trust to be learned when we're walking through the "wilderness". Even when we have to go through a storm, we must learn to trust and be thankful He is with us each step. Today, thank Him for what you DO have and what He WILL do. "Faith, Trust, and Thankfulness." Psalm 100: 4 Enter His gates with thanksgiving and his courts with praise; give thanks to him and praise his name.

June 3

We mustn't be concerned when someone talks about us. To get upset or angry with the intention of retaliating is "drama". Allowing situations and remarks to roll off our shoulders is victory for us. People even talked about Jesus. Let's keep our eyes on God, and don't be moved by what others think or say. Pray for clean hands and a pure heart, loving those who "persecute" us with words. Rise above!!

June 4

If we're looking for God to promote us, then we need to begin to go the extra mile where we are. Some people are sitting on the side–lines waiting for their 'big moment', when they just need to be a good Christian team–player. Let's be diligent and faithful in the small things, so God will reward and promote us to higher levels. If we want promotion, we should strive to have a Christ-like work ethic.

June 5

Decide today that nothing, no matter what happens, or who tries to stand in your way, NOTHING will separate you from the love of your Father! The devil will try many schemes to distract and discourage you! But, we know his schemes! We will not take our eyes off Jesus! We will walk in faith toward God, and we WILL experience victory in our lives!! "Greater is He that is within me, than he that is in the world!" Amen!

June 6

As Christians, we can go to bed at night with peace knowing that if we didn't wake up in this world, we would be with Jesus for eternity. This confidence is a gift that non–Christians don't have. How frightening to know that if we died today, we wouldn't know our future. Thank you God for salvation that is based on faith in you and not on works. We don't have to "earn" salvation; it's a gift for the asking. We love you God

June 7

There's no true happiness outside of Jesus. I remember the old rock song, "I can't get no satisfaction." If we're looking at every avenue to bring us happiness, it won't happen. Only superficial.. When we turn to God and say, "I'm yours", He begins to mold us into the image of Jesus, giving us peace, love, and happiness. If you're tired of being unhappy, turn to Jesus. Another old song that speaks to us is, "Only Jesus Can Satisfy Your Soul."

June 8

Romans 8: 38) "For I am convinced that neither death nor life, neither angels nor demons, neither the present nor the future, nor any powers, neither height nor depth, nor anything else in all creation, will be able to separate us from the love of God that is in Christ Jesus our Lord." Decide today that you will never leave nor forsake God! The sufferings you have experienced will draw you closer to your Father, if you will allow. He loves YOU!

June 9

God's Word tells us that we are made in His image, so why do some people envision God to be a cloud of smoke or some mythical image sitting on a throne? He's real, and we favor Him. He's almighty God, Savior, Daddy, Friend, Redeemer and He desires a relationship with us. Yes, He wants to talk to us and for us to talk back. Today, spend some time with God. He's NEVER too busy for His children!

June 10

It's so important to begin our day with Jesus. It's like taking your morning medicine. If the doctor prescribes medicine to be taken in the mornings to keep us healthy and alive, that's what's what we need to do. Our great Physician has prescribed time with Him in the mornings also. This spiritual "medicine" gives us strength to face the day with victory. Let's take our Jesus meds daily to keep us strong!

June 11

When you're living for God and know His Word, you realize that you don't need to compromise or settle for second best. God's heart is to prosper and give us the very best. We have to change our mind–set from "I probably don't deserve this" to "I'm God's child and He loves and desires to prosper me!" We are children of the KING! Royalty. Let's put to rest the pauper mentality and believe God for the best in every aspect of our life..

June 12

Many times we question God "why" we have to work in certain environments. Can't we see that we are placed in specific situations to shine the light of Jesus? We're probably the only living Bible the lost will read. Yes, our lives. How we live and handle situations is an important witness to others. Instead of complaining about our jobs, let's be thankful God is using us today! Shine your light!

June 13

Sowing and reaping in God's Word applies to every aspect of our lives. Whatever we sow, whether it's prayer, financial giving, the way we treat others, truthfulness, etc., we will reap. So, if we desire to be blessed, then we should sow blessings into someone's life. More prayer equals more results. Today, let's ask God to show us areas of our life to sow. When we obey God, we get to reap the benefits!

June 14

The most spiritual growth we experience is when storms are raging against us. The only way you can become an expert sailor is to learn to guide your boat during a storm. This applies to our spiritual lives. Some believe that becoming a Christian makes you immune to problems. Not so. We must learn to trust God in our storms. Learning to be an over comer is growth! Remember He is ALWAYS with us!

June 15

God is calling us to surrender every aspect of our lives. Many believe this means they will end up with no life, which is just the opposite. When we surrender to our Father, our life just begins! He replaces the yuck with newness and joy! God is a God of 'new beginnings!' Yes, no matter your past, God can and WILL turn it around. The joy of the Lord is new every morning! Start today & give Him your all.

June 16

What are the signs of spiritual immaturity? One that gets offended easily and one who's emotions go up and down throughout the day (moody). To correct the problem, we must grow in Christ through studying God's Word, making it part of our life, and balancing the Word with prayer. Using this spiritual formula, we'll see a major growth spurt so when the storms hit, we will be able to stand stronger. Amen!

June 17

Ps. 115:14– "The Lord shall increase me more and more, me and my children." Wow, what a benefit package offered to the children of God. We must take advantage of this offering and receive it, not allowing the devil to talk us out of it. If you hear a voice telling you that you don't deserve it, please know that it's not God's voice. God's Word is full of blessings and prosperity. Listen to His voice.

June 18

There are times when we mess up, but God in His love forgives us when we repent (grace) and encourages us to continue moving forward. We should learn from our mistakes, with the goal of turning any weakness into strength. That's called spiritual growth. Our wisdom comes from studying the Word, praying, and hearing His voice, which will keep us obedient and on the right path.

June 19

What is our purpose today? God's will is for us to understand His purpose for our lives. His purpose will always involve giving of ourselves. When you allow God to use you, He will provide opportunities for you to touch someone's life. We are called to pray for, encourage, and love one another whether @ work, school, or home. Note: We are happiest when we're giving to others. Today, ask Him to use you..

June 20

Make today count for God. Don't waste a single day. Even when we're on vacation, we should never put God on the "back burner." We need his strength daily to have victory against the devil. 1 Peter 5: 8 Be self–controlled and alert. Your enemy, the devil prowls around like a roaring lion looking for someone to devour. Let's seek Him in prayer and find our purpose. Wouldn't it be hurtful and sad if our family ignored us, so let's not break God's heart by ignoring Him. He loves us. Talk to Him, He's all ears......

June 21

Asking God to bless our "enemies" can be difficult, especially when they have hurt us, but its God will and important enough that it's written in His Word. When you are hurt or angry from the attacks, ask God to bless them. By blessing them, you're saying "God, they belong to you so I place them in your hands." I promise, He will heal you of unforgiveness, and take care of the situation. God has your back! Romans 12:14 Bless those who persecute you. Bless and do not curse.

June 22

What a blessing to look back and reflect over our journey and see the hand of God in each phase of our life. No surprises to Him, God's never caught off guard. He knew the messes we would make before we were even born. Yet He loves us unconditionally. Out of that love, He puts people and situations in our path to help us grow to be like Jesus. Bottom line... our Father's love is for eternity! Trust Him today. Jeremiah 1: 5 Before I formed you in the womb I knew you, before you were born I set you apart. Friends, His plan for us is NEVER a mistake.

June 23

When someone verbally snaps at us, instead of lashing back as our emotions tell us to do, we should first pray and ask God to show us their heart. Many times what comes from their mouth is completely different from what was meant. Harsh words usually come from a wounded heart. Matthew 12: 34 For out of the overflow of the heart the mouth speaks. Let's be more understanding and pray for those with sharp, cutting words. May God heal their hurt. With this understanding and patience, we grow spiritually to be more like Jesus, not allowing words to offend us.

June 24

When we reflect on our childhood years, is there a positive or negative moment that stands out regarding our parents? Do we remember words they spoke or actions they took that affected us? We, as parents, teachers, and others who work with children are called to be Christian examples to them. Not just in what we say or how many times we attend church, but in how we act and react toward situations. Children and teens are always observing and learning from our mentorship. Today let them see Jesus in us. What great evangelism!

June 25

As we face life's storms, we should look for Jesus walking on the water. Yes, large waves can cause fear of drowning, but Jesus is STANDING on those waves in victory! The storm waves are under His feet! Also, many times the storm winds will actually drive us closer to shore where we can dock and "rest". Friends, no storm is too great for God to conquer! He'll make a way where there seems to be no way!

June 26

Today, let's be reminded to be thankful for God's favor. It's easy to grumble and complain about what we don't have. It seems that we always want more than we have. Maybe we should take time to look around giving God thanks for what we DO have, i.e. home to live in, car to drive, clothes to wear, and food to eat. Remember, it's okay to desire more as long as we are grateful. God loves His children and desires to give us His favor. Let's give thanks with a grateful heart for what we have, and by faith expect His favor!

June 27

Let's be reminded to be thankful for God's favor. It's easy to grumble and complain about what we don't have. Maybe we should look around and give God thanks for what we DO have, i.e. home to live in, car to drive, clothes to wear, food to eat. God loves His children and desires to give us His favor. Let's give thanks with a grateful heart, and by faith expect His favor!

June 28

When God places dream/desires in us, we shouldn't allow anything to dampen those dreams. We should get up every morning thanking Him 'in faith' that these dreams/desires WILL come to pass. No matter how big or small our dream is, no matter our circumstance, age, race, or financial situation, God can and will make a way where there seems to be no way. Don't stop believing in your dream! Faith = believing

June 29

Being a Christian isn't always easy in this sinful world. We must not compromise or water down our beliefs but stand strong with our eyes and hearts on Jesus. In His earthly ministry, Jesus walked in love but did not compromise. Friends, God rewards the faithful! As we seek Him in worship and prayer, His strength will rise within us and we will become more Christ–like. Today, keep your eyes and heart steadfast on Jesus and do not compromise His Word!

June 30

Pray for America and Israel. God's Word is clear, "I will bless those that bless Israel and curse those that curse Israel." America must pray for and support Israel if we're going to be blessed. Today, pray for the families that lost from 9/11 and continue praying for protection on this country. We are, and must continue to be "One Nation Under God!" Amen!

July 1

God isn't just interested in the "spiritual" aspect of our lives i.e. church, etc. but also in our daily activities. He desires to bless us and open doors for us to make an impact on the world for Him. Whether it's school, work, play etc. He desires for us to be like Jesus so we can touch lives wherever we go, whatever we do. Yes, He cares about sports, hunting, relationships, job promotions, etc.....If it involves us, He cares.

July 2

It's refreshing to understand God's Word knowing we don't have to earn His love. Nothing we do will cause our Father to love us more or less. It's unconditional. His love is like a big ocean wave that covers over us and washes away the sins that we have repented of. That's love.. That's Jesus.. God desires to set us free from condemnation and guilt. Let's walk in freedom knowing His love is not earned, but a "gift" ....

July 3

Sometimes as Christians, we spend too much time trying to convince others of our faith when we really need to just walk the walk. Many do not care about words. They want to see action. How we live and handle situations like Jesus is more evangelistic than words. Today, let's be aware that the way we live is an open book for others to read. Are the chapters of our book drawing others to Jesus?

July 4

God bless this great nation! What a special day to celebrate freedom, enjoy great home–cooked food, and fellowship with family and friends. Let's take a moment to thank God for all he's done in our country. Even though we can get frustrated and discouraged with our nation or leaders, we still must be thankful we are free and not living under suppression. We have freedom of speech and religion. Many nations don't enjoy that freedom. Today, let's give thanks for our nation, continually praying that God will protect us.

July 5

Worry can quietly creep into our lives without a warning and next thing we know, we're not sleeping well trying to solve our problems! God lovingly instructs us to lay our worries and concerns at His feet, trusting Him to take care of it. His Word says He will lead and guide so why do we feel the need to "help" God solve the problems? God loves us but doesn't need our help. Our job is to trust, obey, & walk in peace.

July 6

Mt 6:33–"Seek first the kingdom of God AND His righteousness, and all theses things will be given to you as well." This verse tells us if we will seek God with our whole hearts and live for Him, He will hear "all" our requests and bless us. It's really not difficult. He loves and desires a relationship with us and nothing is too great or difficult for Him. Do we deserve it? Sure, we're His children! Meditate on this verse and gain victory!

July 7

Sometimes living in a 'NOW' generation makes it difficult for us to trust God and His timing. We get used to wanting instant results regarding technology, etc. that waiting on God's timing frustrates us. We must understand that He is NEVER late answering prayers. Waiting teaches us to trust our Father, knowing that He's doing what's best for us. Taking situations into our own hands without God's leading can cause unhappy results.

July 8

When we pray, we must pray with determination and confidence that God doesn't have a deaf ear and hears every word we speak. The Word says our faith can move mountains! Can we have that type of faith? Yes! Faith comes from hearing and believing God's Word. Jesus said we would do greater miracles than him, so let's "believe" His Word and expect miracles! Never stop praying! Prayer changes everything!!!

July 9

It's amazing to see God's hand at work. Things we're not even aware of, He's doing out of love. How thankful I am that Teri has always had such a strong desire to take family pictures. Over the years we would roll our eyes and groan over her saying, "Just one more picture." Now that Steffan is in Heaven, I'm so thankful that God instilled that desire in her. Its comfort and healing. God is always taking care of us.

July 10

Waiting on God is important. We see in God's Word where Abraham desperately wanted a son, and finally took things into his own hands and ended up with Ishmael. Big mistake! Waiting on God can be tough, but the end result will be His best. After Abraham repented and waited on God, He and Sarah birthed Isaac, God's choice. Whether it's a job, or a lifetime mate, wait on God! He knows best!

July 11

"The Joy of the Lord is My Strength" When we experience major storms, God doesn't expect us to jump & down with a joy–filled laughing heart at that moment, but joy & peace comes from knowing, that "Though I walk through the valley of death (Storm), I will fear no evil, for you are with me.." The Word says that "Joy comes in the morning.." When storms hit, don't feel guilty that your instant joy isn't there..Just rest in God and trust.

July 12

As we weather through our storms, trusting God each step of the way, we come through the storm wiser, closer to God, more compassionate, and Christ–like. We learn to be more experienced each storm we face. God will use us, as a result, to help those experiencing a storm in their lives. As we draw closer to our Father, we will become stronger and the storms less frightning. Remember, He is with us each step of the way.

July 13

"Great is thy faithfulness. Morning by morning new 'mercies' I see. ALL I have needed He has provided, great is thy faithfulness......" I see a loving God who loves His children. He strengthens, comforts, wipes away tears, equips, provides and so much more.

"Oh how I love Jesus, because He first loved me..." May your love for Him put a song in your heart....

July 14

"When We All get To Heaven.." Yes, it will be wonderful... Eternity..But while we're still here, God doesn't want us sitting down 'waiting' to get there..We must make the most of each day, sharing Jesus and living a testimony for Him. We should also make memories each day. Each day is valuable and has purpose. Let's not waste a single day, but love & enjoy family and friends, live like Jesus, and make memories.

July 15

When God calls us to a task, we mustn't quit. In boxing, when the manager throws the towel in the ring, the fight is over...The opponent automatically wins.. Let's not throw our towel in. Yes, it can get weary and discouraging at times, but we must keep our focus on Jesus and finish the race (fight). I long to hear God say, "Well done my child." No matter what you're going through, don't give up!

July 16

"Like a bridge over troubled Water, I will ease your mind..." These lyrics are spiritually true. God will wipe away our tears, comfort us, and will be that bridge. If we'll trust in Him, He will carry us through the roughest storms. Remember the bridge (Jesus) protects us from the water and He will carry us when we can't take another step forward. There is hope, no matter how severe our storm is. Lean on and trust God.

July 17

We should be thankful for those who God places in our lives. There's reason and purpose. It's easy to take for granted family and close friends, but we need to thank God for them and know that God uses them to mold us into the character of Jesus. Thank you God for those you have given us, whether family or friends. Let's allow God to teach us to be more like Jesus by using those around us....

July 18

We've heard the slogan, "Stop and smell the roses." This is a true reminder to take moments in our busy lives to thank God for the many blessings He has given us. Also thanking Him for our family and friends. Time on this earth is short. We mustn't waste a single day angry at those we love. Pray for the special people in your life, & thank God for them. Tell and show them you love them.

July 19

Why do we seem to have a problem hearing God's voice and obeying? Maybe our spiritual ears have become hardened and deaf to the voice of the Holy Spirit. If we will learn to be sensitive to God's voice by spending more time with Him, we can avoid "spinning our wheels" and wasting time. Remember, God doesn't want to confuse us. 'Listen' to His voice for direction. He's an excellent GPS!!

July 20

I think about a child who darts out in the street. If he has been trained to listen and obey, he will immediately stop upon hearing his parents' warning and his life will be saved. But the child who has tuned out his parents' warnings will be in danger. When we allow our hearts to get hardened and tune out God's voice, we put ourselves in dangerous situations. God's voice can save us, if we'll listen and obey.

July 21

We should never neglect our time with God at the beginning of our day. By doing so, we leave ourselves open for the devil to attack. Our guard is down and he takes advantage of the situation.

The next thing we know, we're losing our temper, yelling at others, and making poor choices. God desires to work in us daily, molding us into the image of Jesus, "if we'll allow." Beginning your day in prayer and worship will defeat the devil!

July 22

When we get verbally attacked, falsely accused, etc., by someone, we should stop before responding and ask the Holy Spirit to reveal their heart. Many times, we will see a hurting, wounded individual. Bullies usually have wounded hearts and attack to protect themselves. We should pray for those who say hurtful words, asking God to heal their hearts, and remembering that Jesus died for them also.......

July 23

As we pray, we must pray with determination and confidence that God doesn't have a deaf ear and hears every word we speak. The Word says our faith can move mountains! Can we have that type of faith? Yes! Faith comes from hearing and believing God's Word. Jesus said we would do greater miracles than him, so let's "believe" His Word and expect miracles! Never stop praying! Prayer changes everything!!!

July 24

Today we must choose....We can either begin our day complaining about facing another "yuk" day or we can begin by giving God thanks with a heart of Thanksgiving. It's obvious..Let's go with the second choice. This day will be what we make it. Let's grab a cup of coffee, ponder on the many answered prayers we have received, meditate on how good God has been to us, and get going! I choose to live a blessed life!

July 25

If we say we love Jesus and that God is first in our life, then we must walk the walk and live what we say. Saying one thing but doing another is like the old classic tale Jekyll and Hyde, which were two personalities living in one body. God, help us live our life so others may see Jesus in us. Help us to live what we say.... Amen!

July 26

Holy Spirit, please remind me throughout my day to reach out to someone in love whether it's a student for co-worker. Help us, oh Lord, to be more like Jesus in the way we live. Today isn't about me and my selfish desires, but more about me serving and giving to others who are hurting and without Jesus. Today, let's choose to make a difference in someone's life.. Love unconditionally....

July 27

Why do we tend to hold grudges and unforgiveness toward people when God is so clear in His Word that we MUST forgive? We should follow the example of Jesus as He hung on the cross and asked His Father God to forgive those that had done Him wrong. Wow! Now who are we to get so bent out of shape over trivial matters and hold unforgiveness in our heart? Let's decide to follow the steps of Jesus and forgive. We will have peace in our heart knowing we have obeyed God....

July 28

In the hustle and bustle of our busy lives, let's not forget our loving Father who cares so much about us. We need to make time for Him whether it's in our car, at home, work, etc. It doesn't have to be just at church once a week. Listen, we need His guidance. We're not smart enough to make it successfully on our own (some may think they are). The Word tells us that the Holy Spirit will lead us into all truth....It is a win/win for us.

July 29

Remember the old chorus we used to sing in church, 'Change my heart, O God, make it ever new. Change my heart, O God, may

I be like You. For You are the potter and I am the clay. Mold me and make me, this is what I pray.' Let this chorus be our heart's desire today…May we submit ourselves to the potter's wheel as He molds us, like clay, into the image of Jesus.

July 30

The greatest and most valuable gift we can give to those going through a storm, is love and prayer. Knowing that prayer changes everything, we can help them in a greater way by praying. They probably don't need our sympathy as much as prayer. God can calm the storms if we will seek His face so today, give someone you know and love the gift of praying for them, believing for a miracle!

July 31

If someone is surprised that we're a Christian, especially after being around us for any period of time, we should take a long look in the mirror at our fruit of the spirit listed in the book of James. As a result of spending quality time with God, we should walk in love, joy, peace, kindness, etc. Our fruit is the greatest witness to the lost as they watch us act and react over situations. Walk in the love of Jesus today..The lost are watching..

August 1

Sometimes the devil makes us feel worthless to God's kingdom. We might not have a world–wide ministry, be a corporate president, etc. but we should remember the little boy in the Bible with the small basket of bread and fish that Jesus used to feed 5 thousand. His small gift impacted thousands. God uses 'ordinary' people to do extraordinary feats. Let's offer ourselves to God and allow Him to use us!

August 2

Paraphrased from Charles Stanley: Instead of asking God, "What do you want me to do about this situation?", we should be asking

God, "What are you going to do about this situation?" Honestly, as smart as we think we are, God doesn't need our help in solving our problems. He just needs a surrendered heart and will. If we will trust Him, He'll take it from there and handle it much better than we could imagine.

August 3

If there's something we're not happy about, we should pray instead of complaining. Complaining and criticizing NEVER solves the problem. Let's focus on 'results' through prayer. Mountains (problems) can be removed through praying in faith, 'locked' doors can be opened, miracles can happen, and family members can be saved through prayer! Prayer changes EVERYTHING! So what are we waiting for? Let's begin to pray and expect results. Our Father is listening..

August 4

When God chooses someone for a task, rest assured He isn't concerned about degrees and education, nor moved by extraordinary talent. God always looks at the heart of an individual. David was only a shepherd boy, Moses couldn't speak well, Abraham was elderly, Esther was young and inexperienced, etc. The list goes on....Let's surrender our hearts and will to God, allowing Him to use us today!

August 5

When we make a list to God i.e. "I will never again, or I won't do this anymore" we are setting ourselves up for discouragement & failure. Man–made rules of the flesh ultimately fail, i.e. "dieting." Our main goal should be to strive for holiness by spending more time with our Father, allowing Him to transform us into the image of Jesus. The closer we become to God, the less we lust after the flesh. All things are possible through Jesus..

August 6

Nothing helps erase fear from a child more than being wrapped in their parent's arms and feeling protected. That's a beautiful example of our Father God. Each of us face fear in our lives at some point. We must know in our hearts that we're not alone. Ps 23: "I will fear no evil, for You, my God are with me." God WILL protect us. Today, walk with assurance that Jesus is with you each step you take. "Blessed assurance, Jesus is mine...."

August 7

When we think about our time on earth compared to eternity, which has no end, we realize it's only a drop of water in a big ocean. As a Christian, our struggles, worries, hurts, anger, wounds, etc. will one day vanish, never to attack us again. As we deal today with issues that may seem overwhelming, let's keep our mind on the end result of our journey...Heaven. God desires for us to live in victory never losing sight of Heaven...

August 8

Many people relate to God as they were raised. Some people who grew up under strict rules or abusive controlling parents, may think God is abusive and angry most of the time. It's important to look into the Word and see the true character of God. His Word says He (God) is love...forgiving, and full of grace and mercy. I choose to believe His Word. As a Christian, I should desire my character to be the same as Jesus. Today, study the Word and learn the true nature of God.

August 9

When God places us in a job or situation, we must know it's for a reason. We should look for opportunities to serve Him and be a shining light to those around us. We should also stay in that position until God moves us. No job or situation is perfect, but we should shine while we're there without murmuring or complaining. If we can affect someone's life for Jesus, it's worth it. Today, look for your opportunity to shine!

August 10

God always lovingly speaks truth to His children as the truth sets us free. We could experience more victory in our lives if we would speak and walk in truth, allowing our yes to be yes and no be no. Many are afraid of offending others so they choose to "water down" truth. When it comes to God's Word, we must speak truth in love and not compromise. Many are waiting to be set free.. Today, speak God's truth..

August 11

Have you ever been tormented by the devil on your past? He (Satan) loves to keep reminding us about our sins and "screw ups." But, haven't we ALL sinned and come short of the glory of God? Doesn't God's Word say He (God) forgives us and remembers no more? We musn't listen to the voice of the past. God is concerned about the NOW and not moved on 'where we've been', but on 'where we are NOW.'

August 12

I love the old Hymn, "Let Others See Jesus in You." Today, in everything we do, everywhere we go, let others see Jesus in us. How we decide to act or react regarding a situation is important to our testimony for God. Spending time with our Father, will help us walk in love and "LOVE" (Jesus) changes lives. Let's ask God to fill us with His love so others can see Jesus in us...

August 13

More and more youth are being turned off by religion and denominations. What they are yearning for is a deeper relationship with God. If we, as adults, could get past forcing our denominational beliefs on our children and show them the love of Jesus Christ, we would see more youth saved. It's time

SURVIVING THE STORMS OF LIFE

we began walking, talking, and living the life of Jesus. Truth + relationship = Jesus.

August 14

God's Word is clear and encouraging. He has prosperous plans for each of us. "If" we'll trust and allow Him to lead us, we can be blessed in our jobs, marriage, family, etc. Taking matters into our own hands and making our own decisions can create mistakes that we'll regret. Today, let's choose to trust Him with all our heart, quit trying to figure it out or help God, praise Him for what He'll do, and watch Him bring forth a miracle in our lives....

August 15

Many believe that ministry is reserved for pastors, ministers of music, and youth pastors. God teaches us in His Word that we are ALL called to serve in ministry. Yes, right where we are! God places us in various job positions to be a witness with our lives to the lost. He desires for us to work and live in the world and show the lost, the love of Jesus with the way we live.....Today, shine for Him!

August 16

It's sad to see people without a relationship with Jesus constantly looking for something or someone to fill the void. This could result in numerous job changes, moving locations, or continual relationship changes. There's an old Bill Gaither song, "Only Jesus can Satisfy your Soul". Only He can fill the void. Living a life of love (God) keeps us content and blessed in our walk with our Father.

August 17

Today, let's give God thanks for his goodness and for what He's doing in our lives. A thankful heart creates joy in our lives and the "Joy of the Lord is our strength." Our strength from God will bring victory in our lives, not defeat. Let's begin by "Entering

His gates with thanksgiving and to His courts with praise." Let's choose to celebrate His goodness with a thankful heart...

August 18

It's easy to sit back and become critical of others. Of course, we're NOT gossiping, just "sharing". God has instructed us in His Word to cease from such talk and behavior. When we slander or gossip about someone, we must remember they are God's child and just because they don't do things OUR way, doesn't mean they're wrong. Let's ask God to forgive us for being critical and love, accept, and appreciate one another.

August 19

When a child scrapes his knee or gets hurt in some way, they usually run to their parent, desiring to be held and comforted. That's a beautiful scenario of our Father God. He is always waiting with open arms to hold and comfort us when we're hurt. Many people hunger to know what God is really like...He gives a beautiful description in His Word of himself through the image of Jesus. God is LOVE...and He loves US..

August 20

There is no "past" for believing Christians. We have a present and future, but our past has been washed under the blood of Jesus. We shouldn't worry about our past. Gone....Forgotten.. God tells us in His Word, that He forgives our sins when we repent, and remembers them no more. Gone...Forgotten...We shouldn't allow the devil to remind us of our past nor should we live in guilt of past living. Gone..Forgotten. It's a new day and we are free!

August 21

Our relationship with God should be one of thankfulness and humility. God can't use us when we become prideful about our knowledge and experience. The more we learn from His Word, the more humble we should become. We began to realize that we can do nothing worthwhile on our own, but great feats through Jesus. Giving God the glory, remaining humble about our knowledge will open the door to reach many....

August 22

We should learn to listen and obey God in regards to church membership. As God led the children of Israel out of Egypt to the promised land, He will lead us also. Sometimes that could be to another church, but just because someone offends us or the leadership doesn't do things the way we think they should, is no reason to move. We must listen to God and follow His voice, not our own. Blessings..

August 23

Worshipping, praying and loving others opens doors of opportunity to minister to those around us. Sometimes it's a hug, smile, or greeting that offers hope. God knows what He's doing, and sometimes will use the simple things to touch others. Today, let's worship, pray and allow the love of God to flow through us to touch someone's life. Worship, prayer and love......... Life changing....

August 24

Don't give up believing for your miracle, whether big or small! God is in the miracle working business and desires to bless us with the 'impossible.' When our backs are against the wall with no way out and situations seem hopeless, our trust must "kick in" believing for a miracle. We must never give up trusting God! He loves us and desires to answer our prayers, whether big or small. Today is OUR miracle day!!

August 25

"I am redeemed from the curse of the law. I am redeemed from poverty. I am redeemed from sickness. I am redeemed from spiritual death" (Gal. 3:13). God's Word says we are free! "Jesus paid it all." Since He paid the ultimate price (death) for us, then we should walk in victory and not allow the devil to talk us back into these areas of defeat. Let's keep our eyes on Jesus and walk in freedom! We are redeemed!

August 26

"Yes, even though I walk through the valley of the shadow of death (storms), I will NOT fear evil, for You my Father God, are with me....Your rod and staff comfort me..." This verse doesn't say "if' we will experience storms. We must all travel through storms, but it's comforting to know that Jesus is with us even in the midst of the worst storm. Today, "Reach out to Jesus, He's reaching out to you.." Victory!

August 27

"Acceptance" As a Christian, we should learn through God's Word to love and accept one another. No two people think and act alike. We are ALL different. Sometimes we judge others because they aren't like–minded. Jesus instructed us to hate sin, but 'love' the sinner. To love is to accept them. We don't have to accept sin, but we should love and accept one another with the love of God. Let's be like Jesus!

August 28

God has called the church to be a gathering place to worship Him. It should also be an outreach to the lost. We need to resolve petty and religious, church differences and begin to walk in pure love with one another. We must offer hope (Jesus) to the hopeless. The feeling of 'ownership' of our church should be removed from our mind. It's God's house...Let's purpose to love one another unconditionally.

August 29

Truth (Jesus) is the key to setting us free in a world of lies. We must choose to not compromise or "water down" God's Word in order to please or to not offend others. We shouldn't make exceptions or excuses for the Word. Most people are hungry for the truth. Our churches should speak truth in love. Parents, children, employers, employees, government officials, etc. should speak and live in truth! Choose truth, choose freedom!

August 30

We should walk in confidence of who we are in Christ. We're God's children. With that privilege, comes benefits (Ps. 68:19). We have favor with God and man (Deut. 33:23). Today, let's expect favor from God AND those around us. Ps. 102:13 tells us this is our set time for favor! By faith, let's accept what belongs to us and don't allow the enemy to talk us out of our blessings. Yes, as His children we do deserve it!

August 31

Lord, use me today to love others unconditionally, even the unlovable. Help me make those around me feel special about who they are in Christ. Open my eyes to see the needs of others and the importance of helping. Teach me to lay my life at the foot of the cross and surrender my stubborn and selfish will. I desire to help others with the things I say and do. Use me God....Amen. What a great feeling to help others!

September 1

Prayer brings results! We don't just pray to "get", but we pray because we love God and desire a deeper relationship with Him. But because we spend time praying, believing His Word, and trusting Him, we receive benefits such as answers to our requests and open doors. God loves to bless His children! It's a win/win situation! Today, pray with confidence that God "Will make a way where there seems to be no way."

September 2

Today, we should make a decision to look for the positive in our situations instead of the negative. No situation is perfect. We should look for the good in people and situations instead of complaining. Some talk negative about their job, but still receive paychecks. Being a complainer isn't the character of Jesus. If we're not happy, we can make choices. But first we must adjust our attitude or we'll only repeat ourselves.

September 3

"This is the day the Lord has made, I will rejoice in it." We should learn to be thankful in EVERY situation. Thankful for what we have AND will have (Faith). Let's not waste time moaning and groaning over what we don't have, but rejoice in our Lord (praise). His Word says He will supply ALL our needs! He's our provider in EVERY area! Let's thank Him for what we have with great expectations of His blessings to come!

September 4

Pride has always been the biggest downfall of nations and leaders throughout history. We're familiar with the saying, "Pride goes before the fall." God has called us to be humble knowing that we're nothing without Him, but confident knowing that we can do ALL things through Him. When God blesses or promotes us to a higher level, we should be thankful AND humble. He's our source. Let's rely on Him!

September 5

The will of God is His Word, the Bible. When we pray for God's will to be done, it must align with scripture. The Bible is His will for us. He will not go against His Word. When we need to hear from God, we should meditate over His scriptures and allow the Holy Spirit to speak to us. His Word is powerful and can remove any mountains (obstacles) in our way, if we'll speak to that mountain in faith. Remember, faith is believing His Word!

September 6

"What can wash away my sins? Nothing but the blood of Jesus.." These lyrics are powerful. No matter what we've done, when we ask for forgiveness, He forgives and remembers no more. Our sins are covered with the blood that Jesus shed at Calvary. We don't have to live with guilt any longer. We must not allow Satan to steal our joy by reminding us of our past. We are free! Forgiven! New beginnings!

September 7

When we experience a major storm at sea (in our life), we can give up and never sail again, missing out on many adventures, or we can learn from our storm and continue sailing. When someone gets ready to sail for the first time, they would rather listen to one who has experience and has weathered the rough storms. No matter what you've gone through, allow God to use your experience to help others who are ready to sail.

September 8

We must be careful to not stop the flow of blessings in our lives due to gossiping or slandering others. Yes, our negative attitude can prevent us from walking in the blessings that God desires to give us. Let's hold our tongue and ask God to bless those that persecute us and not be concerned what others say or do. He will hear our heart and bless us. Blessed are the pure in heart......Let's allow His Word to change our attitude...

September 9

When we get wounded over a situation like death of a family member, sudden job loss, divorce, relationship breakup, etc. it leaves a void or a hole in us that ONLY Jesus can fill. Too often we try to fill the void with worldly remedies or substitutes that never work. This only creates a repetitive cycle...."Learning to Lean on Jesus" will fill that void and make us whole again. "Only Jesus can Satisfy Your Soul."

September 10

Some believe that Christianity is based on "do or earn" to be in God's favor. This false teaching can leave one exhausted and frustrated, not being able to match up to expectations. We are God's children and are loved because we belong to Him. It's a relationship built on "Love" (Jesus). His love is unconditional for EVERYONE and we don't have to "do or earn" to receive it. As a parent loves their child, He loves us...Unconditionally...

September 11

Thank you God for teaching us to follow Your ways, not our own. Thank you for teaching us to love others with no strings attached. Thank you for teaching us to accept others, realizing we can't change anyone. Thank you for teaching us to trust Your Word. You can move mountains that stand in our way. You can make a way when there seems to be no way. Thank you for miracles. Thank you for loving, forgiving, and blessing us...Amen..

September 12

When we ignore our time with God we can end up in a bad mood or agitated about everything and everyone. If we will worship and pray, He will mold us to be like Jesus, giving us peace, joy and love. When we're walking in peace, joy, and love, we're MUCH easier to be around. God can use us in a mighty way when we walk with Him. Let's "choose" to spend quality time with Him and allow Him to use us to touch others..

September 13

Our prayer and fellowship time with God is very important but should never be religious. Some days we might pray longer than others. We must remind ourselves we have a relationship with God built on love and faith, not how long we pray. Actually throughout the day we should fellowship with God at work, home, etc., being mindful of Him always. Today, let's not be religious and feel we have to punch a time clock regarding prayer. Just love Him....

September 14

True peace comes from God, and God only. The world tries to manufacture peace in various ways, but it's only superficial. Spending time with Him each morning sets the pace for a successful day. Reading God's Word and building our faith gives us a trust and calmness that helps us deal with people and situations. Today, take some time to seek God's face and walk in peace, joy, and love. He always brightens the day!

September 15

Who can we give attention to today? Who can we smile at and make feel important and worthy? Who can we give our ear to hear someone's problems? The more we learn from God and His Word, the more equipped we are to help someone who needs our help. We should look for opportunities to love others. This is called Christianity....

September 16

In the midst of the worst storms, even when the rain is beating us in the face and the wind and waves are about to wreck our ship, look into the storm and we'll see Jesus. He hasn't left our side for even a moment. By faith, let's grab the hem of His garment and refuse to let go. No matter how bad our storm appears, Jesus is stronger. He WILL carry us through....Let's keep our eyes on Jesus and not the storm.

September 17

It's disappointing to see some Christians unconcerned about others, self–centered, whining and complaining, and priding themselves that they will argue with anyone who crosses them. Christianity is Christ–likeness. We should strive to live the love–filled life of Jesus. If it shocks someone that we're a Christian, we should take a long look in the mirror and re–evaluate our life. It's time that we live the life of a true Christian...loving others.

September 18

Why is it so important to love others? When we choose to love, we're giving them God because "God is love." It's evangelizing, the greatest gift we can give to those who are lost....Jesus (Love). Evangelism has a greater success rate when we witness in love instead of trying to force God on someone. Spending time daily with our Father in worship and prayer is the key to a life of love. God is love.... LOVE someone today....

September 19

Sometimes we hear, "Can't wait til I get away from these people." or "When I start my new job I won't have to deal with this anymore." etc. There's an old saying, "The grass is only greener on the other side on top of the septic tank." Bottom line: There are problems and conflict wherever we go because we deal with people who think different than us. We must learn to accept others, act/react like Jesus and be thankful for what we have.

September 20

As we meditate on God's Word, we see that Jesus paid the price for our freedom. He came to show us salvation and mentor us for a life of victorious living. His suffering from His arrest and death on the cross (which He chose to do out of His love for us) was to give us life and life more abundantly. When we face storms, we should know in our hearts that its only temporary and God has equipped us with His strength to have victory! "Jesus paid it all......all to Him I owe."

September 21

When we think about eternity, we realize just how short our time on earth is. Becoming a Christian is the most important step in our lives! Parents should make it the top priority when raising children. Giving them Jesus, is giving them the gift of eternal life....There is NO greater gift. Let's pray and share Jesus in love to those around us. Remember, we can't force salvation on someone, but we can share the love of God, offering hope in Jesus.

September 22

There have been times in our lives when we questioned our purpose in life. What are we really here for? Yes, we've all experienced those thoughts but God has called each of us for His purpose. Yes, there is a reason that He created us. We have a purpose, a mission. How do we discover this calling? By spending time with Him daily because His Word says the Holy Spirit will lead us into ALL truth. He will lead and guide us to our purpose. Seek Him today!

September 23

If we say we trust God in ALL matters, then why do we feel the need to help God 'make it happen'? Our job is to trust, believe, and praise Him for what He's doing. God, without our help, can "make a way when there seems to be no way." We should submit our self–will to God knowing that He sees the big picture and knows way more than we do. He loves us and has our best interest at heart. Today, let's trust and believe Abba Father cause "Father knows best ...."

September 24

It's a wonderful feeling to know that we don't have to 'earn' God's love. Nothing we do or say will make Him love us more. We are His children whom He loves unconditionally. Some religions relate being a Christian to earning badges or climbing a success ladder to spiritually 'arrive'. This isn't the case with God. Jesus paid the ultimate price so we can go before God's throne and submit our request. What a relationship....What a savior..What a Father...

September 25

Lord, teach us to look at the heart of those who agitate us. Help us to see past the irritating flesh that we have to deal with and see what you see, your child.. Teach us to love the unlovable and forgive those that have hurt us. We desire to be like Jesus and be patient with those who "grind" on our nerves. It's not about us and our way, but about you working their lives. Remind us to daily pray for those around us.. "All things are possible"....Amen...

September 26

"Bridge Over Troubled Water" is such a meaningful and spiritual song. When we experience storms that try to wreck our lives and make us feel all alone, it's important to trust Jesus as He can and will provide situations and people to help us get through our crisis (storm), if we'll trust Him. Many times these people and situations are temporary. God provides them as a "bridge" to help us. Our provider....Yes, He truly loves and cares for us.

September 27

We should be thankful for our friends and family. Life is short, therefore making memories and enjoying each moment with those close to us is important. Too many people waste away their lives waiting for their 'ship' to arrive. Let's savor each day/ moment we have and enjoy each blessing that God gives us. Let's not forgo that hug or smile that someone needs. Remember, a thankful, joyful heart in God is our spiritual strength. Today, be blessed and enjoy..

September 28

A storm in our life, is like a sailor on a ship. When we watch a storm in a pirate movie, we see the sailors working hard to maintain the ship. They follow directions from the captain to keep from sinking. This relates to our lives in our personal storms. We find ourselves through each storm we face, better trained, equipped, and seasoned. The captain of the ship represents Jesus. If we'll listen to His voice and follow His directions, our ship won't wreck or sink.

September 29

When we lose someone in our lives, there is no set time for healing. It's a life journey. There are good moments and some "not so good moments". But as we trust God for healing, He soothes and mends the heart. Even with the "joy of the Lord" we'll always wear a scar from our wound. But Jesus also wears scars from the nails driven through his hands and feet. The scars remind us to keep moving forward knowing that He walks beside us all the way.

September 30

Some people view God according to how they were treated by their fathers. There are some who were abused growing up, who view God as a mean Zeus type God who zaps people when he's angry. Many, who were abandoned by their fathers, feel God doesn't care about them. We need to study His Word and see 'truth" that God is LOVE. Love doesn't abandon or abuse..Love is unconditional.....He is LOVE.

October 1

One of the greatest weapons we have to fight the devil with is praise and worship to our Heavenly Father. Instead of getting mad at the devil, we should worship God with confidence that He will fight our battle and remove the mountain in our way. Satan is real and he comes to "steal, kill, and destroy/." He's like a "roaring lion, seeking who he can devour." BUT, "Greater is He (Jesus) that is in us, than he (devil) that is in the world." Let's praise and worship our Father today. It brings victory to our lives...

October 2

As Christians, we should walk with our eyes completely on Jesus. It reminds us of a horse with blinders. The blinders keep him focused on what's ahead and prevents him from looking to the right or left. There is a lot of distraction around us that could pull our attention away from God, if we're not careful. It's important that we stay focused on Jesus who loves us and has plans for us.

October 3

We mustn't be moved by what others say or do. Sometimes comments from others can cause us to lose our enthusiasm and create discouragement. We must keep our eyes focused on Jesus and the goals that lie ahead. God NEVER discourages. No matter what comments are made, we must believe God's Word. Remember, "Truth" (Jesus) always sets us free and makes a way where there seems to be no way...When others say it will never happen, trust God.. He's the God of Miracles!

October 4

What is our mission for today? The more time we spend with God, the more Love (Jesus) we have to give to others. When you draw closer to God, you develop a heart to love. We also become more mission minded, wanting to help and do for others. This is the heart of Jesus. Making the needs of others a priority helps us stay focused on what's spiritually important. Today, let's pray and ask God to develop a serving heart in us to help and love others. This is great evangelism, to be like Jesus.

October 5

If our entire road was snow–filled and we couldn't get out, wouldn't be easier for us to call for a snow plow instead of taking things in our own hands and attempting to dig the entire road ourselves? This represents us.. If we will learn to call upon the Lord to solve our problems, not only will He do a better job but we won't wear ourselves out. Learning to lean on Jesus.......much better.....

October 6

Today, let's choose to walk in "Victory" regarding every aspect of our lives. Let's believe God for miracles in our work place, family, friends, etc. If we want change, we should pray AND believe. "Prayer changes EVERYTHING!" If we work with someone or have a family member who drives us nuts, we should pray and ask God to bless them, giving us patience and love for them. Believe and have faith in Him that He hears our prayers and WILL answer!!....VICTORY!

October 7

The closer we become to God, the more love we have to share and many times His presence in our life will quite us. Yes, basking in his love will sometimes close our mouths so we can hear His voice. During this time of spiritual fellowship, opinions and questions aren't important. Maybe if we would seek His face more, there would be less arguments and more love and tolerance for one another......... Hmmmm, His presence, a peaceful place to stay.....

October 8

"Mercy there was great and grace was free." When we sin and ask God to forgive us, it's done! We don't have to keep begging and asking because it's done! The blood of Jesus covers over our sins, making us clean. We don't have to walk in guilt and shame.... God's mercy and grace is "new every morning"....No one is sinless, no one is perfect. We've all blown it....Since God shows us mercy and grace with a forgiving heart, shouldn't we do the same to others who hurt us? Let's be like Jesus.......

October 9

When circumstances don't always go our way, we begin to blame God for not coming through, when we actually need to thank Him for a much better plan on the way. His timing is perfect and He knows what's best for us! We must trust Him with all areas of our lives and keep reminding ourselves we are His children. We are cherished...we are loved.....and we are His heirs..

October 10

When we face those times that we feel no one cares and we're all alone with our world seemingly crushing in, let's be reminded that Jesus paid the price on the cross for our feelings and emotions. Because of the cross, we don't have to be defeated! God is with us and will NEVER leave our side. This confidence will get us through the next storm that we face. Expect a miracle today knowing that He loves us. Remember, no storm is too big for our God!

October 11

God loves us just the way we are! We don't have to earn His love by doing. It's unconditional. Of course, as we spend time with Him, He will mold us into His image, but our Heavenly Father doesn't work on a point system. There is NO earning His love. His Word tells us to come as we are. Oh, He loves us so. Let's quit trying hard to be 'good' and just begin to love Him with a desire to know Him better. He'll do the rest. That's His promise.

October 12

God instructs us to love Him and our neighbors. Yes, we are commanded to love those who have hurt us or can't stand us! Rejection and hatred from others is not our concern. We must love the unlovable unconditionally the way Jesus did. If we desire to be blessed, we must choose to love everyone. This decision to love will give us joy and a peace knowing we are obeying God and planting a seed in others.

October 13

We mustn't give up on prayer. God is doing much more through our prayers than what we can see. Don't give up on His promises. The dreams we have that have come from God will become reality.

When we face those times that we want to give up, let's look into His Word and be encouraged. The shepherd boy, David didn't run from the giant Goliath, so we shouldn't run either. Keep believing and trusting Him…He has heard your prayers….He loves YOU!

October 14

God is LOVE…When we get to heaven, we will be awestruck at the love He has for us…It's difficult, living in our earthly bodies, to comprehend the depth of love He has for His children. We will understand that love completely when we join Him in Heaven. But for now, we're still here and are called to share His love with others wherever we go. Yes, even Wal–Mart! Ha! Let's spread the news of Jesus to others with smiles, laughter, kindness, patience, and LOVE.

October 15

Choose you this day, tell me who will you serve? Let nothing stand in your way, give Him the praise He deserves. As for me and my house, we will serve the Lord." An old song with a beautiful declaration. God gives us choices….Let's choose to serve Him as a family with our whole heart. Desire God's plan for your family and don't settle for anything less….Prayer changes everything and everybody!

October 16

Our faith in God and His Word is the key to seeing miracles and breakthroughs on a consistent basis. Matthew 21:22– "Whatever we ask in prayer, believing, we will receive." We mustn't be moved by situations and circumstances around us that could waver our faith. Spending quality time with God builds our faith, keeps us strong with our eyes focused on Him. Let's pray, submit our request to Him, and believe! Remember fear and doubt are our enemy. Believe God's promises!

October 17

If we're asking God to make us a shining light to reach those around us, we must allow Him to change us. People are attracted to light. We must allow the love of God to shine through us. We must also be people (Christians) of excellence whether at school or work. A slothful behavior isn't appealing to the lost. We should work hard at our task knowing, "We can do all things through Christ who strengthens us." Today, let's shine for Jesus and impact those around us.

October 18

The first commandment that God gave the children of Israel in the book of Exodus was to Put Him first. Put God first in our life is loving God...Loving our neighbors. That's God's command. We tend to love whatever we spend time doing. When we put Him first, everything else falls into place. God gives us peace, joy, and love....Make Him a priority today and be blessed.

October 19

A prideful man feels he needs to toot his horn loudly for others to hear. He needs to brag to the world of his accomplishments. He becomes self–reliant and begins to elevate himself to higher levels. But the man of humility is confident in the Word, allowing God to promote him. He isn't interested in bragging to others but gives God the glory for every blessing. Bottom line: Pride goes before the fall..(Look at history). Let's choose humility, a thankful heart, & God promotions and blessings. God first.... Good way to start the day!

October 20

As Christians, we should be motivated to learn all we can about God's ways. God's heart is for us to grow strong. If we are going to celebrate victory in our life and the lives of our family, we need to pray and study His Word. We must believe in the power of prayer and His Word. Mountains can be moved! Family members can be changed! Job situations can turn around! All things are possible when we believe....Let's learn all we can and grow strong....

October 21

I speak to every mountain in my life and command it to be removed and cast into the sea" (Mark 11:23). Yes, we have authority in the name of Jesus to command those mountains (obstacles, hindrances) to be removed from our lives. Let's not allow anything to stand in our way from serving God. Our mountain might look big, but the Word tells us that NOTHING is too big for God! Take authority today, and demand your mountain to be removed from your life in Jesus' name!! Freedom and Victory!

October 22

It's easy to fall into a selfish mode of thinking. It doesn't take much before we begin demanding our own way or getting irritated because some don't do things our way. We must renew our mind daily through prayer and the Word to be Christ–like. God has called us to love and be a giver of ourselves whether in marriage, friendships, or business relations. When we learn to love and care about others' needs, we find that our life has more joy and peace. Loving unconditionally...

October 23

Did you know that the devil loves to use people to "push our buttons?" He just sits back and laughs when we lose our cool with others. Let's choose to win this temperament battle by relying on God's peace. 'Losing it' is NOT going to win someone to Jesus, and it's also stressful. Let's pray for peace that flows gentle like a river. Choose peace and calmness today, not allowing words or actions to upset us. "Peace like a river......It is well with my soul."

October 24

Holy Spirit, show me the ones that I need to give an extra smile to, the ones I should send an encouraging message to, the one I should offer my help to, the ones I should pray for. Let my life (the way I live) be a lighthouse to those who are trying to find the light (Jesus). Let the words of my mouth be exactly what someone needs to hear. Use me, oh God........Today, I choose to make a difference

October 25

Loving one another unconditionally means patience. When someone "barks" at us, we should choose to look into their heart the way Jesus does. Most people do not hear the tone of their voice when they speak, especially when they feel frustrated. Choosing to walk in the steps of Jesus and avoid conflict gives us victory and less blood pressure problems! Today, choose peace and patience......

October 26

No matter what we've done, no matter what our attitude has been, no matter our failures or darkest secrets, God, in His love covers our past with grace and mercy. Yes, He forgives us. Let's thank Him for the blood of Jesus that washes and covers our sins. "New beginnings!" Yes, that's the precious nature of our Heavenly Father. Forgiving..... Friends, it's never too late, it has never gone too far....He's waiting with open arms for us to repent and come back home....What forgiveness......What Love.......

October 27

God cares about each aspect of our lives, whether it's sports, music, careers, family, etc. Yes, He desires to be part of what we do, what we think, and what we say 24/7. Some believe He only cares about us praying and going to church. Nope, not true. It's much more than that. God desires a relationship with His children. His love covers every part of us. Let's grasp that concept and "welcome" Him into each part of our life. He truly cares.

October 28

How comforting to live under God's "grace and mercy". As Christians, we are His children no matter our past. When our sins are forgiven, it's like we emerge from a spiritual washing machine clean. EVERYONE has the opportunity to have a future with Jesus, no matter what kind of life we have led. After forgiveness, we are NOT to live in guilt and shame anymore. Our Heavenly Father believes in restoration! That, my friends, is unconditional LOVE.....Now, let's apply that to those around us....Grace and Mercy = LOVE..

October 29

In the Bible, we read about Lot leaving Sodom and Gomorrah just before it was destroyed. They were instructed to not look back, but Lot's wife turned and looked back at God destroying the wicked city and she was instantly turned into a pillar of salt. God is calling us to keep moving forward, not focusing on the past or what's behind. We must keep our eyes on Jesus during our storm and keep walking one step at a time. If we fall, Jesus will carry us....Today, let's not dwell on the past, but look to a future with God...He loves us...

October 30

If discouragement attacks us, we must fight and not give in to it. Confessing God's Word is the strongest weapon available. His Word will break through the wall of weakness/discouragement. God desires for us to live with "joy." It's our defense against the devil. Let's fight discouragement with His Word, confessing it 24/7 and win the battle. We are God's children and deserve to live happy lives. Let's make it happen!! "JOY"

October 31

Jesus Paid It ALL, "Sin hath left a crimson stain (visible), but He (Jesus) washed it white as snow" (gone, wiped away). That God's grace and mercy. That's the love of God! No more guilt, no more shame...washed away by the blood of Jesus. His suffering and death on the cross, paid the price for us. We are redeemed, restored....No matter what anyone thinks or says about us, we are God's child, God's heir. Let's be confident in the fact that we have a special place in His heart.....

November 1

The closer we become to God the more we desire to give of ourselves. When we spend quality time with Him in worship, we desire to love others. It's a beautiful feeling to hug someone who is hurting. It's a great feeling when we give an ear to someone needing to talk. Even being courteous gives us a good feeling. The ministry of Jesus was about giving and loving others. That's our ministry also. We must take the love of God that's in us and give it to someone today. Evangelism...Loving one soul at a time... Let's begin today.......

November 2

The devil loves to convince us that we're useless and worthless. He works hard to make us doubt our talents that God has placed inside us. "If" we listen, we'll walk in defeat, which he loves. We must recognize who we are in Jesus and that God didn't make a mistake with us and that He has a beautiful plan for each of us, "if" we'll trust Him. Let's not allow discouragement to ruin our day. This is God's day! He loves and desires to bless us. We must ignore the devil and began thanking our Father for what He has, is and will do for us. Live in victory!!

November 3

Being a Christian doesn't magically change our lives to experience perfect days like a fairytale. Everyone experiences good and rough days. The difference for a Christian is God has empowered us to be over comers with a promise to walk with us through the valley of the shadow of death and the mountain tops. God gives us eternal life in heaven and a loving relationship while we're here on earth. He gives us strength to live each day in victory and peace, no matter what we face. He gives us true agape love that none can compare to. Choose Jesus today, and experience real life...You won't be disappointed.

November 4

There are times when we come across people who look hopeless. Their lives are so far from God and their hearts are extremely hard. In the back of our mind, we write them off, thinking they are so mean they will never give their heart to Jesus. No hope.... But as we pray, we should ask God to allow us to see these hard people as He sees them. He loves them, no matter their actions and heart. Let's not give up praying, believing, and thanking God for what He will do in their lives. "ALL things (Yes, even the meanest of people) are possible to him who believes." Never give up believing for the miracle of change!

November 5

Remember the children's church song "Everyday with Jesus is sweeter than the day before"? How true. This should be the goal as Christians to continually be moving forward with God, growing spiritually, depending on Him more each day. God WILL speak to us if we'll listen. Learning to listen to His voice comes from spending time with Him. Most of us recognize our family's voices. This comes from time together. The more time we spend with God, we will recognize that still sweet voice that instructs and leads. He speaks, are we listening?

November 6

God has not called His children to walk in fear. We mustn't be afraid when viewing obstacles or mountains that stand in our way. Fear tries to convince us that it'll never happen, but our God is powerful and mighty and will remove ALL mountains from our path, "if" we'll trust Him. Fear says we do not trust that God can/will do it. Just as a parent protects and fights for their child, God loves us and will fight our battles. Let's trust Him with ALL our heart. We ARE over comers in Jesus' name! And yes, God WILL remove mountains and clear our path! That's Bible! That's LOVE...

November 7

PUSH=Pray Until Something Happens. There is such truth in this acronym. We should NEVER give up praying and believing God for our miracles! If there are obstacles in our way, we PUSH! Too many Christians are living defeated lives. They didn't see results right away, and gave up. God WILL answer our prayers according to His will. He will not ignore His children! Today, believe His promises and PUSH!!!!!

November 8

Forgiven....One of the most cherished words in the Bible for a Christian. We might have "blown it" yesterday with our actions or words, but it's comforting to know that each day is a new day with God. We're NOT to live in the past, but the present. When we go to our Father and repent of sins we have committed, He forgives with an abundance of mercy and grace. Whatever happened yesterday is GONE...Washed away by the blood of Jesus..... Forgiven = HOPE..

November 9

There are times when those closest to us make us angry and upset. This could be family, close friends, or even co–workers. Our "buttons" get pushed to the max and we feel like exploding. This is when we need to step back and think how blessed we really are and how lost we would probably be without them. Friends, time on earth is short. We do not know what tomorrow holds for us so let's lift our eyes to Heaven and thank God, our loving Abba Father, for those who He has placed in our lives. We will discover we are truly blessed......

November 10

Memories...What a beautiful, precious gift from God. The sweet ability to remember good times we have had with those we love. We should take advantage of each day to make a memory that we can look back on. It's important to love those around us, knowing that time on this earth is short. As Christians, hate should never be in our heart. We should leave this world one day with no regrets, knowing that God has forgiven us and we have forgiven others. Today, let's make every effort to love others and make memories that are "keepers."

November 11

Psalm 56:3–"When I am afraid, I will trust in you. In God, whose word I praise, in God I trust; I will not be afraid. What can mortal man do to me?" The devil loves to attack us with fear. Fear can entrap and make us prisoners of our own lives. But keeping our eyes on Jesus and studying His word, we can be set free from fear. Trusting God in every area of our lives strengthens our confidence/faith in Him. We are called to be over comers, not prisoners. When fear attacks, confess and believe His powerful word and be set free.

November 12

It's comforting to know that God forgives us of our sins. We ask, He forgives...done. But when someone hurts us, we tend to want to hang on to the hurt and not forgive. As painful as it can be, we must choose to forgive and move forward. Unforgiveness can keep us bound like a prisoner. Let's be free by forgiving. It's not always easy, but it's God's plan for us. Giving the hurt to Jesus is the first step to our victory. Let's choose to walk in forgiveness, have peace, and sleep better at night!

November 13

Psalm 94:18–"When I said, 'My foot is slipping,' your love, O Lord, supported me. When anxiety was great within me, your consolation brought joy to my soul." This verse brings comfort knowing that we're not perfect and yes, there are times that we feel we're losing our foot hold and are going to fall. BUT, His Word reminds us that He WILL support us. We don't have to worry or allow anxiety to consume us. His love and peace comforts us. He WILL "take care of business" IF we'll give it to Him. Today, trust, rest, and be comforted.......He loves us.

November 14

As Christians we should be willing to reach out to others in need. We are in the "family of God" and families should always be willing to love and pray for each other. When we reflect on the crucifixion of Jesus and how He collapsed carrying His cross and the soldiers made Simon carry the cross for Him. This is an example of how we should be willing to help one another. When a member of our family (Christians) falls under the burden of their cross, we should be there to love, support and help carry their cross. Today, allow God to use you to help others......

November 15

"2 Timothy 1:7–"I do not have the spirit of fear but power, love, and a sound mind." We should NOT be afraid but know that prayer brings results. We MUST believe there is power in our prayers! To make this complete, we should always walk in love toward others. Spending time in prayer AND God's Word develops in us spiritual growth and maturity (a sound mind). This verse is a win/win for Christians. Let's trust God knowing He is working in us and answering prayers. Always remember, LOVE is the greatest gift......

November 16

When a storm hits our lives with large waves crashing over our ship, the natural tendency is to feel sorry for ourselves. Sometimes we even feel our storm is rougher than everyone else's. We must remember to not get angry with God or others. Instead of running from Him, we should run into His arms and hold tight. When we experience the "valley of the shadow of death" (storms) we must keep reminding ourselves that Abba Father (Daddy) loves us. He truly wants the best for us. If the emotional pain is so severe causing us to feel weak, let's begin by telling our Father we love Him, even if we don't understand. It's the first step to victory. We mustn't give up! Our ship has a destiny......

November 17

Being a Christian means taking a stand for Jesus and His Word. We should not "water down" or compromise what His Word says. The Bible is TRUTH, God's spoken Word. It's a manual to live by and strengthens us to be strong in the Lord. People around us should never be surprised that we are Christians. God didn't call us to be "closet" believers but to take a stand! Our words are useless if we're not walking the walk. People hunger to see the fruit in our lives (love, joy, peace, etc.). which gives them hope. Today, let's take a stand for Jesus by living a life full of love, the best evangelical tool to use. Remember when we give people love, we're giving them God because God is LOVE......Take a stand!

November 18

Each of us have close friends or family members who aren't living for Jesus. We see them living in sin, spinning their wheels, wasting away....The key to reaching them is LOVE......Some believe we should get in their face, beating them with the Bible and pounding the name of Jesus into their head, but it NEVER works. Arguing and debating will not bring them to repentance. It's the "love of Jesus" they see in us. Love conquers all. When a sinner understands they are loved unconditionally, their hearts will become pliable and soft. Let's love those around us with the love of Jesus, allowing His light to shine through us, giving hope....God LOVES the sinner.....

November 19

As Christians we must learn to be flexible and giving. Things don't always go the way we want them to. If we're around others very much, we discover that everyone has an opinion about what is right. We must learn to walk in love, not demanding our own way. Striving to be flexible with change, patient with others' attitude, and a giving heart displays the character of Christ and might even keep our blood pressure from boiling to the top. Ha! Life is full of changes. We should learn to relax knowing that God is in control. We can't change others, but with God's help, we can change ourselves. Today, let's "chill."

November 20

Ephesians 6:10–"Be strong in the Lord and in his mighty power. Put on the full armor of God so that you can take your stand against the devil's schemes. For our struggle is NOT against flesh and blood (each other), but against the rulers, against the authorities, against the powers of this world and against the spiritual forces of evil in the heavenly realms. Therefore put on the FULL armor of God.." God equips us to fight back and be strong. We shouldn't cower when attacked but instead praise and worship our Father with the Word of God on our lips....Victory!

November 21

"And if my God is for us, then who could ever stop us? And if our God is with us then what could stand against?" What truth in this song! How powerful is our God...He can literally move mountains in our lives and can make a way for us when everyone else says "No way!" God loves to take the impossible and make it POSSIBLE!!! So, do we listen to doubters or our God? I choose to believe in Jesus, my Savior. "From sinking sand, He lifted me." When we feel there is no hope in our situation, we must trust Him......He will NOT let us down! EVER!!

November 22

"This is the day that the Lord has made (Everyday is God's day), I will rejoice and be glad in it (even when things aren't going the way I want them to).." We have so much to be grateful for. We should stop whining and look to God who loves and blesses us. Life is full of choices. We must decide to allow God full control of our lives. We must rely on Him or else we can possibly become a "god" ourselves, making our own decisions and taking all credit, which is pride. Let's choose a life of surrender and total dependence on our Father. This doesn't make us weak. It makes us wise.......

November 23

King David began his ministry as a teenager facing the giant Goliath. Instead of running from, he chose to run to the problem and conquer. This story in God's Word applies to our lives today. We are faced with many giants (obstacles)threatning us. We mustn't be afraid of situations or even people coming against us. We should keep our eyes focused on God who equips us to win the battle. His Word tells us He can remove mountains (giants) standing in our way. Today when the giant attacks, let's meet him on the battlefield and slay him through faith in God's Word.

November 24

Psalm 97:5–"The mountains melt like wax before the Lord..." What an encouragement to know that NOTHING, no matter how big it looks, can stand under the power of Almighty God. Even the biggest mountains (obstacles) in our way will melt and be removed. That's the power of God! This scripture should remove any fear and doubt that would try to steal our faith. Today, let's look to God to part the sea that's preventing us from entering into our promise land, or collapse the Jericho walls that stand in our way! 2 Samuel 5:20– "Lord, You are the God of the breakthrough..."

November 25

The more time we spend with God praying and meditating on His Word, the stronger we become. When we become grounded in our walk with Him, we are able to face attacks from the enemy. Satan's attacks usually come "out of the clear blue sky" when everything seems to be going smoothly. Yes, he likes the element of surprise to destroy our joy and get us bent out of shape, especially after we have been smiling and full of joy. We must be on guard 24/7, full of the joy of the Lord, and be ready for his attacks by being grounded in God's Word. The question isn't "if" Satan's going to attack, it's "when." Let's be determined to win the battle. Remember, "Love" is our greatest weapon! The devil hates JOY!

November 26

The Bible relates our lives to fruit trees. We all bear fruit. Some fruit is good, some bad. The question is what kind of fruit do we bear? We can rattle all day to others about the Christian life, but it truly boils down to the way we live, handling situations and circumstances. People are looking for hope in this dismal world. What fruit are showing at school or work? Is it love, joy, kindness, patience, etc? Philippians 2:5 "Your attitude should be the same as that of Christ Jesus." Let's shine our light (Jesus) to the world today.

November 27

Sometimes we don't grasp the love that our parents have for us until the moment we hold our own child. The love we have for our children is deep and unconditional. We want the best for them and will do almost anything for them. What a comparison to the love that God has for us. His is deeper and much more unconditional than anything we could compare to. He forgives... because of love. He showers us with grace and mercy...because of love. He opens and closes doors in our path....because of love. He offers us salvation through Jesus...because of love......Love, what a gift.......Today, share the gift...

November 28

There are times when we pray for an answer to our request and seemingly God answers differently. We might become discouraged and even disillusioned that God doesn't care or even love us anymore. Then after some time has passed, our eyes are opened to see it was for our best and that God was looking out for us all along......Friends, it's obvious we don't see what our loving Father sees, so therefore we should "trust Him with our whole heart and lean not to OUR own understanding".......Let's continue to remind ourselves that God wants the very best for us...Next time He answers differently, praise Him for taking care of us! He loves His children..........

November 29

When we choose to forgive someone for hurting us, it might not be a one–time step. After we forgive, it could rise up again, renewing old hurts. Each time we feel unforgiveness toward someone, we should deal with it spiritually, even if it's every day. Old wounds take time to heal so we need to continue forgiving. God's Word tells us to confess forgiveness with our lips and ask God to "Bless those who persecute (hurt) us." This is a big step, but it works. Let's choose to forgive and love so we can walk in freedom.

November 30

Isn't it easy to wake up in the mornings claiming "bad mood" and being critical all day? When we stray from 'abiding in the vine' we become alienated from the power source (God's love). It then becomes easy to get caught up in gossip, critical remarks, moaning & groaning, etc. Most people choose to avoid such complainers. Today, let's stay close to Jesus and allow His love to flow through us so we can live with JOY instead of a bad mood.. Others are noticing..

December 1

When the Beatles recorded the 60's hit "All You Need is Love", they didn't realize how true this statement was. It sums up everything. All we really need is love..Why? Because GOD is love..."All We Need is God (love)." Love (God) completes, heals, restores, and forgives us. Do we need anything else? God desires to complete us "if" we'll allow him to.. Let's offer ourselves to Him, trusting each step of the way and allow Him to finish the work He has begun in us. LOVE=GOD..

December 2

As the Holy Spirit teaches us more about grace and mercy, we find that our biggest enemy is ourselves. We know in our mind that God forgives us with grace and love but we tend to have a problem forgiving ourselves when we sin. The devil enjoys reminding us of our failures and sins. He's thrilled when we continue to beat ourselves up over and over. Nowhere in God's Word does our Heavenly Father keep reminding us of our sinful past. Jesus has come into our lives to set us free from shame. Let's rejoice and be free knowing that grace and mercy is for us and that God desires for us to look forward, not backward......Grace...

December 3

Worry...What a negative word in our language. Nothing good comes from worry, but there are plenty of negatives that accompany. Worry can keep us from sleeping, cause us to wring our hands, and put stress on our physical body. Spiritually, worry says "God, I really don't trust that you can handle my problem alone, so I'll have to help you." God tells us to "Cast every care and worry upon Him." We must learn to LET GO of certain situations and allow God to resolve it. He can and will. Remember the old Hymn, "Tis so sweet (relaxing) to trust in Jesus."

December 4

Why do we feel the need to retaliate for what others have done or said to us? Our human nature craves to get the last word in or "Do unto others as they have done unto us!" ha! This is far from the nature of Jesus. If we'll listen to the Holy Spirit, He'll probably tell us to close our mouth and let things roll off our shoulders. We're not called to get em' back but to love and forgive. Let's meditate on and live by Jesus' words on the cross, "Father forgive them, they know not what they're doing." Today, forgive and move forward in spiritual growth.

December 5

"Be ye kind one to another." God's Word doesn't mention about picking and choosing based on favorites, race, ethnic, etc. We are called to be kind to everyone. If we live in a 24/7 battle with others, we should check our hearts for we have a spiritual problem. We should never be kind to someone with the expectation of them returning the kindness. We give from the love inside of us. Being kind is sowing seed that will give us a harvest. let's give it away today. It's a great feeling to be kind.

December 6

Fear, worry, doubt, and anxiety are enemies of Christians. God has called us to walk in faith, believing His Word. Fear is a creeper. It slowly attacks without warning. The results are sleepless nights, wringing of the hands, etc. The next time we are attacked with fear, begin fighting by verbally using the name of "Jesus" with authority! There's power in His name, so speak it in faith expecting results! Today, let's erase fear, doubt, worry, and anxiety from our vocabulary. "At the name of Jesus, EVERY knee shall bow and EVERY tongue shall confess He is Lord." Yes, even fear has to bow.......

December 7

James 1:5 "If any of you lacks wisdom, he should ask God, who gives generously to all without finding fault, and it will be given to him. But when he asks, he must believe and not doubt..." How hard is this? God tells us to just ask and believe, and He'll give us wisdom. We try so hard to be wise using every worldly tool available. If we would just spend more time with our loving Father, asking for wisdom as Solomon did, God would give us wisdom and supply our other needs as well. "Ask and you will receive."

December 8

Walking with Jesus, means we learn to act like Him in everything we say and do. Jesus reached out to those around Him, loving, caring, and nurturing them. We are called to do the same, even the unlovable. Being kind to others is Christ–like. How sad when we say we love Jesus one moment, and then the next be hateful to those around us. Not good evangelism....Do we live our lives so others will be drawn to Jesus? Are we patient and kind to others who aren't like us? Dear God, may we see those annoying people through your eyes, loving them instead of hating. Oh, to be like Jesus.......

December 9

Are we looking at an impossible situation at the moment? Are we thinking, "There's no way?" God tells us in His Word, that ALL things are possible with God! Nothing, yes nothing is impossible! He loves us! Job 22:28 "I shall decree a thing, and it SHALL be established in my life." We must believe that He can and will do for us. We're not 2nd class citizens, but children of God! Let's have faith in Him, our miracle is on its way! Believe!

December 10

Matthew 6:33 "Seek FIRST the kingdom of God AND His righteousness, and ALL things will be added unto me." There are steps to be blessed. Instead of asking or begging first, we should seek God first (relationship). Also His Word tells us to seek His righteousness (doing what is right in the sight of God). Let's meditate on this verse, follow it.....and watch God bless! His Word doesn't lie, so love Him with all your heart...His benefit package is awesome!!

December 11

When we don't understand God's reasoning regarding a situation, we must learn to trust no matter the outcome. Our loving Father doesn't want to keep us in the dark. If we don't understand why our prayers aren't answered the way we want, we need to press in with worship and prayer, not letting go of the "hem of His garment" till we receive understanding from the Holy Spirit. Most importantly, never give up. Don't throw the towel in the ring! His plans are never wrong OR late.....Trust....Even when our heart hurts.......

December 12

When we pray, God hears. He lovingly listens as we pour out our heart. He's not moved by education, degrees, money, age, race, or speech...He listens to the heart. A child's prayers are just as important as adults. There is power and results in prayer. Today, when the Holy Spirit leads you, pray for others. The greatest gift we can give is our prayers. God listens to our heart. Our prayers DO make a difference. Pray in faith believing God hears and WILL answer. Someone's life may be changed or touched today because we prayed for them.

December 13

In our journey of growing spiritually strong, we say we trust God in every aspect of our lives. But when a crisis hits, we tend to panic. We're not perfected YET, so our soul's emotions do take over at times. We must continue to grow through prayer and God's Word, exercising trust in all matters. Bit by bit, step by step we discover we're getting stronger, more trusting, and peaceful knowing that our Father has it ALL under control....

December 14

If we, as Christians, could truly grasp the importance of praise and worship and the power that accompanies, we would see many more miracles in our lives. God loves to be praised and worshiped. His heart is moved by our love for Him. We shouldn't stress about details involving prayer request. Our job is to remain in His presence as much as possible and allow Him to take care of the rest. NOTHING is too big for our God! Let's cease worrying about "how" it will happen and focus on God, our provider...

December 15

The devil, our enemy, enjoys reminding us daily of our past mistakes and failures. If we listen to his lies, we'll begin to think we're not worthy of God's blessings, that no one has messed up more than us, and it's too late to change. It's all lies to discourage us. Remember, when we're discouraged, our focus is more on us than God. Let's remind ourselves that we sit with Jesus at the "head table", that we are God's own children (heirs) whom He loves and forgives the moment we ask.....Done! Next step, tell the devil He's a liar!!!!

December 16

Matthew 7:7 "Ask and it will be given to you; seek and you will find; knock and the door will be opened to you......Which of you, if his son asks for bread, will give him a stone?.....If you......know how to give good gifts to your children, how much MORE will your Father in heaven give gifts to those who ask him!" We need to stop wringing our hands and stressing and begin by "asking" God, trusting that He WILL lead us to what we're searching for, whether its materialistic or spiritually. He CARES about EVERY part of our life....Amen!

December 17

Most of us have experienced that feeling of yuck when we have purposely chosen to rebel against God's Word (Sin). The guilt and shame really can weigh us down. We even ask ourselves, "Was it really worth it?" God's forgiveness and redemption is given freely to us the moment we repent. Thankfully we don't have to go through a mourning period feeling like scum. When we sin and repent, we should focus on Jesus and continue to tell ourselves the sin is under the blood of Jesus so it's a NEW day! Gone (sin)......and needs to be forgotten.......

December 18

Why do we allow people or situations to sometimes "push our buttons" causing us to lose our temper and exploding? It's not worth it! Losing our temper causes stress on the body and solves nothing. Isn't getting angry a sign of situations not going the way we want them to? Don't we want God's will? We must learn that life doesn't always revolve around us or our way and to remain calm even in the toughest situations. People normally do not respond well to our anger and God isn't pleased with our display of temper. Peace......Today, let's strive for calmness. Life is too short to remain angry all the time. Let's release our situations and people into God's hands and remain calm.

December 19

When we are praying about a matter, we must remember there is power in agreement. Matthew 18:19 "Again, I tell you that if two of you on earth agree about anything you ask for, it will be done for you by my Father in heaven." This verse is powerful and TRUTH! It helps to join with others in prayer over certain matters. "No man is an island, no man stands alone." We need one another in relationships AND prayer. Let's don't hesitate to ask others to pray for us. There's power in agreement!

December 20

If the holidays tend to bring you sadness because of loss or painful memories, please make changes in your plans. Avoid certain Christmas songs that make you have a negative memory. Change your plans regarding gatherings of people that make your heart sad. It's important to be a giver of yourself. The more we give the more joy we receive. It doesn't cost money to give of yourself. Remember, praise and worship will help you retain your "JOY". Don't allow the devil to steal your Christmas joy...Your joy is your strength. Decide NOW to have victory this holiday season!

December 21

Peace, good will toward men." God knew 2000 years ago about our Christmas shopping. Ha! We need peace every time we enter the stores. It's easy to get aggravated at other employees and shoppers, but we must remind ourselves that "it's okay.."

Take a deep breath, and think about the many blessings we have from God.. Being a Christian witness during this season can be a challenge, but God has instructed us to be a shining light.... Today, walk in Peace, joy, and "Love"...People WILL notice.

December 22

It's almost Christmas! Choose to be happy! This is a wonderful time of the year to celebrate Jesus and family. The devil loves to ruin our holidays by making us feel blue and depressed. Friends, we can't change the past, but we can choose to enjoy the present, looking forward to bright days ahead. Remember, life (Christmas) is what we 'decide' to make it... "Count your many blessings, name them one by one..." Choose JOY!

December 23

God is LOVE...When we get to heaven, we will be awestruck at the love He has for us...It's difficult, living in our earthly bodies, to comprehend the depth of love He has for His children. We will understand that love completely when we join Him in Heaven. But for now, we're still here and are called to share His love with others wherever we go. Yes, even shopping malls and groceries at Christmas...Ha! Let's spread the news of Jesus to others with smiles, laughter, kindness, patience, and LOVE..By choosing today to "do" for others, we will bless and be blessed. He (Jesus) is our true meaning of Christmas.

December 24

Christmas! Choose to be happy! This is a wonderful time of the year to celebrate Jesus and family. The devil loves to ruin our holidays by making us feel blue and depressed. Friends, we can't change the past, but we can choose to enjoy the present, looking forward to bright days ahead. Remember, life (Christmas) is what we 'decide' to make it... "Count your many blessings name them one by one..." Choose JOY!

December 25

With food preparations, family gatherings, and travel, today can be a success or failure, depending on our choice. Busy schedules and spending too much time with others can grate on our nerves, causing us to become agitated, losing our "joy". Today's word is "Patience". We should understand it's not about us but about others. No one thinks or does like us, so we should accept their personalities/ways and love like Jesus. Let's choose success today by treating others as Jesus would treat us.......Merry Christmas!

December 26

When we experience salvation, it doesn't stop there. Salvation is a process of changing, molding, and growing us into the image of Jesus. That should be our goal, to be like Him. Let's think of a giant potter's wheel used to make a beautiful vase. The moment we ask Jesus to save us, God's heart is to place us on the potter's wheel as clay to be molded into the beautiful image of Jesus. Day by day He works in our lives, "if" we allow Him. Yes, life is a choice.....Let's choose to allow our Father to mold us to be like Jesus (Holy). The end result is beautiful......and happy!

December 27

"Take Time to love." We're living in a generation of go and do. Technology is rapidly changing and causing many to be stressed trying to keep up. Our lives on earth are short compared to eternity so we need to take time regularly to relax and enjoy life. God speaks to us about a day of "rest" but many have forgotten. There are more people having illnesses of various types due to stress and exhaustion. It's good to be productive, but God expects us to "chill" and relax some also If parents don't take the time to enjoy their children while they are young, they will turn around and their children will be grown and gone ...Today, let's check our calendar and schedule some special time to enjoy those we love. Its God's will to "stop and smell the roses" along the way.

December 28

God is teaching us unity in the body of Christ. He intentionally brings people across our path that are our complete opposite showing us how we must love each other unconditionally. Patience and tolerance are key words for Christians. Remember, Jesus told us to hate the sin, but love the sinner. We must remove our judgmental clothing and love the unlovable. God doesn't love them any less and doesn't play favorites.

December 29

Let's don't waste a single day following God's plan for us. Listening to His voice and following His plan keeps us at peace and in His will. God's will isn't for us to witness on the streets 24\7. He understands our hearts. He DOES desire for us to be ready to minister when He speaks. Let's "choose" to obey, be at peace, and be productive when He speaks. Enjoy this day with God!

December 30

Responsibility is given to each of us to help us grow as Christians and to prepare us to be givers. Responsibility has no age requirements, it's given to all. As Christians, we should accept our responsibilities whether home, work, school, or relationships. What we do with it defines our character. It's time that each of us step up to the plate and do our part. We should never pass it on to someone else to handle.

December 31

Have you ever fussed at your GPS? Sometimes you can type in an address and it seems to give you the longest route to your destination. This is much like our lives. We tend to map our lives "our" way which causes us to take detours and wrong roads that could be avoided if we would trust the Holy Spirit to guide us. If we'll listen to His voice and obey, we can make wiser choices regarding our life. God's plan is ALWAYS the best. No, we can't always see what's down the road, but we can experience complete peace if we'll trust Him. His map is NEVER wrong! Let's walk in faith, believing His path is the best to follow.